THE
AIRBORNE
SOLDIER

A formation of US Army Iroquois helicopters is approaching a landing zone a few miles north of Trang Bang, in the Republic of Vietnam. The choppers made four round-trips to ferry Rangers into combat against the Viet Cong attacking in force.

THE AIRBORNE SOLDIER

by

JOHN WEEKS

Colour Artwork by John Batchelor

BLANDFORD PRESS

Poole   **Dorset**

First published in the U.K. 1982
by Blandford Press, Link House,
West Street, Poole, Dorset,
BH15 1LL

Copyright © 1982 Blandford
Books Ltd.

British Library Cataloguing in Publication Data

Weeks, John
  The airborne soldier.
  1. Airborne troops
  I. Title
  356'166   UD480

ISBN 0 7137 0918 9

Distributed in the United States
by Sterling Publishing Co., Inc.,
2 Park Avenue, New York, N.Y. 10016.

Typeset in 10/11pt V.I.P.
Palatino and printed and
bound in Great Britain by
Fakenham Press Limited,
Fakenham, Norfolk

CONTENTS

The Douglas C-47 'Skytrain' (British name: Dakota Mk I). A military adaptation of the DC-3 airliner, the C-47 was essentially a freight carrier but from the North African Campaign onwards was the mainstay of the Allied airborne forces as both parachute aircraft or glider tug. C-53s are also included in this photograph of Dakotas in service with the Royal Air Force.

Introduction

Airborne warfare has one of the shortest histories of any kind of warfare, for it only started after the beginning of World War II; and, although it is still very much a potent method of fighting, it will never again reach the peaks of intensity to which it rose in the last years of that war. Today it has changed in its characteristics and in its methods. In World War II the emphasis was on huge armies delivered by parachute and glider on to large areas of flat land. The ground troops then followed up to meet the airborne forces, and a junction had to be achieved in the shortest possible space of time. Delay was fatal and expensive. Although the technique was refined and improved throughout the entire war, the idea seemed always to be that 'Bigger was Better', and the size of the operations grew and grew so that the Arnhem and Rhine operations of 1944 and 1945 required almost the entire resources of the Allied Transport Aircraft Fleet to lift the troops and gliders into battle. Such massive effort was bound to be self-defeating, and it is interesting that since then there has been nothing on a similar scale, though greater loads have been carried and greater numbers of troops have taken part in the more drawn-out helicopter operations in Vietnam.

Before one can be drawn into any discussion of the technical and equipment aspects of any type of warfare, it is necessary to have some idea of how that particular method came into being, for so often in human history what went before shaped what came after. So it has been with airborne war; probably more so than with many other ways of waging war. Many methods of waging war evolved naturally with the normal process of man's education and advancement. This was so with the early days of the airborne method, but it quickly turned into evolution by imitation born of desperation and overwhelming haste, with two main results. The first was a marked lack of initial originality of thought. The idea was to do something as quickly as possible, and the easiest way to do that is to copy whatever it is that is known to work at the time. This stage is rapidly followed by original and often danger-

Napoleon's proposed invasion of England involved the use of balloon troops or Aërostiers. This illustration by Conte depicts a balloon bag in the making, seam by seam.

This illustration, which appeared in the Publiciste *in Paris in Year XI of the Napoleonic Calendar and captioned* La Thiloriére, ou Déscente en Angleterre *was accompanied by the claim that 'the project was capable of lifting 3,000 men'.*

6

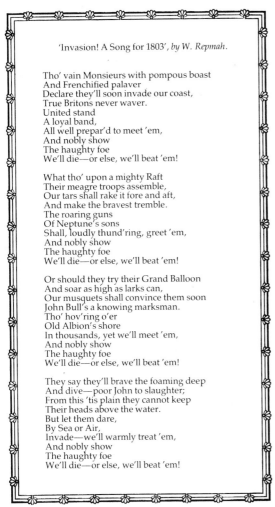

'Invasion! A Song for 1803', *by W. Repmah.*

Tho' vain Monsieurs with pompous boast
And Frenchified palaver
Declare they'll soon invade our coast,
True Britons never waver.
United stand
A loyal band,
All well prepar'd to meet 'em,
And nobly show
The haughty foe
We'll die—or else, we'll beat 'em!

What tho' upon a mighty Raft
Their meagre troops assemble,
Our tars shall rake it fore and aft,
And make the bravest tremble.
The roaring guns
Of Neptune's sons
Shall, loudly thund'ring, greet 'em,
And nobly show
The haughty foe
We'll die—or else, we'll beat 'em!

Or should they try their Grand Balloon
And soar as high as larks can,
Our musquets shall convince them soon
John Bull's a knowing marksman.
Tho' hov'ring o'er
Old Albion's shore
In thousands, yet we'll meet 'em,
And nobly show
The haughty foe
We'll die—or else, we'll beat 'em!

They say they'll brave the foaming deep
And dive—poor John to slaughter;
From this 'tis plain they cannot keep
Their heads above the water.
But let them dare,
By Sea or Air,
Invade—we'll warmly treat 'em,
And nobly show
The haughty foe
We'll die—or else, we'll beat 'em!

The challenge of a Bonaparte balloon assault had clearly caught the imagination of the English people. The first popular song to refer to airborne troops?

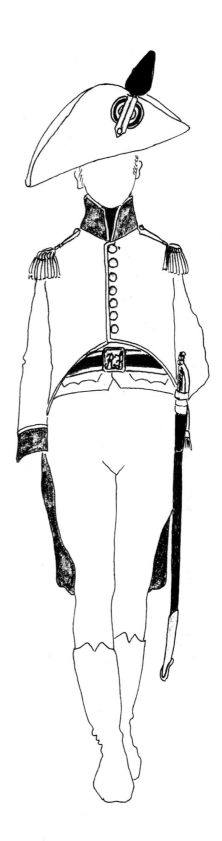

A present-day reconstruction of the uniform of a field officer, Compangnie d'Aërostiers, 1800. Formed on 23 March 1794, four balloons were brought into service, each with its own detachment of Aërostiers: 'L'Entreprenant', 'Celeste', 'Hercule' and 'Intrepide'. Coutelle, captain of the 1st Aërostier Company took 'L'Entreprenant' to Maubenge, reporting on enemy locations; attracting the first anti-aircraft fire in history when Austrian roundshot grazed the basket.

Top   *Observation balloons were widely used on both sides in World War I as observation posts (OPs) for artillery batteries. They presented vulnerable targets for aircraft and the average operational life of a 'kite' balloon was said to be no more than fifteen days. Primitive parachutes were used for split-second emergency jumps and this photograph shows a German officer about to descend earthwards.*

Bottom   *'Guardian Angel' parachute. The test parachutist is a woman, 1918.*

Right   *Leslie Irvin, whose name is synonymous with the development of the military parachute, fitted with his 'A' Type Parachute and about to make his first free-fall descent at McCook Field, Ohio, 19 April, 1919. The exit was made from a DH-4 biplane travelling at 100mph: jump altitude 1500ft: opening altitude 500ft. The official report notes under 'Misc.: Irvin broke his ankle on landing.*

The American Civil War and the Franco-Prussian war saw the practical use of observation balloons in battle. England was to make use of them in the Boer War. A new military balloon issued to the Royal Engineers in Aldershot, 1899.

Top and Centre Top   Although the defeated German nation was not allowed an Air Force under the Treaty of Versailles, scenes such as these were common in the 1920s and Hitler's Luftwaffe owed much to clandestine training with gliders and sailplanes. These photographs taken at Trebbin in 1935 show Hitler Youth taking lessons in the principle of flight from an instructor and a military sailplane being manoeuvred into position for launching.

Centre Bottom   The US Navy Flying Corps between the Wars maintained a school for parachute jumpers at its base at San Diego. Here two parachutists are about to descend high over San Diego harbour. After pulling their ripcords, the wind will fill their 'chutes and they will be dragged away into the slipstream of the aircraft.

Bottom   A school existed at RAF Henlow before World War II for training RAF pilots to jump to safety by the 'pull-off' method. The aircraft is a Vickers Vimy.

9

ous ideas for which there is frequently too little time for proper trial. The two are welded together and put into action. There is then a much longer period of evolution in which the wilder suggestions are thrown out and the less satisfactory adaptations modified and brought into line with the conventions of the new sponsor.

The first part of this evolution, that is the copying and local improvisation, is usually achieved in a short time, often surprisingly so. The second part, the sorting out and pulling into shape, takes much longer, especially if the original pattern for the copying was defective in its fundamental thinking. The history of airborne warfare is a fascinating study of this thought process happening within different nations and different military hierarchies.

The start of it all lies in almost ancient history. The myths of the Greeks have fables of flying men and surprise attacks by individuals with the

Top *At the outbreak of the Spanish Civil War in 1936, General Franco air-lifted Spanish and Colonial troops from Morocco to confront the Nationalists in Northern Spain and was greatly assisted in this task by a fleet of Luftwaffe Ju 52s.*

Bottom *Libyan parachutists at Castel Benito in 1938. Italy's contribution to the development of military parachuting in the late 1920s and 1930s was not exploited by the Italians in World War II.*

power of flight, but it was not until the balloon became a realistic way of flying in the last years of the eighteenth century that there seemed to be any chance at all of actually carrying soldiers into battle through the air. When Napoleon was waiting for the right wind to blow his invasion fleet to England, there were some suggestions for the use of balloons instead of ships to carry the troops. This is not such a far-fetched idea as it might seem at first sight; but it has all the classic hallmarks of the improvised local invention, so it will not be a complete waste of time to pause for a moment and examine the proposal in a little detail.

The first practical balloons were made and flown in the 1780s, using both hydrogen and hot air. An attempt to combine the two methods showed the foolishness of lighting a fire within reach of a combustible gas like hydrogen, and so they both pursued separate lines of development. Hot air soon lost way to hydrogen, partly from a lack of understanding of the use of hot air and a misguided belief that there was some mysterious lifting gas generated from the fuel, provided that this fuel was made up from the more repugnant farmyard residues. Another reason was the frequent incineration of the balloons from uncontrolled burning of the fire beneath. Hydrogen became the accepted lifting medium and it was this which was considered in the troop movement proposals put forward to Napoleon.

A balloon can carry four or five soldiers. Let us say for the sake of argument that it can carry five, since this is a convenient figure for calculations. A battalion of 1000 men would need no less than 200 balloons and, since one battalion would not achieve much against a country prepared and warned to expect it, it would be sensible to send at least three battalions. So 600 balloons would be needed. The balloons of that period were made of silk, an expensive and scarce product. They could probably have been made from fine linen or cotton, but there were few machines for making such large quantities of material; and so the resources of France would have been strained to the absolute limit to provide the raw material. Indeed it was impossible, for Napoleon's campaigns were already making huge demands on the French economy.

Let us suppose, however, that it could have been done. Let us also suppose that sufficient seamstresses could have been mustered in the various centres to make up the balloons, and remember that they would be working with needle and thimble, for the sewing machine had not yet been invented. Let us stretch our imagination even further and suppose that the supplies of iron and sulphuric acid, then the favoured way of making hydrogen, could have been raised and could have been so brought together in one place that there was a more or less simultaneous generation of gas to fill the balloons, all within a few hours. Filled balloons cannot be held on the ground for long as they are at the mercy of the winds—the lightest breeze imposes a huge force on the envelope and to try and hold it down by anchoring the basket to the ground merely invites the wind to pull at it until the one parts from the other. So it would be practically impossible to arrange a simultaneous take-off. It would mean that the flights would be spread out over several hours.

Finally, let us imagine that all these difficulties have somehow been overcome; the equal difficulty of finding sufficient level space to lay out 600 envelopes has been surmounted, and the inflation is under way. By a miracle of organisation, and it would need a miracle, the 600 balloons are ready to take off at roughly the same time. Into each basket climb the five passengers, all of them trained infantrymen, but not, we presume, trained balloonists. The ropes are released, and off into the clouds go 3000 men, to drift across the English Channel with no control over their route, and left to land in a hostile country.

Naturally, however, they have no idea of where they are, nor how to land the balloon. It was on this point that the whole idea would have foundered before it ever started, for piloting a balloon is a skilled business, and in 1805 there were only four or five men capable of doing it in the whole of France. Landing a balloon is the most hazardous part of the entire flight, and it is where the injuries occur, so a substantial proportion of the force could be expected to be casualties before ever getting into a battle at all. Finally, just to round off this whole fanciful idea, Napoleonic armies were trained and equipped to fight in large, close formations. Scattered groups of five men, or less according to the landing injuries, would have done little more than cause alarm and fright.

This detailed examination of the Napoleonic balloon invasion has perhaps been taken a little too far, for one can see from the very start that it

11

Bir el Ghnem 1939. Marshal Balbo's 1st Battalion of the Air in action. The suave and competent Governor of Libya's 300-strong battalion of paratroopers was recruited from Italian officers and native Colonial volunteers.

could never have taken place at all; but it is worth going through it as an exercise in logical thought because, later in the history of airborne warfare, we shall see how more modern military men were equally blinded by the novelty of their ideas so that the obvious drawbacks, and sometimes the obvious impossibilities, were blithely overlooked or pushed aside. Napoleon was sharp enough to have no truck with balloons, even for propaganda purposes.

After that there was no real suggestion of using airborne delivery methods for troops until the closing stages of World War I, when the monotony and appalling casualty rates of trench warfare were enough to allow the wildest ideas to be tried out, or at least given a hearing. In 1918 a certain Colonel W (Billy) Mitchell commanded the United States Army Air Corps in France. His suggestion for overcoming the deadlock of positional war was to fly over the obstacle and

land a force behind it, using aeroplanes to carry the force and parachutes, a significant idea, to land them in action. This suggestion was the first real milestone in airborne history, for it was the first time that a suggestion for the use of the parachute as a means of military movement was made. Parachutes were not new (fairground acrobats had used them for over a century to thrill the crowds), but parachuting from aeroplanes was quite a novelty. From about 1916 onwards a small number of agents had been dropped behind the German and Austrian lines using static-line parachutes, some of them made of black material for better camouflage at night. Nevertheless, the numbers of these drops was tiny, the planes were only two-seaters, there was no requirement to fly in formation with other machines, and once dropped the agent was on his own. So Mitchell was reaching out into the darkness with his imaginative idea.

Nevertheless, Mitchell pursued his idea and put a staff officer on to the task of preparing the detail of the plan. This was a Lieutenant-Colonel Lewis H Brereton, whose name will reappear in

French units of the l'Infanterie de l'Air were formed in 1937 only to be disbanded by the Vichy Government in 1940. They received their parachute training at the Centre d'Instruction de Parachutisme at Avignon-Pujaut, which was also responsible for training Air Force pilots in emergency escapes. This photograph is of instructors from Avignon-Pujaut training at Toutchino in Soviet Russia in 1939.

Top   A well-known photograph of a Tupolev Ant-6 bomber of the Red Air Force converted for parachuting. This shot from a newsreel in the 1930s shows Russian paratroopers climbing through a hatch in the roof of the aircraft before descending by free-fall.

Bottom   Soviet Army manoeuvres in the 1930s revealed that Marshal Tuchachevski's airborne forces were well advanced in military parachute and air-landing techniques. Here Red paratroopers are handling a 76 mm Recoilless gun on a drop zone during one of these exercises in the mid-'30s.

Jumping by the 'pull-off' method from a Soviet biplane; another French instructor-parachutist at Toutchino.

airborne history some twenty-four years later. Brereton realised that to carry a useful force he would require the biggest planes then made, the British Handley-Page 0/400 and V/1500 twin-engined and four-engined bombers. These could certainly have carried quite a large force had they all been made available, and one of the conclusions reached by Brereton was that he would need the entire holding and factory output of Handley-Pages to gather enough aircraft for his assault. The idea was to land part of the US 1st Division behind Metz and attack it from the rear.

13

Right   British paratroopers with Polish comrades in training at
RAF Ringway, Manchester in October 1940. Thompson SMG
M1928s and a Bren light machine-gun are in evidence.

Top   Jumping through the hole but these British paratroopers
training in a Whitley mock-up in the hangar at Ringway in 1940
do not have far to fall.

Right   British paratroopers emplaning in a Whitley at Ringway
in 1940. Like their French, Russian and American friends they
wore pilots' helmets, of no special benefit on impact with the
ground.

The first German parachute training school at Stendal near Berlin; where in 1936 the newly formed 1st Parachute Rifle Regiment had its headquarters. German paratroopers were not encouraged to land feet first as were their Allied counterparts. Rather hands and knees first.

April 1940. German mountain troops being conveyed in a Ju 52 for air-landing in Norway.

It may be instructive to look for a moment at the possible size of that part of 1st Division that could have been committed to the battle of Metz. On 31 October 1918 the Royal Air Force had 258 0/400 bombers on charge and a further 1500 were on order in the USA. If we presume that the US order could have been delivered in time for the assault, and if we further assume that the existing 258 are discounted as representing the inevitable wastage that will occur from crashes and other causes, then there are a possible 1500 planes. The 0/400 could carry twelve passengers in some discomfort, so the most that it could possibly be expected to lift with parachutes and full equipment would have been no more than ten. Even so, that is a force of 15,000 men. There were to be far fewer V/1500s, as only 255 were on order in November 1918, and so it would be reasonable to suppose that no more than 200 would have been flying when they were needed for the assault. The number of parachutists that a V/1500 could carry is problematical. In one publicity stunt in 1919, forty passengers were lifted to 6500 feet (1980 m.) over London, but a maximum of twenty men seemed likely if there was to be enough room for them to move about and somehow make a parachute jump. Here again, the number of men that could be carried appears to be high. It would have been another 4000, making a total parachute force of 19,000, and Brereton cannot have imagined that he was going to get that number into the air. More likely he had heavily discounted the building programme and was counting on something between 5000 and 10,000 men being lifted into

the battle zone on the day.

General 'Black Jack' Pershing, Commanding General of the American Expeditionary Force, shelved the idea and sent the planners back to work on more mundane tasks more nearly connected with winning the war. Within a few months they had done as he wished, and the great airborne offensive of 1919 was thrown into the waste basket, as everyone turned to grapple with the unfamiliar problems of peace. Pershing was undoubtedly right, though not perhaps for reasons stemming from the difficulties of airborne war. He vetoed the plan in 1918 because it used too many valuable resources and he also felt that it was too novel to risk. We now know that, like the Napoleonic balloons, the Handley-Page assault could scarcely have succeeded. For one thing, and this is a most important factor, it would have been impossible to keep the operation a secret from the Germans. The extra aerodromes, the extra aircraft, the parachute training, all these would have been noticed and the information fed back through the spies which each side had in plenty, and the Germans would have been warned and to some extent prepared. Next, the troops could only have dropped with light equipment (even to drop a machine-gun would have strained the ingenuity of the parachute and aircraft makers) and the proper training of a large number of men would have been almost impossible in the short time allowed by Mitchell. It seems likely that the Handley-Pages were in any case highly unsuitable for parachuting, which would have led to difficulties in getting the parachutists on to the drop zone in

15

A variety of Luftwaffe aircraft including Ju 52s and He 111s at Oslo-Fornebu airport during the invasion of Norway.

The following month, German gliderborne troops landed on top of and captured the Belgian frontier fortress of Ebian-Emael, which is adjacent to the Albert Canal forming a junction with the Maas Canal.

Operation Mercury, the battle for Crete commenced on 20 May 1941. The Germans committed some 22,000 parachute, gliderborne and mountain troops to the operation involving 500 transport aircraft. 6000 Germans were killed and 250 aircraft destroyed. Here the Fallschirmjaeger round up a few of the 12,000 British, Australian and New Zealand troops taken into captivity.

German paratroopers in Rotterdam. General Student's devastating airborne assault on the Low Countries on 10 May 1940 paved the way for the swift capture of Belgium and Holland.

compact sticks. Finally, the inadequacies of wireless communication in 1918 were such that the force would almost certainly have lost contact with the base after jumping.

Nevertheless, Mitchell was far closer to originating airborne warfare than the Napoleonic balloon enthusiasts. The use of balloons was a manifest absurdity; but in fact Mitchell could have been given all those bombers, he could have loaded them with men wearing parachutes and those parachutes could have been made in the time, he could have flown his men over to Metz, and he could have dropped them by parachute and the world would then have witnessed its first ever real airborne assault just twenty-one years before it actually did. The possibilities were becoming practicalities.

Throughout the 1920s parachutes became more commonplace, so too did aeroplanes, and both were gaining strongly in reliability and simplicity. Flying became a sport and a hobby, though only on a very limited scale. Gliding was started soon after the Armistice and in Germany in particular it was encouraged and supported by the government, since it was one of the ways of

One of the 280-ft jump towers at Fort Benning, Georgia. These replaced the original jump towers at Benning which were 34-ft tall.

making the population air-minded in defiance of the Versailles Treaty. Parachuting was not regarded as a sport for ordinary people, and it was confined to a small body of experts in all countries except Soviet Russia where for some unexplained reason it was taken up quite seriously. By the late 1920s there were parachute towers in most of the larger Russian cities, and

Men of the 501st Parachute Battalion jump training at Fort Benning in 1942. The aircraft is a C-53 Skytrooper.

the citizens could join a club and learn to jump. It was the only country in the world where there was such a spread of parachuting expertise, yet others were experimenting and trying every bit as hard.

Italy must take pride of place for being the first nation to see the full military implications of the airborne arm and to be bold enough to experiment for herself. In 1928 there were already Italian parachute troops, only about a company it is true, but nevertheless trained parachutists, and practised ones too. They used a version of a wartime British parachute, as will be more fully related in its proper place, but apart from the parachute they had little else to show that they

were in any way different from any other soldier; nevertheless they showed the way, and others were on the way to follow.

By 1929 Soviet Russia selected men for parachute training, and in the next year a battalion was trained and some of the men were dropped on a large exercise with some success. In 1931 there was another exercise and then there were no more public announcements until 1933 when in the Ukraine a complete battalion was parachuted *en masse* from the huge TB-3 four-engined transports. The next year there was an even more startling manoeuvre in the same region when a regiment dropped in front of all the foreign military attachés. The British attaché was Major General (later Field Marshal the Earl) Wavell, and in his report he said:

18

Lieutenant Wm. T. Ryder's Parachute Test Platoon pose in front of a B-24 Bomber at Fort Benning in 1941. The 'chutes are T-4s. This team pioneered experimental military parachuting in the USA prior to Pearl Harbor.

'We were taken to see a force of about 1500 men dropped by parachute; they were supposed to represent a "Blue" force dropped to occupy the passages of a river and so delay the advance of the "Red" Infantry corps which was being brought up for the counter-offensive. This parachute descent, though its tactical value may be doubtful, was a most spectacular performance. We were told that there were no casualties and we certainly saw none; in fact the parachutists we saw in action after the landings were in remarkably good trim and mostly moving at the double. They are, of course, a specially picked force and had had some months training. It apparently took some time to collect the force after the first descent began landing; about one and a half hours after the first descent began a part of the force was still being collected, though the greater part had already been in action for some time. The personal equipment seemed to consist of a rifle or a light automatic with a small supply of ammunition. The less experienced parachutists, we were told, landed without rifles, their rifles being parachuted separately. No mechanical vehicles were landed by plane as was done at Kiev in 1933.'

The response to this demonstration by the Soviet Union is interesting. In Britain the War Office considered that there was little scope for any serious employment of airborne delivery of troops, and in this they may have been swayed by the fact that at both the 1933 and the 1936 Russian manoeuvres the troops could only carry light weapons. Another very potent reason must have been the fact that there were not the aircraft to lift the men, nor was the acquisition of any foreseen at that time. The re-armament programme was just starting, and in the aircraft field the emphasis was firmly on fighters and bombers, with no provision for transports to carry troops. In any case, the RAF and the Army were not particularly close in their planning; both tended to go their own way and make their own plans, and the one thing that an airborne force requires is combined planning and co-operation between the two arms of the service. Another possible reason is that at this time there were any number of new ideas being bandied about, most of them more or less fanciful, and it would have been easy to have dismissed the use of parachutists as just one more of these. Finally, the country was not by any means airminded, except in a

Determined American paratroopers march through Washington, D.C. in 1941 but the United States was only beginning to learn about the principles of airborne assault.

19

defensive sort of way. There was a real fear of bombing, and a more extreme fear of the effects of gas, and where there was any preoccupation with the air war it was largely directed towards defence from enemy bombers which might be loaded with high explosive and mustard gas.

The Germans reacted differently, for all their manifold distractions in other fields. They saw that the airborne delivery was a practical and a possible method of waging war, and without much delay they took it up. It offered great possibilities for the surprise attack, which was something that was occupying the minds of the German Army planners, and it looked to be a suitable way of speeding up the armoured thrust of the *Blitzkrieg*. In addition, it had distinct possibilities for lowering the morale of the opponent by surrounding his troops; the Germans were going to be operating from interior lines in any case. They therefore had large and useful bases within their own boundaries from which to launch an airborne attack. They set about the training and development of such forces with some energy.

The Germans were not the only nation to see the advantages of airborne war. The Polish Army opened a Parachute Training School within a few months of the Russian demonstration and ran it on much the same lines as the Soviets. They also studied the counter-moves needed against an airborne invasion of their own country, and in this they were undoubtedly ahead of anyone else. However, although a few hundred men were trained in parachuting, the Poles never actually formed a proper and effective airborne unit in their own country, though at a later stage in the war they fought most gallantly in the Polish Independent Parachute Brigade Group as a part of 1st Allied Airborne Army.

In the USA there were some desultory experiments with parachute delivery in the 1920s, but these were never followed up and no serious trials were ever performed. The Soviet demonstrations seem to have aroused the same reaction in Washington as in London; France was a little more forward-thinking, and in 1938 two companies of *Infanterie de l'Air* had been formed, totalling 300 men. An offer for British officers to visit this unit and observe its training and techniques was received with almost total indifference and was finally cancelled just after the war started.

In Italy, where the idea of military parachuting had really started, there was only slight progress, with the emphasis on the parachuting of lightly-armed men, but almost no effort was directed towards delivering any heavy equipment once they had landed. They were very much seen as a raiding force with limited objectives.

The real development of airborne forces took place in Germany from about 1938 onwards, and it happened in some secrecy, concealed from the world. By a happy and sensible choice the new arm was placed under the command and care of the *Luftwaffe*, and this one move straightaway ensured the minimum of friction between the providers of the transport fleet and the men who would use them. As all the Allied armies were to find out in later years, this is the main stumbling-block in the formation of any airborne force, for the Air Force is wedded to the idea that it can win the war on its own and the airmen are usually convinced that flying transport aircraft is of less importance than the glamorous and exciting business of handling fighters and bombers. Since the Air Force usually has control of the budget for building new planes, it is unlikely to allocate money to machines meant for use by soldiers. In Germany, however, none of this happened and the senior officers of the infant airborne arm were all men with an understanding of the uses of airpower and a sympathy for the many problems involved in its proper use.

The first major step forward in German Airborne development came on 4 June 1938, when Major General Kurt Student was charged with forming an airborne division from the miscellany of men who had been parachute-trained up to the time. Student was a natural-born airborne leader. Trained as an Air Force officer, he had been involved with the building programme of the infant *Luftwaffe* and he had a lively awareness of the value of air transport for military operations. He quickly made up his mind as to the way he wished to see the German airborne forces expand, and he set himself to make sure that it happened in his way. With a gambler's instinct he accepted everything he was given and frequently asked for more. Nothing was too unconventional for him to try out and he radiated an infectious and irresistible confidence that communicated itself to everyone in his command. He had need to possess these qualities because the main task given to him was to have his new division ready for action within three months in

A Japanese paratrooper making a simulated parachute descent (1942). Jap airborne forces were trained by a German military mission but the Japs were to find little use for their Army and Navy paratroopers as the Pacific war got under way.

order to support the planned invasion of the Czechoslovakian Sudetenland border country.

Student raised the 7th Flieger (Air) Division consisting of a mixture of parachute battalions and air-landing battalions, all with their own integrated air units. He also brought in, however, a unit of twelve DFS 230 gliders, a most significant step in view of what was to happen in the invasion of the Low Countries two years later. This division was ready for action on 1 September, but it was not used as the Czechs gave way to the German demands, and Student had to be content with a demonstration landing of the non-parachute elements. Afterwards his division was all but disbanded by the Army who withdrew the men. Student wasted no time and rallied the support of both Goering and Hitler to re-activate his division, and he was given clearance to go ahead and raise both a parachute

division and an air-landing one. There was sufficient air-lift for this to be a practical possibility, the result of some very clear thinking and far-sightedness in the early 1930s. Hitler took a personal interest in these preparations, proof of Student's skill in co-opting Goering as his commander, for Goering was the favourite of Hitler at that time. His *Luftwaffe* had not yet failed, and its reputation was high. Hitler now gave some very interesting and sensible instructions for the planning of airborne operations, and one wonders if they were really his or whether Student had a hand in their drafting. The two main ones related to command of the airborne drop. The *Luftwaffe* was to command until the airborne troops made contact with the main ground forces. After that all command passed to the Army commander. Whereas these two ideas may seem simple and obvious, they were not to

21

General Hermann Ramcke with Italian paratroopers. In 1941 Ramcke, one of the German group commanders in Crete, was appointed chief instructor to the Italian Folgore Division, which was assigned at that time to seize Malta. Ramcke subsequently formed a German 'Brigade' in the Western Desert and created havoc with the Eighth Army at the Qatarra Depression; the lightly-armed Folgore deprived of transport by the Germans formed the majority of the graves at El Alamein.

German and British paratroopers came face-to-face in North Africa (November 1942—May 1943), where the latter earned from their German adversary the nick-name 'Den Roten Teufeln'—'The Red Devils'. In this unusual photograph 'Red Devils' of 1st Parachute Brigade are being emplaned in a Ju 52 as prisoners-of-war bound for Italy.

12 September 1943. Skorzeny's 'Commandos' having landed on the Gran Sasso plateau in the Appenines in twelve DFS 230 gliders approach the Hotel Albergo-Rifugio to rescue Mussolini. A daring feat that was totally successful.

Russian paratroopers emplane. A large element of the Red Army in World War II was parachute-trained but fought not as airborne soldiers but in the elite Guards Divisions.

be adopted by the Allies until late in the war, and the lack of them brought about many troubles and delays.

Hitler also issued special instructions to the individual soldiers which apply equally well today, though there is a good deal of political rubbish mixed in with the good sense.

I. You are the chosen fighting men of the *Wehrmacht*. You will seek combat and train yourselves to endure all tests. To you the battle shall be the fulfilment.

II. Cultivate true comradeship, for by the side of your comrades you will conquer or die.

III. Beware of loose talk. Be incorruptible. Men act while women chatter. Chatter may bring you to the grave.

IV. Be calm and thoughtful; strong and resolute. Valour and the offensive spirit will cause you to succeed in the attack.

V. The most precious thing when in contact with the enemy is ammunition. He who fires uselessly, merely to assure himself, is a man of straw. He is a weakling who merits not the title of *Fallschirmjaeger*.

VI. Never surrender. To you death or victory must be the point of honour.

VII. You can only win if your weapons are in good order. Ensure that you abide by this rule—first my weapons and then myself.

VIII. You must grasp the full intention of each operation, so that if your leader is killed you can fulfil it yourself.

IX. Against an open foe fight with chivalry, but to a guerrilla extend no quarter.

X. Keep your eyes wide open. Tune yourself to top condition. Be as agile as a greyhound, tough as leather, as hard as Krupp steel; and so you shall be the German Warrior incarnate.

Student's airborne divisions continued to recruit throughout 1939 and trained hard. They stood by to take part in the invasion of Poland, but the advance was so rapid that they were not needed, and the frustrated Student turned his mind to planning his part in the projected invasion of France and the Low Countries. Just before this took place, his troops were used as the spearhead of the remarkable and daring assaults on Denmark and Norway. When these are examined in detail, they show more clearly than anything else the tremendous faith that the airborne force had generated, and the belief in their ability to take on any task, however impossible it looked at first sight.

This tremendous confidence, and the success that accompanied it, nearly brought about the end of the airborne divisions in their next battle. The Scandinavian venture had alarmed the Allied nations, and without delay those who saw themselves as being next in line for the same treatment took suitable precautions. On the other hand, the Germans were tempted to think that nothing could stop the parachutists, and they risked all their new force in the invasion of Holland in May 1940. It very nearly did not come off, for the Dutch had deployed to meet such invasion and they fought with a skill and courage that surprised the Germans. By a lucky chance the aerodrome at Waalhaven was kept open and the assault was reinforced by the air-landing units, but it was a near thing and the losses were heavy. Had there been any hold-up in the advance of the ground troops from the Dutch frontier, the story might have ended very differently. There were also some deficiencies in the command of the whole operation, but these were all lost in the celebrations that followed the victory and in the splendidly daring and successful glider assault on the fortress at Eban-Emael and the bridges along the Maas.

In May 1940 there was no doubt that the airborne arm had come to stay, and it had come in a dramatic and frightening way. In England there was near panic at the thought of thousands of German parachutists dropping at any place in the country, and the precautions that were taken did little to lower the level of alarm. Signposts were uprooted, place names obliterated on notice boards, fields were blocked with cars and farm machinery lest gliders should land on them, road blocks were set up and the countryside was patrolled by belligerent but untrained volunteers carrying shotguns. Few of these measures would have done much to stop a determined airborne attack, but they brought home to everyone in the country the dangers inherent in being on the receiving end of such an assault, and there was a general demand for the raising of a similar British airborne force. Churchill, now Prime Minister, wrote on 22 June his historic memorandum, calling for 5000 parachute troops, and the task began immediately.

The formation of the British airborne force is an almost classic example of copying and improvisation. With no precedents to guide them except German ones, it was inevitable that the first methods and even the equipment should closely follow those of the Germans. It took some time for these to be modified and changed, and the infant force had enough trouble even to survive in the face of mild opposition from the Army, who hated to see good men taken away for special units, and also from the RAF who had no resources to spare for a transport force. Progress was slow and only partially encouraging throughout the winter of 1940/41, but the invasion of Crete in May 1941 gave a spurt of almost panic proportions. From then on there was no doubt at all of the need for as many airborne troops as could be raised and trained. From that time onwards the numbers of men and their associated equipment was always well ahead of the aircraft to carry them, and it was this lack of planes that led the British into their detailed examination of gliders, and their highly successful design and use of them.

Crete also stirred up the United States into putting some effort into their infant force, though in fact the first purely parachute unit had been formed at Fort Benning in the summer of 1940, and in May 1941 the 501st Parachute Battalion actually existed, though it was greatly under strength. However, the US Army possessed a great advantage over Britain, and indeed (as was to be proved) over all the other combatants. In early 1940 the Chief of Infantry had been asked to study the use of air transport of all kinds and he had reported in favour of the use of the aeroplane as a means of moving both men and equipment. Shortly afterwards the Army Air Corps placed orders for the building of 11,802 transport

Right   D-Day, Normandy, June 1944. A Horse glider has made a safe landing; the tail having been blown off with a cordtex charge for easy release of troops and equipment.

Right   An American prisoner of the 82nd 'All American' Airborne Division taken in the Cotentin peninsula after the huge American assault forward of Utah beach, June 1944.

Bottom   A Short Stirling tows a Horsa glider in to the air, en route for Holland, 17 September 1944.

Brigadier-General James M. Gavin, commanding general of the US 82nd Airborne Division emplanes in a C-47 for Holland, 17 September 1944. At 37, he was the youngest general in the Allied Army at the time.

aircraft; these began to arrive with the units in the end of 1941. These machines were not only for parachuting, they were intended for all purposes, but they did mean that almost from the start the American parachutists, like the Germans, had a suitable aeroplane.

It made a fundamental difference. Training was easier because only one aeroplane drill had to be taught, and loading tables for the air-landed element were easier. Spares, servicing and every other support activity was simpler, and the US airborne force expanded rapidly. By 1942 there were four full-strength battalions; a year later there were two divisions. By the end of the war there were five divisions, all up to strength.

Japan never made the full use of airborne forces, although she more than any other belligerent country had need of them. Her pre-war expansion plans for the Pacific cried out for preliminary assaults by airborne troops, but the resources of the country were strained beyond all reasonable limit by the demands of the Army and particularly the Navy, and all hopes were put into seaborne attacks. Quite what difference a large and well-trained airborne army would have made to the overall result in the Pacific is now hard to say, perhaps very little, but in the beginning there seems no doubt at all that the Japanese conquests could have gone even faster and more cheaply if each invasion had been preceded by the landing of large bodies of troops from the air. It was only done twice on what may be considered a large scale, at Menado airfield and the Palembang oilfields and refinery in 1942. In both cases the Dutch fought hard and well, but the Japanese quickly prevailed, and the stories that circulated had almost as good an effect as the ones about Germans in Holland. Morale dropped among the Allied troops in the East Indies and there was much nervousness about parachute drops. Nevertheless, the Japanese never managed to follow up their advantage; and although there were several operations in the Pacific, the only successful ones from then on were American. The Japanese airborne force deteriorated until in 1944 their efforts were completely farcical and did nothing whatsoever to help their war effort, and nothing to stop the American advance at all.

The Japanese were taught by the Germans, and it must have horrified the instruction teams to see how their teaching was wasted.

A British SAS officer with the Maquisards in eastern France in the autumn of 1944. Altogether the SAS Brigade conducted 43 missions behind the lines in France from June until the end of the year.

The Italians, who had been the actual beginners in the use of parachute troops, never advanced much farther, though by 1940 there were two very under-strength divisions of parachutists with light equipment. Italy had never fully recovered from the economic effects of World War I and the country remained a poor one, though the façade of Fascism did much to hide the fact. Behind the scenes, there was little finance to put into industry and investment was low. Natural resources were uneconomically used, and the country was incapable of supporting a large modern Army, Navy and Air Force all at the same time. The parachute force was one of the desirable though not essential adjuncts to the Fascist cause, and so it never received the support that it needed to become effective. As a result the troops were frittered away in infantry battalions and never actually used in the rôle for which they had been trained. This is one of the

difficulties which every army has to face when it forms units of special troops. If they are to be effective they must be kept for the particular rôle. If the need for that special rôle does not appear, then there is the agonising decision of whether to hold them in reserve for yet longer in the expectation that they will be needed, and accept the probable drop in their morale as they watch the rest of the forces fighting while they wait, or to use them in an unspectacular rôle, usually as infantry, and recognise that this will in time mean the loss of all the trained men. For Italy the decision was forced upon her by the turn in the fortunes of the war after 1941, and the parachutists all but disappeared.

In Soviet Russia, the country which had started and shown the way to use airborne forces in the mass, the story was in many ways like that of Italy. In 1940 there was a somewhat artificial quarrel with Romania, and the Soviets occupied

the northern provinces of Bessarabia, using air-landed troops in the process. This seems to be the last time that their elderly four-engined bombers appeared in public and they made a spectacular curtain call by landing with a few light tanks slung between the wheels of the fixed undercarriages. After that there was almost complete silence on Soviet airborne operations, though we know from Russian and German sources about at least three brigade-sized drops were made in 1943 and 1944. All were failures through heavy opposition and the lack of what appears to have been the most elementary precautions, and all were pure parachute drops without any attempt to provide support weapons or even fighter cover. The Germans had little difficulty in rounding up the few survivors. More successful were the Soviet re-supply and reinforcement drops to the partisans, and in these they seem to have used reasonably sophisticated techniques for that time, and to have delivered their loads with tolerable precision and regularity. The official Soviet War History, the *Great Patriotic War*, tells of the tens of thousands of Russian parachute-trained troops who fought in increasing numbers from 1943 onwards in the Red Army's elite Guards Divisions but purely as infantry of the line.

At the end of World War II those who still lived were exhausted, none more so than the Allies for whom the final battles had taken a huge toll in money and resources, and in this toll the airborne assaults on Normandy, Holland and the Rhine had had a large share. There was some unspoken, and more than a little spoken, resentment of the amount of effort and publicity afforded to airborne forces, and the airmen were particularly anxious to point out that their bombing campaign had been of much more value than the use of airborne troops, and that these same airborne troops had taken aircraft and men who could have made the bombing even more of a war-winner. After the war, the US Army rapidly reduced its five divisions to one, and the British did the same. Only the French built up a new force, and they found that it was ideal for their colonial war in Indo-China. In the Far East, in the remote humid atmosphere of the swamps and rice-paddies, they set about teaching themselves how to use the smallest possible numbers of troops to gain the greatest advantage on the ground, a philosophy that was in direct opposition to that used by the Allies in 1944 and 1945 when it was at all times a policy of 'Bigger is Better' and 'Much Bigger is Much Better'. The French, however, found that in their kind of war a small number of men placed in a tactically sound position with the least loss of time could produce an effect out of all proportion to their number.

Korea seemed to offer a use of airborne forces when the advance was moving up to the Yalu in 1951, but it was found that the ground forces were quite capable of covering the distance without help, and the two large US airborne operations that were mounted were little more than demonstrations of progress in technique since 1945, and indeed there had been real progress. There were now aircraft with rear-loading doors and the ability to drop heavy loads by parachute. The glider had disappeared from the skies, though the familiar shapes of the DC-3 and C-47 were still in evidence. Five years later in 1956 at Suez the French showed that they too had moved on, and their troops and aircraft made a copybook drop and advance using modern aircraft and specialised techniques. The British, on the other hand, showed that they had scarcely moved at all since 1945 and their operation was little better than a public humiliation, saved only by the gallantry of the men involved.

A year later the Soviets revealed that they had once again trained a large airborne army, and throughout 1957 they showed off different aspects of it in army exercises, Red Square parades and the Tushino Air Show. It was a disturbing show for the Western Allies, and it made clear that the Soviets had overtaken the West by producing specialised self-propelled guns, heavy-lift tail-loading aircraft, a variety of special dropping platforms, and had trained at least six divisions of parachute troops. All of this had been done in total secrecy and it must have taken several years. Within a few months there were further Soviet revelations of the use of

Top Left *Korea, March 1951. Members of Coy E., 187th Airborne RCT prepare to board a C-119 at K-2 Airstrip for a practice jump in the Thegu area. Sgt. Dellgado has an M1 Garand Rifle slung over his shoulder.*

Top Right *French paratroopers on patrol in Algeria, 1954.*

Bottom *The siege of Dienbienphu, 20 November 1953—7 May 1954. Reinforcements, both French and Vietnamese are parachuted into the defended zone. The fall of Dienbienphu virtually ended French control over Indo-China.*

helicopters for troop movements, and almost overnight there was a marked change in the attitude towards airborne forces and the use of them, as the West made what efforts it could to catch up. Meanwhile, almost unnoticed in the general excitement, the French were fighting a deadly and losing fight in Algeria; once again they were using their parachutists, but they were also employing helicopters in the offensive rôle and using considerable imagination and flair in the process. It was in Algeria that they scored a notable first-time triumph by mounting the SS 10 wire-guided missiles on to light helicopters and firing them in flight.

Airborne forces, or rather parachute forces, suddenly became popular throughout the world and all the emerging countries started to form them. In Israel there had been a well-trained brigade for some years, largely using French ideas and equipment, and in the 1957 war it had done good work. Now every other country seemed to want a similar body of troops, and from South America to Japan men were to be seen in elaborately camouflaged combat dress wearing distinctive berets and badges and sporting high boots with thick rubber soles. The number of parachute badges proliferated and now there are over 1000 different versions all indicating that the wearer has made whatever is the local requirement for a basic training minimum, and generals and African rulers are only half-dressed unless they have parachutist's wings on their uniform. Germany re-formed her *Fallschirmjaeger* at the pre-war training school at Stendal, but she did so with care and precision, keeping the numbers of men in the units to within the limits that could be carried by the transport force.

In Vietnam the local war was hotting up, and in the early 1960s the US Army trained some Vietnamese battalions as parachutists to form a mobile reserve, just as the French had done ten years before. This phase, however, only lasted a short time and within two years the helicopter had arrived in strength.

The use of the helicopter was a deliberate policy decision by the US Army and it stemmed from the report of the Howze Board. The Howze Board was a body specifically set up to investigate the use of air-transported troops and to recommend the best way both to carry and to employ them. The chief recommendation of the Board was that the helicopter offered far and away the best method of moving troops about the battlefield, and that there should be some form of armed helicopter to protect the transport fleet. The US Army promptly ordered the 1st Cavalry Division to assume the rôle of airborne cavalry, and from that point on the rise of the helicopter as a battle-winning weapon began in earnest. Helicopters provide highly flexible tactical transport on the battlefield in a way that parachutes can never do, and in Vietnam the overwhelming need was for tactical movement of large bodies of men and their equipment. The US Army brought the employment of the helicopter to an astonishing pitch of excellence within a very short time, though the cost in financial terms was enormous. As a result of the Vietnam operations, the theory and practice of the use of airborne troops has gone ahead by huge leaps, and for those who can afford them, helicopters are the modern version of the wartime C-47 for many battlefield tasks.

But the parachute force is still necessary for the long-range tasks, and this was no more dramatically demonstrated than by the French intervention in Zaire in the Spring of 1978 when a regiment was sent in to rescue white Europeans who were being massacred by invaders from Angola. The French parachutists were flown in aeroplanes from Corsica to Zaire within twenty-four hours, something that no helicopter can yet do, and their arrival was decisive. Despite the gloomy prophecies and the effects of continually rising costs, airborne forces are still required and still a potent force in any army. The short survey of the background that this introductory chapter has covered will suffice to show how the airborne method of war has been built up and perfected. From now on, this book will concern itself with the tools of the airborne soldier's trade, the special equipment, weapons and vehicles that he needs to complete his task. The tactics, strategy and planning we leave to others to explain.

Parachutes and Parachuting

What first inspired the parachute is now entirely lost in folk-lore, mythology and guesswork, but it is a fact that the ancient Assyrians actually used a form of sunshade or parasol over 2500 years ago. Perhaps, just perhaps, one day when a strong wind was blowing someone had the idea that a bigger parasol could be used to slow down a long fall. If they did have such an idea, they did nothing about it, or nothing that has come down to us; and the next source of invention seems to have been the ordinary boat's sail. Leonardo da Vinci, that fruitful originator of so many modern ideas, left a sketch of a man descending supported by what he called a 'tent roof', a sort of braced framework covered in canvas and about 36 feet (11 m.) wide across the opening. Like so many of Leonardo's ideas he never tried it out, but it looks to be a perfectly sound basis on which to develop something more useful, and the dimensions make it possible that it could have worked. There is another and less well drawn variant of the same idea in the British Museum, and a hundred years later a book published in Venice contains a sketch of a man falling supported by a square sail stretched out above him and connected to him by lines from the corners. It is in fact an elementary parasheet, and is exactly like the ones small boys make with their handkerchiefs and pieces of string.

After these flights of fancy, for there is no proof that anyone tried them, there is a pause of a couple of hundred years, until 1782. In that year the brothers Montgolfier began their celebrated series of experiments with hot-air balloons. In 1783 they were flying themselves, and straightaway began a similar surge of parachute trials. In fact they may have started about ten years before, but conclusive evidence is lacking. It seems that a certain Canon Desforges made a contraption from wickerwork with a large cloth canopy, but he injured himself when he was launched from a tower in 1772. Seven years later Joseph Montgolfier, one of the ballooning brothers, parachuted a sheep safely from a tower at Avignon, or so it is said. There is a fearful danger in trying to parachute from a tower, as

32

Methods of parachute training were similar in all armies. Here pupil paratroopers at Ringway watch a demonstration of a backward roll, c. 1943.

countless brave and unfortunate experimenters can avow. It arises from the fact that the height is too low to allow a canopy to develop and produce its full retarding effect, and secondly it arises from the fact that the walls of the tower are uncomfortably close to the jumper as he falls and are highly likely to interfere with the deployment of the canopy, if not actually injure the jumper himself by high-speed abrasion as he scrapes past the stonework. The balloon, of course, overcame these evils at a stroke and the fact that it introduced others, equally deadly, was not realised for a little time.

In 1784 and 1785 Jean-Pierre Blanchard dropped animals from his balloons, not always with success, but with sufficient margin of safety to show that the idea was perfectly feasible, though nobody seemed keen to take the place of Blanchard's sheep and dogs. Late in 1797 another Frenchman, Garnerin, actually made the first recorded parachute jump which can be confidently ascribed as being successful and genuine. He did it with a 23-foot (7-m.) diameter parachute shaped like a large umbrella. A long pole ran right through the assembly, the top of

Top Left   *A German Fallschirmjaeger practises flight control in a hangar at Stendal Parachute Training School early in World War II.*

Top Right   *An Italian paratrooper is experiencing what it is like to swing on the end of a parachute, Tarquinia Parachute Training School, 1940.*

Bottom   *French paras in the making at the French military Parachute Training School at Pau in S.W. France, c. 1960.*

the pole being attached to the rigging of an unmanned balloon while at the bottom of it was a small basket for Garnerin. The canvas canopy had short ribs at the apex, again an umbrella idea, and the rigging lines were gathered in to one point on the pole above the basket. There are many features of the Garnerin parachute which are still used in today's models. One notable one is his system of rigging lines and shape of canopy, though he was obviously groping in the dark with other aspects (and one wonders what

Top Left *British paratrooper equipped with the Irvin X-Type parachute in the early days of World War II.*

Top Centre *A feature of British parachute training was and still is jumping from a balloon cage. Here a World War II version of the cage can be seen as it is about to be winched by cable to a height of 700 feet. The jump exit is a hole in the floor of the cage.*

Top Right *The first jumps from Whitleys at RAF Ringway in 1940 were made from this platform erected in place of the rear turret. This was a slow method of despatching paratroopers and the introduction of the hole in the floor of the fuselage enabled ten men to jump in quick succession.*

it was like to land in a basket with a pole in the middle of it). None the less, on 22 October 1797, in front of a large crowd in the Parc de Monceau in Paris, he rose in his basket to a height of 3000 feet (914 m.) and then cut himself loose from the balloon. To add drama to the occasion the balloon shot away from him and burst with a loud report that so startled the spectators that some women fainted with the shock. Garnerin fell some way before his canopy opened fully, but he then dropped at a safe speed, oscillating wildly, and landed unhurt. He and his family went on to make a series of jumps using a similar arrangement, and all of them were apparently violently and continually sick for some time after each landing, from the effects of the uncontrolled swinging on the way down. As these early parachutists were inclined to release themselves at what we should now consider to be generous altitudes, their flight time was several minutes in duration, and there was plenty of time for the stomach to be thoroughly upset by the time they landed.

In 1837 Robert Cocking attempted to demonstrate that the umbrella shape of canopy was naturally unstable and that the saucer, or inverted cone, was the natural and safe way to parachute. He drew on the example of seeds and thistledown to support this theory, and other eminent thinkers were equally certain of the rightness of his approach. Unfortunately Cocking overlooked the Laws of Physics and Mechanics which implacably point out that whereas an umbrella-shaped canopy keeps itself inflated

34

with the pressure of the supporting air, an inverted umbrella spends all its time trying to fold up and it exerts a push inwards along the outer seams, rather than a pull as with the conventional type. Thus, Cocking had to brace his entire canopy with a large hoop round the outside and then run rigging lines from that hoop to his basket. The result was inevitable. On a warm summer's evening in July 1837 he dropped from a large balloon at a height of 5000 feet (1524 m.) over Lee Green in Kent and within seconds his parachute collapsed with a loud crackling of woodwork that was clearly heard by the pilot of the balloon. Cocking's body was exhibited to interested members of the public by a local publican at a charge of sixpence (2½ p.) a head until vigorous protests put a stop to such ghoulishness a few days later.

After Cocking's unhappy demonstration,

parachuting dropped in popularity. It underwent only marginal improvement for the next four or five decades, during which time it was used as an added interest to the spectacle of a balloon ascent. Sometimes an acrobat risked injury by dropping with one; more often only dummies were used. Nobody thought of the possibilities of parachutes being life-saving devices. In 1880 the first unribbed canopies appeared, invented by two Americans, Tom Baldwin and Van Tassell. The extended parachute was hung down the side of a balloon, the rigging lines terminating in a trapeze level with the balloon's basket. Van Tassell swung himself into the trapeze when 4000 feet (1230 m.)

off the ground, cut himself loose, and landed perfectly safely, though with some alarming oscillations. From then on the flexible parachute was used more and more extensively as a showground stunt, using balloons as a jumping platform, but always having the entire canopy and lines stretched out down the side of the balloon, or in a few cases hanging underneath.

In 1907 the next step forward occurred. Another American, Stevens, invented a packed parachute in which the whole 'chute was folded into a back-pack which was opened by a ripcord, and the canopy was thrown out by compressed strips of whalebone. It remained a curiosity for some years, but it was a significant move in the right direction. However, nobody had yet jumped from an aeroplane. It was soon to happen.

On 1 March 1912 Captain Albert Barry, a balloonist and parachutist, climbed through a hole in the fuselage of an aeroplane flying at 1500 feet over Jefferson Barracks, St Louis, and sat himself on a slender trapeze bar. His parachute was packed into a metal tube clamped to the undercarriage. Barry tied himself to the bar and dropped away, his weight pulling the parachute out after him. It was a perfect drop, and a copybook demonstration of how to do it safely. Next year Alphonse Pegoud became the first man in Europe to jump from a plane, and in England

Bottom Left   *A German Fallschirmjaeger equipped with the RZ-Type parachute. The original RZ-1 was superseded by the RZ-16, RZ-20 and RZ-36.*

Bottom Centre   *A night descent with Parachute Type 'X' Equipment. The canopy consisted of 28 panels and measured 28 feet across when laid out on the ground. 28 rigging lines each 25 feet long were brought together below the periphery in four groups each of 7 lines. Having assessed his drift the parachutist by manipulating his left webs could steer himself on to the ground from six directions.*

Bottom Right   *An American T-10 'chute in use by a trooper of the 82nd Airborne Division, Exercise Crusader, West Germany, September 1980. 32 feet in diameter, it has a large canopy and the T-Types have always had an unhealthy reputation for oscillation.*

William Newell shuffled off the landing skid of a Graham-White over Hendon on a cold May evening in 1914, holding a folded Calthrop 'Guardian Angel' parachute in his lap. The newspapers scarcely mentioned his jump, but the London Aeronautical Club gave him a silver medal. By this time Stevens had improved his parachute to the point where he was calling it a 'Life Pack' in anticipation of the fact that it might be adopted for aerial life-saving, and it was already working reliably in the hands of stunt-jumpers.

When World War I broke out, parachutes were still fairground novelties, and for aeroplane crews they remained so throughout the war, the only exceptions being a few German pilots and observers who were issued with a practical and effective seat-pack in late 1917. These were static-line operated parachutes with silk canopies, and their obvious usefulness enraged the Allied pilots who were prevented from having such life-savers by government policy. Even the American pilots were denied parachutes, and there was an outcry when Raoul Lufbery, the first US ace, jumped to his death from a burning plane. The only parachutes allowed to the Allies were those for balloon observers. These were generally 'Guardian Angels', a round canopy 28 feet (8.5 m.) in diameter with rigging lines running to a single suspension point from which the man hung by a rope to his harness.

The canopy was packed into an aluminium cylinder or cone which was carried on the side of the basket with its mouth downwards. A lid closed the opening, and through it ran the attachment rope. The observer wore his harness all the time while in flight and if he had to jump he hooked the rope to himself and stepped over the edge. His weight pulled out the parachute in sequence, rigging lines first, carefully folded, then the canopy, apex last. The canopy inflated gently and took about two seconds to do so. It was perfectly reliable, and in order to publicise its capabilities two officers jumped from a

Bottom Left   *Japanese World War II parachute.*

Bottom Right   *The Italian Salvatore parachute, which is a descendant of the Guardian Angel used by the British and the Italians in World War I.*

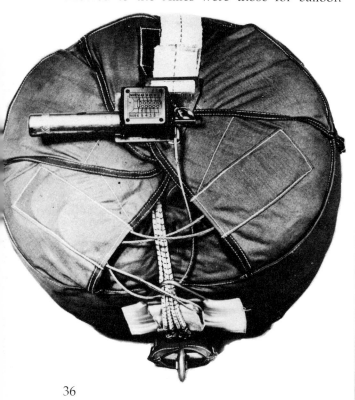

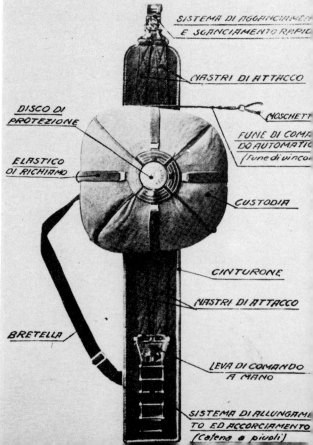

Max Schmeling, the famous German heavy-weight boxing champion leads a stick of German paratroopers to their Ju 52 in 1941. Schmeling took part in the Battle of Crete.

A Whitley in flight, 1941. The third man on the left is sitting next to the hole.

Men of the British 1st Parachute Brigade emplaned in a C-47, North Africa, November 1942, await the order to 'prepare for action'. Note the knee-pads worn in the North African and Middle Eastern theatres.

Top Left   *A German Fallschirmjaeger in position to exit from the port door of a Ju 52.*

Top Right   *This next photograph demonstrates the diving technique the Germans learned to adopt in direct contrast to Allied paratroopers who jumped in an upright position.*

Bottom Right   *The German paratrooper made his descent suspended by two lines attached to the rigging lines of his RZ-Type 'chute so he had scarcely any control of his canopy. He was thus liable to land 'doggy fashion' on 'all fours' resulting if he was unlucky in injury to knees and elbows.*

platform above Tower Bridge, landing safely in the Thames.

The Guardian Angel could also be used from aeroplanes, though the arrangements were clumsy and very similar to those used by Berry in 1912. However, with such a method several brave men were dropped behind the Austrian and German lines to operate as agents. They were dropped at night, and a macabre touch was given by the fact that their canopies were made of black material for better camouflage against the sky. Despite these dramatic and exciting uses, the design and development of parachutes did not advance very far during the war, and it was not until it was over that there was any real progress made.

In 1919 the US Army Air Corps set aside funds for parachute research and set up an investigating team at McCook Field, Ohio. To this team came a civilian enthusiast, a man who was a balloonist and film stunt man. Leslie Irvin was his name, and he made history. On 19 April 1919 Irvin made the first free-fall jump in the world, using a parachute developed by the McCook team. The parachute had a back-pack and a harness carefully designed to spread the shock of opening over the whole body. The Guardian Angel and all similar harnesses were based on a substantial webbing waist belt which not only bruised the jumper, sometimes severely, but also rode up under his arms with the opening pull. At McCook the harness was comprehensive and adjustable and it hung the man from the shoulders. With minor modifications it is still used today.

Development of life-saving parachutes now went ahead with plenty of momentum. Irvin set up his own company and in 1926 moved to Letchworth where he based himself for the remainder of his working life and where the UK Irvin factory still is. Other designs appeared and were tried for the military and civilian markets, but all of them were aimed at the life-saving aspects of the parachute.

A parachute is a means of slowing down a falling body, a fairly obvious statement, but one that is necessary to accept before looking at how they work. A flexible surface such as a parachute canopy is one of the most efficient ways of providing the required air-resisting brake, though the requirements called for are at first sight quite demanding. There has never been a better specification for a parachute than the one given

to Major Hoffman at McCook Airfield in early 1919, and although it is intended for the development of a life-saving parachute, it is worth repeating here since almost every requirement applies equally well to a military parachute.

1. It must make it possible for the aviator to leave the aircraft regardless of the position it might be in when disabled.
2. The operating means must not depend on the aviator falling from the aircraft.
3. The parachute equipment must be fastened to the body of the aviator at all times while he is in the aircraft.
4. Operating the parachute must be simple. It must not fail nor be liable to damage under service conditions.
5. The parachute must be of such a size and so disposed as to give the maximum comfort to the wearer and allow him to leave the aircraft without difficulty.
6. It must open promptly and be capable of withstanding the shock incurred by a 200-pound (90-kg.) load falling at 400 mph. (844 kph.).
7. It must be reasonably steerable.
8. The harness must be comfortable and very strong, and designed so as to transfer the shock of opening without injury to the airman. It must be sufficiently adjustable so as to fit large or small people.
9. The harness must prevent the airman from falling out when the parachute opens, and it must be possible for him to remove it quickly on landing in water or a high wind.
10. The strength of the 'follow through' must be uniform to the top of the parachute.
11. The parachute must be simple in construction and be easily packed with the least time and labour.

Faced with a list like that anyone might be excused if he faltered, but Irvin satisfied them all with his design, and probably the easiest way of explaining the working of a modern military parachute is to follow these requirements one by one and explain how they are met with in today's models.

The first two are obviously specialised requirements for a life-saving parachute, and the second one was no doubt aimed at the Guardian Angel type of parachute which was definitely sensitive to the direction of the pull of the rigging lines. A Guardian Angel that was placed so as to be opened when a man fell below the plane would not open reliably if the man fell out when the plane was upside down. For a military parachute, however, it is highly desirable that the opening should be independent of the man.

The military parachutist does not want to do more than the barest minimum to operate his parachute, and he also needs it to work as quickly as possible so that he wastes no height while it opens. The static-line is therefore ideal, since it can start the opening sequence within a few feet of leaving the plane. The Russians used ripcord parachutes for their first demonstration jumps, and it was noticeable that they had to fly in at above 1000 feet (305 m.) to allow every man time to pull the ripcord. There is a famous photograph of Russian jumpers sliding off the wing of an ANT-3, controlled by a man in the nose holding a flag. However, this method did not last after the 1930s, and now all military jumps, except for a tiny number of highly-specialised free-falls, are made with static-lines.

The fourth requirement is obviously paramount – the parachute must open without fail. The best way of doing this is to keep everything simple, and that is now the accepted practice. There are two main ways of opening a parachute: the canopy-first and the canopy-last. Canopy-first is the usual way with life-saving parachutes, as it is quicker, uses less height, is well suited to a compact pack and packs into a small pack.

Canopy-first, as its name implies, withdraws the canopy as soon as the pack is opened. This may be done by a static-line, or by a small pilot parachute which is sprung open by a spring. Whichever method is used, the apex of the main canopy is pulled out, followed by the entire canopy, which then rapidly starts to inflate in the airstream. The rigging lines are stowed in the base of the pack, and once the canopy is clear of the pack they are pulled out from their stowages by the man falling away. He is stopped fairly abruptly by the lines tightening, and then the canopy fills completely and normal flight begins. Some parachutes filled their canopies almost before the rigging lines were taut, and with those the jerk on the falling man could be enough to leave small bruises on the body, often at the shoulders where the main force comes.

Canopy-last is the method pioneered by the Guardian Angel, the original Salvatore, and others which had their basis in the ballooning days. Here the opening sequence is the reverse of the Irvin. The rigging lines pay out as the man falls away and only when the lines are fully deployed and running in a straight line above his head does the canopy start to emerge from its stowage. It comes out with the periphery, or outside edge, first, so that it presents an open mouth to the airstream and starts to fill with air the moment it appears. The apex is usually held in the bag with slight tie so as to be sure that it comes out last, when for a brief moment the entire parachute is stretched out above the man. Then the apex tie breaks, or it slips off, and the whole parachute is free with its canopy filling fast. It then slows down progressively and steadily, taking a second or so to do so, and exerting an even pull on the lift webs so that there is none of the jerk associated with the canopy-first arrangement, but there is a greater loss of height.

For a life-saving parachute speed of opening can be critical, and a man whose life has been saved is unlikely to carp at a few bruises. A soldier, on the other hand, who has to make many jumps in his life and who has to carry weapons and equipment requires the least opening shock and the most comfortable jump that can be made. He can afford another hundred feet or so in his jump height, if that is needed, and in return he is able to offer the parachute designer the fact that he will jump from a stable platform, travelling at a known and fairly low speed and will always be in one position in the air when the parachute is opening. This makes the designer's job far easier, and both sides can be satisfied. Almost without exception military airborne forces around the world use a parachute with the same broad principles of working.

A modern military parachute is so designed that all the wearer has to do is to jump through the door of the plane in the correct manner and fall away in a reasonably upright position. No parachute in the world can be expected to open properly if the man is tumbling head over heels as the lines pay out, so much time and trouble is taken in the training period to get the men to jump well clear of the sides of the plane and to keep a rigid and straight posture in the air until the canopy develops. Keeping straight also helps to reduce the opening shock, because the harness is meant to work best when the man is upright. If he is standing on his head when the lines tighten then he is jerked up, and his load will be pulled away from him.

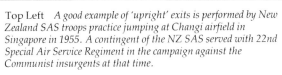

Top Left   *A good example of 'upright' exits is performed by New Zealand SAS troops practice jumping at Changi airfield in Singapore in 1955. A contingent of the NZ SAS served with 22nd Special Air Service Regiment in the campaign against the Communist insurgents at that time.*

Top Right   *A trooper of 22nd SAS demonstrates the abseiling equipment used for descending to the ground after parachuting on to the matted surface of the trees in dense jungle. The photograph was taken at Coronation Park, Kuala Lumpur, 1957.*

Bottom Right   *A Laotian parachutist in French service in Indo-China in 1952 calmly awaits 'Action Stations'.*

Top   *Interior of an RAF Blackburn Beverley in 1962; the nets had recently been introduced for the safety and comfort of the troops.*

Top   *The Irvin PX.1 Mk4 which has now replaced the famous Irvin X-Type. The PX.1 is 32 ft flat in diameter and has 32 gores. As its precursor, it is a static-line-operated parachute assembly.*

Bottom   *A mass waterjump off Tel Aviv's shore line, August 1969. The torpedo boat is picking up the parachutists, including 35 women, whose principal concern was to release themselves from their parachute harnesses on impact with the water.*

Bottom   *1974, Fort Stewart, Georgia. A Ranger floats in to the Drop Zone (DZ).*

Military parachuting started in Italy with a derivative of the Guardian Angel. The Italians had used this parachute in the war and had adopted it for their own use afterwards. They improved it to some extent by fitting it with an alternative opening arrangement so that it could be either ripcord or static-line. They also put the canopy into a back-pack so that the jumper carried the parachute on him, but in making this change they were forced to alter the opening characteristics of the canopy and it now came out first, inflating before the rigging lines were fully deployed and giving the parachutist a sharp jolt as he took up the slack. This is why they were forced to change the opening characteristics and go to canopy-first. It was to be another thirty years before successful canopy-last. They thus lost some of the more attractive aspects of the Guardian Angel, and in fact they also lost another useful facet, which was the relatively modest rate of descent. By putting the canopy into a back-pack there was less space and the diameter was reduced to 23 feet (7 m.) across the uninflated diameter, and it flew with a diameter of roughly 15 feet (4.6 m.) giving a dropping speed with an average man of 20 ft/sec (6 m./sec). This was not bad, though modern military parachutes tend to drop rather more slowly than that, and there was the difficulty of the harness, which was modified Angel pattern, with the emphasis on the waist belt and a single point of suspension from the back of the neck to the collecting point of the sixteen suspension lines. This parachute was known as the Model D-30 and it was made, as were all its successors, by the firm of SAA (Societa Aerostatica Avorio).

The D-30 was replaced by the D-37 which had a much improved harness based on the Irvin. However, it was still rather too small a canopy for military jumping, and it too was replaced in 1940 by the D-40 which had a canopy of 20 per cent greater area and a correspondingly better descent rate. The opportunity was also taken to improve the static-line operation and the opening characteristics of the canopy, as there had been a disturbing number of failures with the older models leading to injuries and some deaths. In fact the D-30 was not an easy parachute to use. The opening shock was transmitted direct to the main webbing belt and thus to the middle of the body, so that it was not unusual for the man to be almost winded from the effects of his parachute opening. After that

beginning he had to prepare himself for the landing, which was fairly fast and not easily controlled. In any wind speed above 10 ft/sec. (3 m./sec.) the risk of minor sprains or broken ankles was high. The most serious defect of the D-30, however, was that the man could not carry any weapon with him beyond a pistol. It was the same position as with the German parachutists, the opening shock, rate of descent and landing attitude all dictated that the man must be as lightly loaded as possible and left with arms and legs free for the gymnastic feat of rolling as he hit the ground.

In Russia parachuting started with ripcord types, and they all seem to have been a copy of the original Irvin pattern. A feature of the Russian parachuting is that from the very beginning they carried a reserve, and to all intents and purposes it seems to be permanently attached to the harness in much the same way as the main canopy on the back. The main set of harness webs were doubled, one set was attached to the main canopy and the other to the reserve, which made for great strength and reliability in the harness, but it complicated the packing of either canopy. Many of these Russian canopies were square, a shape that looks as though it might be easier and simpler to make, but in fact it is not so, and it also suffers from the drawback that the opening is slower and so takes more height. The advantage of the square canopy is that it is stable in flight and gives a remarkably smooth descent. The Soviet versions left two rigging lines out at the middle of the back edge so that the material of the canopy arched up when it was flying and allowed some air to escape, giving a slow forward push. Nevertheless, round canopies were used just as frequently, and quite often the two types were mixed on one harness, square for the main and round for the reserve. Another Russian peculiarity was that they taught jumpers to use both canopies at the same time, and it is common to see pre-war photographs of Russian parachutists descending on two canopies, with the front one flying well out in front.

Static-line opening did not seem to come into general use in Russia until the very late 1930s, but it was well established when the Soviet Army made its few operational drops during the war. By this time the technique of jumping had become very similar to that of other countries, and planes with doors were used in preference to the uncomfortable pre-war habits of climbing out

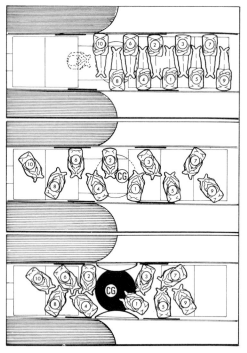

Whitley V jump positions.

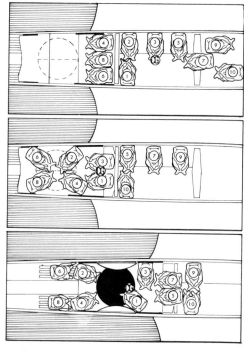

Wellington jump positions.

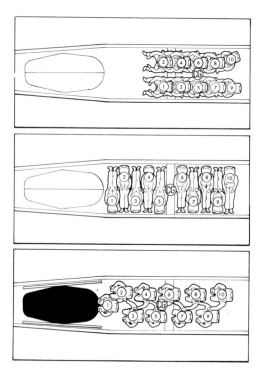

The Albemarle jump positions. The paratroopers hopped like bunnies to the coffin-shaped exit hole.

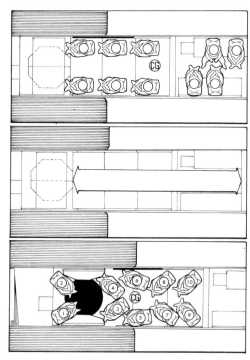

Halifax jump positions.

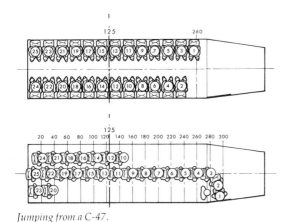

Jumping from a C-47.

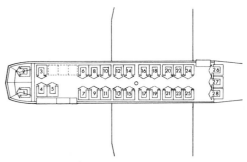

Horsa I seating plan.

of cockpits or hatches. The great bulk of the Russian canopies arose from the fact that they were made from rayon or silk. Silk is an ideal material, as it packs well and unfolds without retaining any creases, but it is bulky, and with a large canopy such as one of 28 ft (8.5 m.) diameter the size of the back-pack becomes all but unmanageable inside the plane. For this reason many pre-war 'chutes were smaller. Rayon is nearly as bulky and it was not until nylon was perfected in the late years of the war that the ideal material was found.

Modern Russian parachutes are much like any other in the world, and the square shape has disappeared entirely. As we now know, square canopies are no easier or cheaper to make than round ones, so any apparent advantage in that direction was lost. Nevertheless, some peculiarly Russian features are retained with their military 'chutes. The habit of combining main and reserve into one complete equipment still persists, though their sport jumpers use modern and sophisticated gear. The military parachutist may also have a ripcord as well as a static-line, though all photographs of men jumping on exercises show the dropping height to be well below what we would consider as safe for a ripcord opening and it is obvious that static-lines are used on these occasions. So there is a slight mystery about the ripcords. It may be that the ripcords are part of an automatic opening device. For many years the Soviets have fitted a safety device which is meant to open the parachute if other means fail, but even this theory is difficult to square with a dropping height of around 1000 feet (305 m.) for this simply is not the time for any

safety gadget to work. Anyway, the man carries a reserve for those occasions. As the Soviets keep their airborne troops well out of sight of Western observers in the middle of the country, the chances of solving these little queries are not good.

When the German airborne forces were started in 1936, there was a small reservoir of knowledge on which to base the equipment design. The German Air Force had kept in close touch with the Russians throughout the 1920s, as one way of avoiding the restrictions of the Versailles Treaty; there had been some exchanges of information and some training was undertaken in Russia also. The Germans therefore must have had some basis from which to start, yet they chose to develop a parachute that was radically different from any used by the Russians. In fact, the first German military parachute, the RZ-1, has more in common with the Italian D-30 than with any other. It was a small diameter 24 ft (7.3 m.) canopy with single-point suspension, canopy-first opening and a harness that was a variant of the World War I broad webbing belt. There were two substantial D rings on the belt, one at each side, and hooked to each was the end of a rope which ran to the main suspension point, just above the top of the head. The effect of this arrangement was that the man hung slightly face-downwards in a curve, looking, as some classical wag immediately remarked, just like the Golden Fleece or a large sack of potatoes.

It was the ideal position for a face-first landing, and the standard German teaching was to take the landing with a forward roll. The parachutist jerked himself round as he neared the ground so that he faced downwind and so looked towards the direction of drift. The motion of this turn was not unlike swimming, and it took a little skill to

45

get the timing right. He then prepared to take the shock of arrival on feet and hands and go straight into his roll. It was a fair gymnastic feat, and it required the man to be fit, alert, agile and strong, but more significantly for the military purpose of the jump it completely denied the possibility of carrying anything about the body without running the risk of painful injury. At first the Germans jumped with a pistol and two grenades, but after their experiences in Holland they also carried sub-machine-guns which were tucked into the front of the harness, together with three or four magazines.

The RZ-1 was replaced by the RZ-16 in 1941 and the RZ-20, the latter being the one used until the end of the war, and both of these variants had changes made to the pack and the opening method of the static-line. The German static-line was a length of rope which ran from the centre of the pack, and in some photographs the men can be seen climbing into their planes with the rope held in their teeth so that they have both hands free. One disadvantage of the RZ parachutes was that they were not well suited to use by anyone who had not been thoroughly trained in how to jump with them. To make a safe landing the man needed to be fit and also to be in training with his reflexes tuned. In fact, the RZ parachutes were just about out of date when the war started, but by then there was no time to change and they limited the full use of the German airborne soldier in all his operations. It is interesting that in the post-war German parachute army the equipment and parachutes are predominantly American in origin and, of course, canopy-last opening.

The Japanese entered World War II with aircrew safety parachutes derived from the Irvin, and for their first experiments they simply added a static-line to the ripcord extension, and promptly suffered the same series of mishaps and failures as did anyone else who used that method. Their first military parachute was the Type 1 of 1941 which was specifically designed for the job and probably owed something to the German RZ series. The canopy was 28 ft (8.5 m.) in diameter and shaped so that it flew with a pronounced hemispherical appearance. There was a large vent and a prominent skirt so that it is reasonable to suppose that it was stable in flight. The harness was a modified Irvin, but the later Type 3 abandoned the lift webs of the Irvin and brought the rigging lines to a single point just

46

A photograph of an SAS trooper issued by the GQ Parachute Co., Woking, Surrey, fitted out with High Altitude Low Opening (Halo) jump equipment. His 'kit bag' is carried to the rear. With the decline in the rôle of conventional parachute troops, the free-fall military parachutist assigned in small parties to Special Forces represents the parachute soldier of the future.

behind the man's neck, where they met in a large steel D ring. On this parachute the pack was closed by a single pin which was attached to the static-line, a surprising way of arranging the opening, because the Japanese must have known that this method is dangerous and liable to failure. The static-line pulled the canopy out by means of a light line tied to the apex, and the opening must have then been a mixture of canopy-first and canopy-last in which, presumably, the canopy opened as the lines paid out, but for safety's sake would need to remain on the static-line tie until it was well out of the pack. It all sounds a bit odd, and it is noticeable that the few operational jumps made by the Japanese were all at a good height.

Each man carried a 24 ft (7.3 m.) reserve in a chest-pack, although the naval parachutist training programme called for jumps at 500 and 300 feet (150 and 90 m.), neither of which gave a chance of operating a reserve, or for that matter allowing for any hesitation in the opening of the main canopy.

When the Japanese airborne troops were started up again in the early 1960s, they were entirely equipped with US parachutes, and they have remained with this equipment ever since. They are therefore jumping today with American parachutes from American planes and, generally speaking, carrying American weapons.

The American Army started late in the parachute business, but, as with so many things in that country, once they realised the value of the airborne method of attack they took to it wholeheartedly. In the very beginning a Test Platoon was formed at Fort Benning and under the command of a Major William Lee it first of all trained from the tower left from the 1939 World Fair in New Jersey using the parachutes provided for the public. This was unrealistic, though it was an excellent introduction, and the next move was to take the existing aircrew Irvin T-4 and modify it for static-line. The harness was very good for its day, and was fully adjustable for any size of man. It fastened in front by three snap hooks and, whilst it was not the easiest harness to get out of in a hurry, it was a long way ahead of any other at that time. The canopy was a 28 ft (8.5 m.) diameter flat circular design of no special features, and to the harness were permanently fixed the lift webs for the reserve which was worn by every man from the start of all training. These early reserves were bulky and heavy and flopped about on the front harness, and in contemporary photographs the jumpers are usually holding them in with one hand as they move about.

With these modified aircrew 'chutes there was no effective way of carrying more than a pistol and the very minimum of personal equipment, so all other gear, including rifles, had to be dropped in containers. This was unsatisfactory as by now it was clear that the weakness of the German system was that the men had to search the drop zone for their container before they were effectively armed for a battle. With this in mind, and also because the T-4 was not proving reliable, another parachute was produced in 1941. This was the T-7, and it was a distinct improvement since it was specifically meant for military parachuting and for operation by a static-line. It kept the three-point harness because that was successful, but it also kept the canopy-first opening, which it might have better avoided. However, the opening shock was not too bad and it allowed men to carry equipment on their bodies. The rate of descent was reasonably slow and the harness comfortable. The Irvin reserve was carried high up on the stomach, and it allowed enough room for a small equipment bag to hang below it and not get in the way on landing.

The T-7 opened quickly and on one or two occasions it needed to. For instance in July 1944 a battalion of the 503rd Parachute Infantry was dropped on to Noemfoor Island just off the north-west tip of New Guinea. Both men and aircrew were lacking in training and the planes flew in over the drop zone in a loose straggling formation and at any height from 200 feet (60 m.) upwards. The T-7 saved the lives of the low jumpers by opening in time, and because the men had no leg bags or any other sort of container to lower below themselves they survived, but a few had almost reached the tree tops before their canopies fully opened. Others, less fortunate, fell into high trees, and they were all casualties; but the majority must have agreed that the shock of a T-7 opening was worth while.

Probably the most common criticism of the T-7 was that it was not easy to get out of the harness when being dragged on the ground. All three snap hooks had to be undone, and a slightly concussed or flustered jumper often found it beyond him. By the end of the war there was a modified harness with one quick-release box, copied from the British X-type, and the reserve was a much neater and smaller size which clipped to the front of the harness and the long clumsy extra lift webs were abandoned.

After the war came further improvements and the T-10 was in service by the late 1950s. This was a canopy-last opening parachute, the first to be on issue to US forces, and it also had a larger canopy. It was now up to 32 feet (9.7 m.) diameter with a further reduction in descent speed and the capacity to carry even heavier loads. With the T-10 the US jumper could, and does, carry quite considerable weights of equipment, and he can also lower equipment bags beneath him. This is the parachute which is still in use in the US Army and in many other countries around the world, including a substantial proportion of NATO. It now has a single release box for the harness, and another useful innovation involves the shoulder releases which allow a

man to rid himself entirely of his canopy if being dragged on the ground. This is a quick and safe way of preventing dragging, and because the canopy can be separated from the rest of the harness it makes for easier packing and general handling in the parachute sheds.

As with so many other vital war equipments, the British had taken no steps to prepare an airborne force, although in 1936 Geoffrey Quilter (later knighted) offered a practical static-line parachute to the War Office. He was brushed aside, however, and told that there was no need for such things. So it came about that when Sir Winston Churchill called for his 5000 volunteer parachutists in the summer of 1940 the only parachutes for them were a few hundred ripcord types from the RAF. These were converted to a static-line and soon there was the usual crop of accidents and fatalities. Within five days of the first fatality a modified version of the 1936 GQ design was being tried and it proved itself to be an ideal parachute from the very start. It was the first practical canopy-last opening parachute to be used from a plane, and in many of its basic principles it was the same as the Guardian Angel; though with the Statichute, as it was called, the entire parachute was in the pack on the man's back, and the only connection with the plane was by the static-line. This, it will be remembered, was the reverse of the Angel method.

The Statichute operated in the way that has already been described for canopy-last opening, and it gave a smooth, progressive opening with little shock and few twists and an encouragingly high safety record. This was necessary, for the British never jumped with reserves. There are various reasons for this, none of them very good, but all of them applicable to the emergency times in which the whole idea was conceived. British parachutists had to use the unsuitable Whitley bomber and jump through a 3 ft (1 m.) diameter hole in the floor. With just one parachute it was difficult enough; with two it would have been impossible. Having started without a reserve and found it to be not entirely necessary, there was no compelling reason to adopt one when the

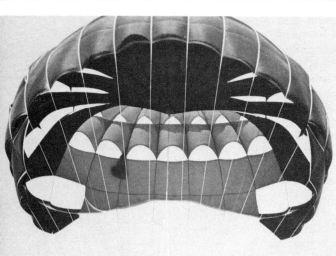

Two types of Tactical Assault Parachute designed for the SAS and SBS.

Whitley gave way to the Dakota. In any case, there was always a shortage of war materials of all kinds in Britain throughout the war, and to have to make two parachutes for each man would have delayed the training and formation of the airborne units even longer.

There is another and less obvious reason for the lack of reserves at least in the early stages. When the British started their training centre, they only had the example of the Germans to follow, and the first developments all look suspiciously like German ones. Since the Germans never carried reserves, neither did the British, and it is just possible that this was the original thinking behind the single British parachute. Anyway, the Statichute, or its derivatives, worked amazingly well and their accident record is astonishingly low. It was so low in fact that up to the mid-1950s, when the reserve was introduced, the instructors at the RAF Training School used to solemnly aver, and produce statistics in support of this, that it was more dangerous to cross the road in London on foot than make a parachute jump. They were probably lying, but they had the grace to say it with a straight face, and the author made the best part of 500 jumps with only one parachute and never felt the slightest qualm.

The Statichute soon became the X-Type, a slightly improved version, and in this form it stayed almost without modification until superseded by the larger PX in the early 1960s, a longer run than any other military parachute ever produced. It had its drawbacks. For one thing, it was not the easiest parachute to pack, though this was a skill that could be learned to perfection with practice, and the WAAF packers could produce a first-class job in about twenty-five minutes. A Guardian Angel took two hours with a skilled man. The X-Type occasionally gave a 'lazy opening' which might take the parachutist to within a few feet of the ground before the canopy fully inflated, and there were several other ills which could occur from the canopy developing in the airstream. Chief among these was the notorious 'Mae West' or 'Blown Periphery', in which the canopy turned itself partially inside out by passing through some of the rigging lines before they had taken up the tension of the load, and so there would be a 'thrown line', as it was called, over the top of the canopy. This produced the characteristic double hemisphere from which came the vernacular

'Wait for me, Sergeant York!' A Lady paratrooper of the 82nd Airborne Division clears the Sicily Drop Zone at Fort Bragg, N.C. in impeccable order after the first ever all-female parachute jump. (Even though a 'leg' or non-airborne man, Alvin C. York and his adventures at Châtel-Chéréry in the Argonne in the fall of 1918 still make him the most-famous soldier of the 82nd of all time.)

name, and it also reduced the effective area of the canopy so that the jumper came down that much harder. Mae Wests were not popular.

Probably the greatest drawback of the X-Type was that it was sensitive to dropping speed, and though it could be used at speeds of 120 mph (193 kph) the risk of Mae Wests and other similar malfunctions went up, and the best dropping speed was at around 100 mph (160 kph) or less if possible. The Whitley, for all its other faults, could fly at around 70 mph (112 kph), and the Dakota was not much faster on the run-in; and these were most forgiving machines. The Dakota especially would allow the most appalling exit to be made and still the 'chute would open without trouble. Try that now in the modern high-speed planes which drop at 130 mph (209 kph) or even more, and see what the blast of air in the slip-stream does to you!

The development of the X-Type took some time, and it was not finally free of all vices until early in 1942, the last of its troubles being a tendency to twist the rigging line when dropped from a plane. At times this became so bad that it collapsed the canopy altogether with unfortunate results to the man, but it was cured before the first large airborne operations. The next substantial contribution that the British made to parachuting was in the method of landing. With only the German example to follow, the first courses had all tried to hit the ground in either forward or backward roll, and the risk of injury was high—in fact very high. Trainees of that time have left their impressions of what it was like to make a landing using the roll method: one likened it to falling off a galloping horse, another to skiing, but the most colourful description comes from a man who said it was like jumping backwards off the top deck of a London bus travelling at 20 mph (32 kph). He was quite right too; there are times when it feels like that. With the German type of roll landing, however, a top deck bus jump is dangerous, and men were hitting the ground with a hell of a bang. The ambulance was the busiest vehicle on the dropping zone.

Flight Lieutenant Kilkenny of the RAF Physical Fitness Branch is the man who altered the entire philosophy of landing from a parachute. He carefully analysed the physical stresses involved in a man's body hitting the ground, and stipulated that the objective should be to develop a controlled collapse of the body either to the right or the left, with the impact being spread over the longest possible stretch of those parts of the body best suited to receive it. The first contact was to be with the two feet pressed tightly together to form a single column with the legs, then on the side of the thigh and hip, and lastly over the rounded shoulders with the head and arms tucked in out of the way. It was not a standard exercise found in any PT book, but strangely enough it had been known and practised for years by stage and film stuntmen without their realising that they were using the most efficient method of falling. They just knew that that was the way not to get hurt.

Kilkenny put his ideas into practice during the winter of 1941 and 1942 and it is now the almost universal way of landing from a military parachute. Every country has introduced its own minor changes, but in the essentials it is Kilkenny's landing that soldiers are taught from Canada to China and from Bangladesh to Brazil.

Fallschirmjäger in Battle 20–24 May 1941

Top Left
DFS 230 glider approaching the ground.

Top Right
Men of the 7th Air Division tumble from Ju 52 aircraft.

Centre Right
Approaching the ground.

Bottom Right
The paratrooper in the foreground has located an equipment container.

Bottom Left
A paratrooper lying dead on the ground with his 'chute collapsed after landing in a tree.

Top Right
Riflemen take aim in a posed shot for the benefit of the cameraman.

Centre Right
Troops of the 5th Mountain Division land from a Ju 52 after the seizure of Malème airfield.

Bottom Right
Riflemen using a low wall for cover.

Bottom Left
Recce party with MG 34 Machine-gunner in the centre.

Personal Weapons and Equipment

Landing the soldier by parachute is only half the story. Once he is on the ground he has to fight like any other soldier, and for this he needs his weapons, a supply of ammunition and some means of communicating with his own units and with the aircraft that are bringing in more men and supplies. He needs some sort of supporting fire, whether by mortars, artillery, machine-guns or all of these; and finally he needs some means of moving or carrying all these diverse pieces of equipment, for their combined weight will run to many tons. So, although the arrival by parachute of an airborne force is always exciting and dramatic, it is only one part of a logistical operation that involves the tiresome humping of large quantities of military stores from one place to another and the highly specialised delivery of these stores to the battlefield and the men meant to receive them.

However, the lowest possible factor in this movement exercise is the man himself. He needs to have his personal weapons with him when he lands and starts the battle, and even this comparatively modest demand was almost more than could be managed with the first airborne armies. In 1936 Major General Wavell commented that the Russian soldiers who took part in the public demonstration were only carrying light weapons, and that some had not carried anything at all. The Germans found themselves in the same difficulty. The restrictions of the RZ parachute and the awkward door of the Junkers 52 made it almost impossible for the man to carry more than a pistol and a couple of grenades, and all other weapons and equipment went into long box-like containers which were carried under the wings of the plane and dropped by the navigator, using a standard bomb-switch. Each container was 5 feet (1·52 m.) long and about 16 inches (0·4 m.) square in section. Fully loaded it weighed 260 lbs (118 kg) and was dropped on one parachute canopy which packed into a pack on the top. On the bottom was a metal crash pan which collapsed on hitting the ground. The container opened along its length and the contents were packed with thick felt or some other shock-absorbing material (often it had to be straw).

A German platoon needed fourteen containers for all their weapons and ammunition, which meant that there was a lot of running about on the drop zone while men looked for their containers and unpacked them. This explains the little groups of men which occasionally appear in genuine action photographs, and which rarely appear in posed training pictures! In Crete the British and Commonwealth troops were already familiar with the need for the parachutists to rally round their containers before they became an effective fighting force, and they merely watched for the coloured canopies of the containers and laid their machine-guns on them after they had landed.

Not every container had to be unpacked on the spot. Mortar ammunition for instance could be left intact, and in these cases the container had a pair of small wheels inside the lid which could be quickly fitted and with the aid of a small tow-bar two men could drag the container off the drop zone to where it was needed. The same was done for radios and the light guns that were tried for artillery support. Nevertheless, however the containers were moved, they were a severe handicap to the German airborne units, and they undoubtedly limited the tactical flexibility of the troops, and increased the casualties on the drop zone. The difficulty for the Germans was that they had started with the Junkers and had built so many of them that there was simply none other, and the restrictions of the small door were a large factor in preventing much experiment. The other factor was the parachute, and to enable the man to carry a load the entire stock of RZ parachutes would have had to be scrapped and a new design made. Neither Goering nor anyone else was prepared to admit that the design was so far wrong that it needed that sort of revision, and the *Fallschirmjaeger* had to put up with it.

Although the parachutists were armed with standard weapons of the *Wehrmacht*, they also developed and used some of their own. It was the parachutists who first took to the sub-

53

Typical German equipment container.

machine-gun in quantity, and in 1940 they made the MP 38 as well known as is the Kalashnikov today. The *Fallschirmjaeger*, however, realised at a very early stage that their main requirement was for maximum firepower as soon after landing as possible, and this was not easily gained with the existing small arms of the *Wehrmacht*. The old bolt-action Mauser carbine was particularly ill suited to parachute operations, but there were no others. A specification was therefore drawn up for an automatic rifle especially for parachutists, and because they came under command of the *Luftwaffe* the parachutists were able to push it through against Army opposition and get it made. This remarkable weapon was the *Fallschirmjaeger Gewehr* 42, or FG 42, and it was intended to be a combination of rifle and light machine-gun, capable of being used as either. Unfortunately it fell between the two stools and was never entirely successful, though it showed astonishing ingenuity in its design and was well ahead of all contemporary thought and

54

practice. The main difficulty was that it needed metals that were not then developed fully, and the ammunition it fired was too powerful so that the mechanism broke too easily. One interesting feature of it is that it was obviously never intended that it should be carried on the man when parachuting since there were no arrangements for folding the butt or taking it to pieces, and one presumes that from the start it would have arrived in battle in a container.

The other weapon specifically intended for parachute troops was the light recoilless artillery pieces. Krupp had been experimenting with the recoilless principle for some years before 1939, and in 1940 they made their first practical light gun, the *Leicht Geschoss* 40. It was in 75 mm calibre and only weighed about 300 lbs (136 kg) complete. It broke into three loads for parachuting in the standard containers and its two wheels gave it reasonable mobility. It could be man-handled or towed by a motorcycle combination. It was quite a useful support gun and it fired a 12½-lb (5·7-kg) shell out to 6800 metres a well as having a solid shot for anti-armour work. It did not fire from a trail like a normal artillery gun, but let down three legs to make a tripod very similar to that of a machine-gun, and it was strictly meant for the close support of infantry in difficult conditions.

Mountain troops used it as well as the parachutists, and it was first tried in Crete. By all accounts it did well, but since there were no sizeable airborne or mountain operations after Crete it faded from the scene. There were two other recoilless guns, both meant for parachute troops and both showing plenty of promise, but they came after the LG 40 and so were probably not made in any numbers at all. One was a lighter version of the LG 40 weighing 95 lbs (43 kg) and firing an 8½-lb (3·9-kg) shell to 2000 metres, and the other was a 105 mm version weighing 1150 lbs (522 kg) and firing a 27-lb (12·2-kg) shell out to 8000 metres, but it was abandoned before it was perfected. In any case, it was probably too heavy for its main purpose, and perhaps the lightened LG 40 was too light and short in range.

The ordinary 81 mm mortar of the *Wehrmacht* could do rather better than the little recoilless gun, so perhaps it was a blind alley of development.

The Japanese Army and Navy both developed their own airborne forces and there is some evidence that right from the beginning neither

Top Right   *Mauser Kar 98K Carbine and Stick grenades.*

Top Left   *A Fallschirmjaeger in action in France in 1944 with an MP 40 Machine-Carbine.*

Left Centre Top   *MG 42 machine-gunners sight a target in Sicily in 1943.*

Left Centre Bottom   *Monte Cassino, 1944. German paratroopers operating a 10 cm Nebelwerfer 35 Mortar.*

Bottom Left   *A German paratrooper armed with an Italian Beretta M 38/42 Sub-machine-gun: 'Invasion front—Normandy', June 1944.*

55

Top Left *Sten machine-carbine demonstrated by British paratrooper.*

Top Right *MG 34 Machine-Gun team in Holland in 1940.*

Right Centre Top *RAF Lysander aircraft about to take off to drop a supply container to the Resistance in France.*

Right Centre Bottom *A 'Red Devil' mans a Vickers Mk 1 Machine-Gun in the North African Campaign in early 1943.*

Bottom Right *3-inch Mortar layout ready for airborne despatch.*

Bottom Left *British bombcell weapons container with a .303 Lee Enfield Rifle and Bren gun on the right.*

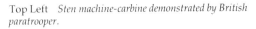

French SAS in action in Holland in the winter of 1944–45 with a PIAT and its Hollow Charge Bomb.

service was quite clear how to use them. The Navy plumped for short-term raids intentionally in support of amphibious landings, and never intended its parachutists to do more than create a diversion inland from the beaches while the main assault came in from the sea. Carried to its logical conclusion and properly used, such a tactical policy had a lot to recommend it in the Pacific and on the very few occasions when it was used. The airfield at Menado in January 1942 is the best example: it was entirely successful. In 1944 the idea was repeated on Leyte with the express intention of disabling airfields so that an amphibious landing could be made free from US air attacks; but by now it was too late for simple raiding forces with only light arms, and the American defenders massacred the parachutists. The Japanese Navy failed to keep up with the changes in warfare and the equipment and tactics of 1941 were fatal in 1944. As with so many other aspects of World War II, the Japanese war machine was not geared up sufficiently to fight a major war, nor could the country's industry cope with the volume of arms and equipment that was needed. Something had to give way, and with all the concentration on the Army and the Navy, airborne forces were pushed to the back of the queue.

There was, however, some concern for the parachutists' weapons, and almost from the start of their airborne force the Japanese tried to give it weapons suited to its special rôle. The difficulty was that in Japan there was little if any spare factory capacity for new designs and the only course open was to adapt the existing ones so that they could be carried on the man while jumping. The Japanese realised that containers were a weakness in any airborne assault and though they were forced to use them throughout the war they tried to parachute each man with his own weapon and a basic amount of ammunition for it. To do this the standard platoon weapons were adapted by making them fold into the smallest possible space. The Type 99 rifle was hinged at the small of the butt, as was the light machine-gun and the sub-machine-gun. The Type 99 rifle was arranged so that it came into two separate pieces by taking off the barrel from a point just forward of the breech. The Type 99 light machine-gun was made to fold at the small of the butt as was the sub-machine-gun. These weapons, together with their respective bayonets, were capable of being carried in a large flat pack strapped to the man's chest. A reserve parachute could be clipped over this pack, though it cannot have been a very comfortable arrangement, and the man was ready for battle. Landing must have been rough, but it would have been worth while enduring it for the comfort of having one's weapons immediately to hand.

In addition to these folding small arms there was the Grenade Launcher, which was really a small mortar. It packed into the chest-pack without any modification, but the man carrying it could then only protect himself with a pistol. All other weapons had to be dropped in containers, and apart from the early assaults in 1942 it is clear that Allied AA fire invariably scattered the aircraft so that the drop was spread out over a wide area and the containers were lost. However, the reports of Japanese airborne operations against the US and Allied positions after 1943 are little better than catalogues of disasters, and whether or not the containers had been recovered would not have altered the outcome.

An American parachute officer tests a Johnson M 41 Machine-Gun at Quantico, Virginia, in 1941. The inventor Melvin M. Johnson is the civilian in the foreground.

The American Bazooka M 9 in action in France in 1944.

.30 Browning Machine-Gun manned by Airborne men at Bastogne, winter 1944.

This American World War II airborne layout includes the T-Type 'chute and Reserve, Springfield Rifle with Grenade launching attachment, Anti-tank rifle grenades M 8, Colt .45 pistol M 1911, Hand Grenades M 1, Field Ration 'D' and a Machete.

There is one clue to show that the Japanese did at least experiment with other methods of carrying their weapons, and this clue is in a newspaper photograph found in a Manila office in 1945 showing parachutists sitting in an unidentifiable plane holding what are quite clearly weapon sleeves, apparently made of some sort of canvas. Whether these were lowered below the man when he jumped cannot be discovered from the picture, but it is an interesting indication that there was some development into the carriage of weapons after 1941.

In Italy the parachutists carried exactly the same weapons as the infantry, and there was the same difficulty in arranging for their delivery on to the drop zone, but the *Folgore* Division carried out experiments and as early as 1941 the individual parachutist was able to carry his rifle or light machine-gun in a strong canvas sleeve which he lowered below him after his canopy developed. He held the weapon to his side for the actual jump, with the lower end stuck in a canvas bucket on his ankle and the upper end under his arm. The sleeve was attached to his harness by a rope braided up into slip knots; these gave a degree of shock-absorption when he dropped the sleeve in flight and the knots pulled out. This method of carriage was a significant step forward, and was ahead of anyone else at that time, but the other difficulties of the D-40 parchute and the apparent lack of interest in Italian airborne forces prevented the idea going much further.

The Italian marine parachutists of the Regia Marina carried their equipment in a novel way. They were armed with a large proportion of

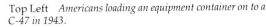

Top Left Americans loading an equipment container on to a C-47 in 1943.

Left Centre Top Japanese Ariska airborne rifle in World War II.

Left Centre Bottom 7.62 mm German MG 3 Machine-Gun; the post-war version of the MG 42.

Bottom Left An 81 mm Mortar team of 1st Parachute Battalion on exercise in the Berlin area in 1975.

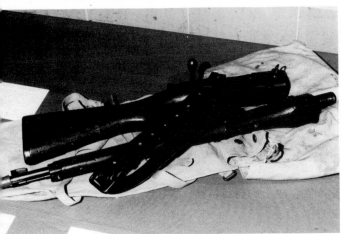

Beretta sub-machine-guns, the gun being carried in the weapon sleeve, but to carry the magazines they had a special corset. This corset was in effect a sleeveless jacket with a belt and a short skirt below the belt. In the front were pockets for five magazines, stowed horizontally across the chest and secured in place with press studs. Below the belt was a row of small pockets which could take six hand grenades, or a similar load of other munitions. A short knife or bayonet could be slung on the left side. It was a sensible way to overcome the restrictions of the parachute, and it apparently worked, however it did mean that the man was very lightly equipped when he went into action and he needed more ammunition fairly soon after landing.

By 1945 the existing Italian parachutists had adopted British equipment entirely, and they continued to use this for some years after the war. Nevertheless, in 1953 the small numbers of Italian paratroopers were back to a completely Italian parachute, including the reserve, and they had once again moved away from the idea of carrying equipment in containers slung below the man in flight. The reasons for this were mainly the fact that the Air Force had been forced by limitations of finance to go back to using pre-war SM-82s for parachuting, and the interior and the doors were too small to allow a fully-equipped parachutist to move about. When C–47s became generally available after the Korean War ended, kit bags and equipment containers were immediately adopted once more. With minor exceptions the carriage of weapons and equipment is now very similar to that of the British, though it is all Italian-made, as are the parachutes.

During the war, the Allies showed little concern for the specialised needs of the airborne

Two versions of the German Heckler and Koch HK 33 (A2 and A3) Sub-Machine-Gun.

soldier in regard to his weapons, and it was axiomatic that they carried the same as the rest of the Army. This was sensible because the requirements of the airborne force are always far smaller than the remainder of the Army, and so it is always uneconomic to make up these small batches; it also means that without great care and careful planning the spares supply will falter at the wrong moment.

For the British, the weapon which made all the difference to the airborne troops was the Sten. It came just in time to be adopted by the first units to be formed, in late 1941, and it was carried in its various different forms until replaced by the Sterling in 1953. The Sten had the great advantage that it could be taken to pieces with no trouble and to carry it tucked into the harness only required the butt to be taken off. It could be carried like that even in a Whitley. However, because of the size of the Whitley hole, there was no hope of carrying much more, and from the very beginning of the British parchute experiments the main weapons and equipment of the men had to be dropped separately in supply containers very similar in size and shape to the Germans. These were dropped in the middle of the stick, the navigator of the plane controlling the release switch. Naturally they brought about all the restrictions that the Germans suffered, for the man was dropped in a separate place from his arms. Worse than that, he might be launched into battle with no arms at all, his container stuck in the aircraft that carried him, and taken all the way back home again. It might collide with him during the descent, which happened to some unfortunates, or it might easily land miles from

the drop zone and to all intents and purposes be totally lost. Various ideas were tried, but the one which worked and immediately made all other systems obsolete was the kit bag. Its introduction was a significant landmark in the development of airborne forces, a landmark which is all too often forgotten today.

Before going fully into the development of the kit bag, this may be a convenient point to interrupt the general flow of the story and pause to examine containers in a little detail, for they are a phenomenon of the war which, like the glider, has long since disappeared. The Germans really pioneered their use and still had them in service in 1944, but the initial idea that brought them into being was actually British. Throughout the 1920s and 1930s the RAF had been dropping small quantities of supplies to isolated army units in the operations against the tribal revolts in Northern India and Iraq. These stores were packed into bundles or boxes and hooked on to the external bomb racks of the biplane day bombers. Using these crude containers only very small loads could be dropped, but the idea seems to have prompted the Germans to improve on it. They also had the Russian experience to start from, and the Russians had used similar arrangements for their own airborne troops. Whatever the source, the result was a distinct improvement on what had gone before, for the Germans soon introduced a standard container (*Waffenhalter*) which slung on to the external racks under the wings of the Junkers 52.

The final design was a long box, about 5 feet (1·5 m.) overall, and 16 inches (0·4 m.) square, of which one complete side formed the lid. It

61

dropped vertically and landed on one end, which had a domed metal shock-absorber that crushed on the impact. At the other end was a canvas bag holding the parachute, often a time-expired man-carrying canopy, or on other occasions a specially made cargo 'chute. A short static-line ran to the plane, and the container was carried horizontally under the wing. Fully loaded, a container weighed 260 lbs (118 kg), but that was the absolute maximum, and it was advisable to keep within 200 lbs (91 kg) to avoid a hard landing. A German platoon required fourteen of these containers when it was at its full strength of forty-three men, and it can be seen that there was a good deal of running about on the drop zone while all of them were located and unpacked.

The greatest difficulty about any load that is dropped separately is the finding of it. The German containers were marked with bands of paint and coloured canopies, but it is surprising how easily a container and its parachute can hide themselves in the tiniest fold in the ground, and at night they simply disappear. This may explain why the Germans were so careful not to mount night parachute operations, for very little could have happened until morning when the containers could be found. The experiences of the first British airborne operation certainly bear this out.

Operation 'Colossus' was an attempt to blow up the Tragino Aqueduct in Italy, and on the night of 10 February 1941 six Whitleys dropped thirty-eight officers and men together with their containers, but not all the containers dropped. Due to faults in the mechanism, two aircraft loads were carried all the way back to base. Such minor disasters were unhappily common at that time, but of course the men on the ground had no idea that it had happened. All containers had been fitted with an elementary light signal to help to locate them on the drop zone, but not all of them worked, and three hours later only a partial load of explosives and the weapons from one container had been picked up. The group therefore carried out their task with what they had. 'Colossus' was a failure, and the lost containers undoubtedly contributed to that failure. A year later, when the Bruneval radar station was raided and its vital set captured, the container dropping was much better and the lights worked properly. Even so there was some delay while they were unpac ed or pulled off the drop zone.

1st Parachute Battalion on exercise in West Germany in 1975. These troopers are armed with Sterling sub-machine guns.

The Parachute Regiment: Suez drop, 1956. 3.5 inch Rocket Launcher broken in half and clipped together for transit.

The British containers were all very much a copy of the German ones. They were produced by the Central Landing Establishment, known as the CLE, and hundreds of them were dropped to the resistance movement in France by bombers, who could carry them inside their bomb-bays, and for this special purpose there were also very large containers which would only go into the four-engined aircraft. Nevertheless, the standard CLE model was heavy enough, and when it contained ammunition it was often not necessary to unpack it until it was actually needed for use; there was then the difficulty of getting it off the drop zone. The Germans overcame this to some extent by putting a pair of small wheels into each container, together with a short handle. With the wheels clipped on to one end and the handle at the other the container could be pulled by two men on hard ground without too much trouble, though ploughed land and ditches posed a problem. The British decided against this use of wheels and adopted instead a folding wheelbarrow which could take a container, but was better when loaded with the contents themselves. Barrows had to be pulled by teams of men on ropes because the man on the handles could not possibly exert enough push, and this need for barrow pulling is one of the reasons for one of the distinctive items of British airborne equipment, the toggle rope. Every man carried, and still does so carry, a coiled rope looped on to his equipment. The rope is 6 ft (1.8 m.) long, with an eye at one end and a wooden toggle at the other. They had other uses, of course, but when joined together they made a splendid way of pulling the little barrows.

To return now to our original theme, the kit bag rapidly became an indispensable part of the parachutist's equipment, and design in various guises was modified to take a variety of stores. The bag was made of canvas reinforced with leather, 2½ ft (762 mm) long and one foot (305 mm) in diameter, opening at one end, and sometimes also opening all down one side. Inside could be packed any stores that would fit that space, a Sten-gun with the butt folded, a wireless set, ammunition or any similar load up to a maximum of 60–80 lbs (27–36 kg). The opening was then closed by lacing a length of rope through eyelets, and the complete bag strapped to the man's leg with webbing straps held by quick-release buckles and locking pins. The bottom of the bag was thickly padded and there

American M 72 40 mm Grenade Launcher.

was a hollow in the padding for the man's boot, the idea being that the weight of the bag would then rest on the floor and not directly on the foot. A 20-ft (6-m.) length of suspension rope was fastened to the leg strap of the parachute harness, and tucked into a pocket on the side.

The parachutist could stand up quite easily holding his bag; to walk he picked it up with one hand and swung it with his leg. The result was a curious clumping step, and a line of trainees learning to walk in unison looked for all the world like some unearthly caterpillar with arthritis as they clumped across the floor of the hangar, left hand on the shoulder of the man in front, right hand holding the top of the bag, right leg tied to the bag, and chanting in time 'kit bag, kit bag, kit bag' as the right foot went forward. In the Dakota they would do the same thing, moving steadily towards the door, swinging their bags at the same time—or near enough—and at the door throwing it through and following on with it. Once learned it was an easy way to get a load out of the plane, and the modern methods are nowhere near as comfortable or convenient.

Once his parachute had opened, the man pulled the quick-release pins and lowered the bag on the 20-ft (6-m.) rope, an operation that was sometimes easier said than done since the bag could easily take charge and fall away. If it did the rope almost always broke, invoking the furious cry of 'KIT BAAAAAG' which was the warning to those on the drop zone to look up and

dodge. A free kit bag was no joke; it could squash a man flat. Later in the war a shock-absorber was built into the suspension rope, using a metal strip which was coiled in a box and pulled out by the tension. It was a great improvement and saved a lot of time in the air.

Rifles were carried in a long sleeve made of thick felt and suspended from the centre point so that the weapon did not strike the ground at one small point such as the muzzle but landed horizontally and took the shock along its length. The sleeve was known as a 'valise', and it was held to the man for jumping by a neck and leg strap locked by quick-release pins. Strangely, a suspended load gives the parachutist a quieter flight since it takes the swing and leaves him an almost undisturbed descent. The combination falls faster than a man alone, but the bag hits the ground first and allows the canopy to 'breathe' or flex, and at that instant the man lands, quite slowly and quite gently. It takes a bit of believing, but the heavier the load, within limits, the better the flight, and it was not unknown for soldiers to load up their lighter rifle and Bren valises in order to get a better landing. Kit bags started while the Whitley was still being used, and to wriggle along the narrow, cramped fuselage and drop through the hole with a bag strapped to one leg was a nightmare. Luckily the experience was usually restricted to one training jump only, all others being from either a larger hole in, say, a Stirling, or the door of the Dakota.

This general method of carrying a personal load has now been copied all over the world, and practically every parachute force uses a variation of it. The general principle remains the same, however: the load is dropped after the parachute opens and it hangs below and absorbs part of the landing shock before the man arrives. Nowadays

Top Left   *American M60 Machine-gunner* (left) *and M16A1 Rifleman* (right).

Left Centre   *101st Airborne team with a 3.5 inch Rocket Launcher (Super Bazooka).*

Left Centre Bottom   *American TOW anti-tank missile launcher; signaller with M16 Rifle on right.*

Bottom Left   *Israeli paratrooper armed with a heavy barrelled FAL FN 7.62 mm rifle on manoeuvres in the Negev Desert (1973).*

the kit bag fastened to the leg has gone out of fashion and the load is now carried under the reserve, hooked to the waist straps of the harness. This makes it easier to walk and easier to release the load, since it is only held by metal quick-release hooks; but it means that the entire weight is taken on the harness, and to stand up carrying a full load of 60 lbs (27 kg) or more pulling directly on a strap that runs around the small of the back and the kidneys can be utterly crippling. The old kit bag had its merits. Suspension ropes are now made of extendable nylon, and the load can be kicked away in flight without having to worry about breakages and injuries to men below.

Even with the leg-bags the British wore their personal equipment for jumping. In the early days in Britain the main ideas had been taken from the Germans, and one predominant German idea was to present a smooth outline in the slipstream. This was faithfully copied by a sleeveless jump jacket, under which the man wore his equipment. He generally twisted such items as pistol holsters and hanging map-cases so that they were above the belt rather than below it, and the jump jacket held everything in place. The small pack was hung round the neck by one shoulder strap, in which position it hung at waist level. The resulting silhouette looked, to say the least, pregnant or even worse, and over this ungainly figure went the X-Type parachute harness, often with the straps extended to their limit to get them over the hump. Like all these overall type garments, the jump jacket had to be taken off after landing and discarded, but it was much quicker than the German idea because under the jump jacket the man was wearing his equipment over his smock, and all he had to do was to sling his small pack on his back, pick up his weapon from his valise, and set off.

The US Army suffered the same lack of experience as did the British, but they were less prepared to copy the Germans blindly since they had more time to experiment with their own ideas. Even so there appeared to be no alternative to some sort of underwing container for weapons, and the first parachutists carried their weapons in large canvas bundles wrapped up with padding and slung on release points under the C-47. These had to be unrolled on landing and they were both heavy and clumsy; they were soon dropped. When the T-5 parachute came into service it allowed a fully-equipped man to drop at a reasonable vertical speed, and the Americans decided that they could afford to land carrying their weapons, something that no other nation had tried until them. A light felt sleeve, known as the Griswold container, was developed and it was usual to carry the Garand rifle in this, slung off the shoulder and hanging by the side throughout the flight and landing. There was no special version of the rifle for airborne use, and in retrospect this seems a pity, since it must have been an awkward burden at times, and a folding butt would have made it far easier to carry. The Thompson sub-machine-gun was nearly always carried tucked behind the reserve, with the butt removed.

The other favourite weapon of the American airborne was the M1 carbine, a light rifle originally developed for use by supply and rear echelon troops, but which was rapidly adopted by all arms and made in very large numbers throughout the war. The M1 was ideal for parachutists; it was light, handy and had a good volume of fire. It was only a close-range weapon, for its light bullet was ineffective at more than 300 yards (274 m.), but this was enough in most actions, and it was taken to battle by everyone who could lay his hands on one. A special version was made for parachutists, incorporating a skeleton folding butt, and when so folded it could be carried in the same way as the Thompson.

By 1944 the American parachutist was carrying an extraordinary amount of weaponry and equipment on his person when he jumped, and contemporary photographs show what looks to be a horrifying quantity and weight of gear hanging off the men climbing into the C-47s for the Eindhoven and Rhine drops. They all apparently landed without hurting themselves, though one wonders how some of them did. Nevertheless, at least they had all they needed immediately to hand and could start fighting within seconds of arriving on the ground; and that is one of the secrets of a successful airborne drop. American parachutists never wore any special jump jackets or overalls, and apart from the jump boots and a certain panache there was little to distinguish the American parachutist from an infantryman of a line division. The likeness still holds, and modern US airborne soldiers are equipped and dressed in a very similar manner to all other troops of the Army.

The Soviets appeared to lose interest in their airborne troops after 1940, for very little was

Israeli paratrooper takes cover with his UZI sub-machine-gun on manoeuvres (1973).

A trooper of 2nd Parachute Battalion on Border patrol, Berlin 1973 looking east. His weapon is the 7.62 mm L1A1 FN Rifle.

done to improve them or indeed to use them. It is now thought that the huge purge of army officers after the fiasco of the Finnish War took away all the experienced and dedicated airborne leaders, and in the year that was left before the German invasion there was too much to do to build up just the elementary basis of the Army, without sparing effort on such sophistication as airborne forces. Of course, once the invasion started, it was all too late, and most of the men were thrown into the ground battle in just the same way as the Germans were. The result was that the Soviet airborne troops seem to have entered World War II with very elementary methods of carrying their equipment, and apparently with no special weapons at all. They used simple canvas bundles for rifles and light machine-guns, though they may well have jumped carrying sub-machine-guns. There was no attempt to develop any form of suspended load, nor any proper personal load-carrying gear. The result was that in the three small operations which were mounted the men dropped with no support weapons at all, and often separated from their rifles. The Germans had no difficulty in dealing with them and there were scarcely any survivors.

Since the war there has been a marked change in Soviet equipment and the first indications of this came in 1956 when the first post-war airborne troops were shown at the Red Square Parade. There are still some unexplained anomalies, one of which is the fact that even now there appears to be no way of the individual soldier carrying any more than a very small amount of equipment under his harness, and it is still not clear how he carries his weapons while parachuting, nor how his support weapons reach him. On the other hand, the Soviets are as advanced as any country in heavy dropping and the use of platforms, large parachutes and methods of retarding large loads. All of these abilities will be examined in detail in other chapters; it is sufficient to note here that in some respects they seem to have made less progress than might have been expected.

Top Right
Il Duce with the Paracadudisti.

Centre Right
One of the eight DFS 230s that landed under the command
of Obersturmbannführer Otto Skorzeny on top of the Gran
Sasso plateau northeast of Rome to rescue Mussolini from
the Hotel Albergo-Rifugio where he was held prisoner by
the Badoglio government.

Bottom Right
Another of the gliders, which were manned by a mixed force
of paratroopers and Waffen SS Special Forces.

Bottom Left
A shot from the mountain lair. The foot of the funicular was
guarded by a Fallschirmjaeger Battalion.

67

Top
German paratroopers with 37 mm PAK 37 anti-tank gun at
Nettuno in the Anzio beach-head, February 1942.

Bottom
A state of Civil War existed in Italy—known in present-day
Italian terms as 'The War of Liberation'—from the date of
the Italian Armistice in August 1943 until the end of the war
in Europe. The 'Folgore' Division was largely inducted into
the British Eighth Army and made several parachute
assaults behind the lines but the 'Nembo' Division
remained pro-German. Here a 'Nembo' paratrooper is
engaged in street fighting in northern Italy in May 1945.

Aircraft

Germany

Any airborne force is only as effective as the aircraft that carry it, and without sufficient planes a parachute army is no more than an army of specialised infantry with light equipment. The Germans realised this full well, although in 1944 they set about raising parachute divisions that had no hope of ever being flown into action, but this was an expedient way to form high-quality infantry formations who could be relied upon to fight well whatever the odds. As a recruiting scheme it worked and the fighting qualities of the men were undoubtedly the best that were available at that time. Nevertheless, they were not real parachute formations, any more than many others are today which have virtually no aircraft to lift either men or equipment.

When the Germans set about forming their airborne force in 1936 they had the basis of a successful transport aircraft fleet already in existence in the country. As with so many other organisations in Germany after the Versailles Treaty, what appeared on the surface to be a civilian airliner company was in fact a carefully controlled air force in disguise. *Lufthansa* used airliners and transports that had their origin in the bombers and supply planes that the future military *Luftwaffe* was going to need, and the designs allowed a change in use without much trouble. The mainstay of the *Lufthansa* was the three-engined Junkers 52, a product of the fertile and ingenious mind of Professor Junkers who had been designing aircraft since 1915. Certain features were a speciality of his, one in particular being the use of a steel tubular construction with metal cladding. To prevent the cladding from buckling and rattling he corrugated it with the corrugations running in the direction of the airflow. This is a highly practical and sensible way of using light alloy sheets, and it has been copied with equal success by the well-known Citroën light cars of recent years.

The Junkers, known as 'Auntie Ju' to the parachutists, was an ideal machine for the new airborne army. It was designed in the late 1920s when engine-output was not high and the three-engined layout gave a useful reserve of power. It was typical of its time with a fixed undercarriage, large square-cut wings and a narrow and none too large fuselage. A special Junkers feature was the long flaps behind the trailing edge of the main planes which helped to give extra lift for take-off and landing. There was plenty of drag, but the top speed was only 180 mph (290 kph) so that built-in wind resistance was not terribly important. The Junkers was strong and simple. It could be operated from almost any surface that was not actually boulder-strewn, and maintenance was straightforward. In the air operation to supply Von Paulus' besieged army in Stalingrad Ju 52s operated from rolled snow runways in Russia and stood out in snowstorms and sub-zero temperatures for weeks on end. Those machines that flew to the city did so under incredible conditions. Many of them came out with twice the normal load of passengers, bumping and bouncing across the snow to get airborne, then flying over the muzzles of the Russian guns to lurch on to the base aerodrome, only to return a few hours later and repeat the whole performance. Proper maintenance was impossible in the open without hangars, yet the serviceability was never less than 50 per cent.

The fuselage was adequate for passengers, but not too large for freight. It allowed 590 cu ft (16 m³) of cargo to be loaded, or 10,000 lbs (4540 kg) in weight which offered a fair variety of loads, but a difficulty lay in the fact that the only doors were in the sides and everything that went into the fuselage had to be turned through 90°. This made it impossible for heavy loads to be dropped in flight, and parachutable loads were carried on strong points beneath the centre-section where they had originally been provided for bomb-carrying. These strong-points restricted the size of the dropped loads to containers only, and the Germans were never able to drop such items as small howitzers which the C-47 could do, albeit in many small bundles. For

Junkers (Ju 52s) or 'Tante Ju'
as they were known to the
Fallschirmjaeger fly into Tunis
with reinforcements and
supplies, February 1943. This
famous transport aircraft was
the 'work-horse' of German
airborne troops.

passengers there were canvas seats and for parachuting the interior was cleared out, seats put down the sides and a strong point for the static-lines fitted in. A hooter was put in at the door to act as the jump signal and that was about all. It was very basic and quite adequate. Thirteen paratroops, eighteen air-transported troops or 10,000 lbs (4536 kg) of freight could be carried, all to a maximum distance of 700 miles (1126 km). As a glider tug the Ju 52 could pull two DFS 230s or one Go 242. For safety reasons it was generally only used with one DFS 230, which was uneconomical in terms of pay-load.

As a civilian passenger machine, the Junkers was no more crude and simple than many others when it was first introduced in 1931, but it soon became out of date; and it would probably be fair to say that shortly after the war began it was obsolescent. However, as in the case of so many other German equipments, large-scale production had been started before the war, and it was too late to change it when the design was overtaken by more modern machines, so the Junkers went on until 1945, by which time it was little better than a flying anachronism. Even so its life was not finished, because the French took a number in war reparations and used them to set up their own parachute force. They then took them out to Indo-China, and until about 1952 most of the re-supply and sorties were flown by Ju 52s and all the early French air drops against the Viet Minh were made from them. Probably the last ones to be in daily military use were a few that were kept by the Spanish Air Force, who certainly were using two Ju 52s for parachute training in the early 1960s. One of the difficulties with the Junkers was the low height of the fuselage roof and the small size of the door. Jumping through the door required a low crouching method of exit and a head-first dive was devised as the best means of getting clear, but this was not an easy feat and it required a good deal of training and expertise to get it right every time.

In 1934 *Lufthansa* had 231 Junkers on strength and was flying them on all its routes; in 1935 there were 680, and already some of these were in the hands of the *Luftwaffe*. By the time that the first airborne experiments were started in Stendal, there were sufficient Junkers to lift more than 7000 parachutists, could they all have been got into the air at the same time. From then on the Junkers was the aircraft of the *Fallschirmjaeger*, and they had very few other types. The

marriage between the men and the machine lasted the whole life of the German airborne force and it was a formidable combination; it could have been better, however, since the Junkers placed some restrictions on the freedom of action of the troops. The main drawback was the inability to drop large loads and this meant that the assault troops had to be lightly equipped; for any heavier weapons they had either to link up with the ground troops or seize an airfield and have their needs flown in by aircraft which landed on a prepared strip. This explains the early techniques of General Student. He had to have an airfield early on in the assault or else his parachutists were helpless against counter-attacks by the defence.

In Holland the battalions which dropped north of Rotterdam never captured their airfields, and the Dutch Army all but mopped them up. South of Rotterdam the assault managed to hang on to Waalhaven airfield, and despite the fact that it was under artillery fire the air-landed infantry were flown in by Junkers to secure the area. In Crete the objectives were the airfields; after they had been secured the rest of the infantry could arrive and spread out along the north coast, but without an airfield the assault was lost.

There is an interesting similarity between parachuting aircraft and landing craft. An amphibious assault has to have landing craft with bow ramps if it is to put vehicles ashore, but men can be landed from quite small boats. If there are no proper landing craft then a jetty or harbour must be captured quickly so that ships can come alongside, and though this simile should not be taken too far it does give an idea of the tactics that the Junkers forced on the Germans. If parachuting had been easier and if small guns could have been dropped, then it is likely that the desperate need to seize and hold an airfield would have been less pressing and might have allowed a little more flexibility in the choice of the objective.

The Junkers was the workhorse of the *Luftwaffe*, and in this it was exactly similar to the C-47 on the Allied side. Although it must have seemed that the pre-war manufacturing run had more than enough for all needs, the planes were always in demand and were worked continuously. The date of the Crete operation, to give one example, was fixed by the need to move the Junkers back into Poland for the invasion of Russia and, before the surrender of the Commonwealth troops on Crete, the air fleet was already on the move, off to the next job. So it is not surprising that before the war had been running for very long more aircraft were being sought to carry parachutists, tow gliders and land air-transported men and freight.

An obvious source of aircraft capable of carrying heavy loads was that provided by bombers, and as we have seen with the Ju 52 there were often only the slightest differences between the early models of transports and bombers, but the latest bombers in 1938 and 1939 were much more specialised and had little room inside their fuselages for bulky freight. They were made to carry a small high-density load at speed, but like the British who were in similar straits the Germans tried.

By late 1941 and early 1942 the twin-engined Heinkel 111 was losing its importance as a bomber. It had originally been a civilian machine in the late 1930s, though it was never very impressive in that disguise, so it was an obvious choice for a troop transport. It was converted to paratrooping by cutting a hole in the underside, close to where the lower gun position was, and to get through this door a short slide was fitted and the men slid out feet first. Up to eleven parachutists could be carried and dropped in this way though the Heinkels were never apparently used for operations. It was more use as a supply-dropper and could lift up nine-ton fully-loaded containers, roughly equivalent to 9000 kg of supplies, and drop them with considerable accuracy. Finally it was a useful glider-tug and was used to tow the larger gliders that were built in 1942 and onwards; but in this particular aspect the Heinkel reached a peak of aeronautical peculiarity when it was impressed to tow the Messerschmitt 321 glider.

The method of towing this huge glider is described in the glider section, but the Heinkel contribution belongs here. General Ernst Udet was put in charge of the air assault for the invasion of England in 1940 and his programme had evolved the giant glider. What he then needed was a tug, and he suggested that a couple of Heinkels would be one way of obtaining sufficient power. Experiments with triple-towing using Me 110 fighters soon showed that to use more than one plane at a time was simply asking for trouble, though it was a good enough way to carry out the flight trials of the glider, and it proved the system. The difficulty with using two or more separate tugs was that the pilots found it

very hard to co-ordinate their actions, and trouble in one plane involved all three very quickly. The sensible solution was to have all the power under the hand of one man, and Udet put forward the idea of joining a couple of Heinkels together. It was done, and it worked. Two Heinkel 111 H 6 bombers were joined at the wing roots, making one large plane with two fuselages, two tail units, two sets of undercarriage and five engines—five because an extra engine was added at the wing junction.

The pilot of this extraordinary machine sat in the port cockpit, and in the starboard cockpit, 40 feet (12 m.) away, was the co-pilot. They had over 5000 horsepower at their command which was more than enough to pull a 321, but some delicacy was required to fly the *Zwilling* (twin) Heinkel. Twelve were built by early 1942 and remained in squadron service in steadily reducing numbers until 1944 when the unit was disbanded. By that time only four Heinkels were still airworthy and they appear to have been broken up and their components used for spares. As aircraft they appear to have been a success: they apparently gave little or no trouble, no modifications were called for, reliability was good and, despite the fact that there was a good deal of flexing in the wing which joined the two fuselages, none of them broke or required more than normal maintenance. They towed at 140 mph (225 kph) for six hours on the fuel carried in the tanks, but did require help from rockets when taking off with a fully-loaded glider. Without rockets the run was very long before flying speed was gained.

There were few actual transport aircraft apart from the Ju 52 that the *Luftwaffe* could use, and attempts to build more modern machines had not been entirely successful. The Focke-Wulf 200 and the Junkers 90 were both large four-engined machines with good pay-loads, but both of them were plagued by minor troubles throughout their service lives and both needed hard runways and fairly sophisticated maintenance equipment to keep them going. The Focke-Wulf was used as a long-range maritime reconnaissance aircraft in which rôle it had priority over transport needs, and the Junkers was simply never made in enough numbers to be of much use. Both were kept for special tasks such as VIP flights, which did little to help airborne units. Throughout the war there was a powerful need for a plane with a good load capacity and the ability to operate from

rough strips, and though several designs were drawn up one reason for their failing to come into service was the chronic overloading of the aircraft industry in Germany. As an expedient the service gliders were fitted with engines which was a policy of despair, though it worked in ideal conditions. The Me 323 is mentioned in more detail in the glider section, but it performed a useful function provided that there was no opposition and the weather was good. An attempt to fit engines to the Gotha 242 was less successful and the Go 244, using two radials, was underpowered and difficult to fly and never entered service.

Japan

The Japanese airborne forces were in a far less satisfactory position with regard to aircraft since there had been only a small national airline in peacetime and the majority of the aircraft output had been directed towards specific war planes such as fighters and bombers; though from 1939 onwards there was a definite move to build ordinary transport planes, and a direct copy of the DC-3 was one of the priority tasks. This machine was in practically every respect identical with the original design, and was known as the Nakajima L2D2, Type 0, with the Allied code name of 'Tabby'. Tabby was a familiar sight over the islands during the fighting in 1943 and 1944 and there were some unhappy mistakes by AA gunners who could not see the US markings on the friendly ones. As far as is known, however, Tabby was not used for parachuting, perhaps because it was too valuable as a transport, and the parachute assaults all seem to have been carried out using native Japanese designs—or nearly native, since there was always an element of copying in pre-war aircraft in Japan.

The main parachute plane was a twin-engined transport known as 'Topsy'. Topsy was the Mitsubishi Ki-57, Type 100 and she appeared in 1939 as a commercial machine and was impressed into

Top Left   *Mitsubishi Ki-21.*

Centre Top Left   *A Mitsubishi Ki-57 arriving at Rangoon Airfield with Japanese surrender envoys.*

Centre Bottom Left   *Nakajima L2D4.*

Bottom Left   *Japanese paratroopers emplaning in 1942 in a Kawasaki Ki-56 (Lockheed 14 Super Electra).*

military service with no alteration. In broad terms Topsy was three-quarters the size of the DC-3, which she resembled in general outline and layout. She was a low-wing monoplane with two radial engines, single fin and rudder and a two-wheeled undercarriage, and the engines were nearly as powerful as those in the DC-3. It would be reasonable to expect Topsy to have had something like the same performance and load-carrying capacity of the DC-3, but this was not so, due no doubt to some failing in the aerodynamics of the design, and she only carried eleven passengers or 3000 lbs (1360 kg) to a distance of 900 miles (1448 km). This was about half the load of the DC-3 and about half the range, which was not a good return for an airframe which must have cost the same to make. Topsy was used for all the early Japanese parachute operations and was clearly identified at Palembang and Menado. She was the only Japanese plane to have been used for parachuting to any great extent, though others were tried from time to time, especially for training.

Like the other combatant nations, when Japan ran short of transport planes she took obsolete bombers and tried to use those as passenger and load carriers, and the success rate was no better in the Pacific than it had been in Europe. The Mitsubishi Ki-21, Type 97, was none too young when the war started, though it was a good bomber and had seen a lot of service in China. As the lack of transport machines became acute during the middle period of the Pacific War, more and more examples of Sally, as the Mitsubishi was known, were taken for load-carrying and they did very well, but the space was restricted and only nine men could be fitted in, or 2000 lbs (900 kg) of freight. It was uneconomical, but Sally was used for some of the smaller airborne operations later in the war.

Finally, there was a Japanese-built Lockheed Lodestar, a machine that was used by both the US and the British. In British service it was known as the Hudson and a few were converted to parachuting, though with only limited success. The Japanese tried the same conversion, and used it in the February 1942 parachute drops on Palembang and Menado, but the reports are not clear as to whether it was carrying men or cargo. Although as the Lodestar the Lockheed had been a good long-range passenger machine, it had only ever taken a small number of people in its small interior, and it had been intended for those customers who could pay for speed. This was hardly the chief consideration in the Pacific in 1943.

Since the war the Japanese have used American planes for their airborne troops, and at the present the mainstay of the fleet is the ubiquitous Hercules C-130, a plane which seems to have taken on the same range of tasks as the old C-47.

Italy

The Italian transports were mostly variants of the existing bomber designs, or rather variants of the last bomber designs, since it was the outdated ones which were converted, though this was by no means the rule with the planes of the early 1930s when a bomber was often little more than a transport with bomb-racks. By 1939 the standard parachuting aircraft was the Caproni 133, a high-wing three-engined monoplane with a fixed undercarriage and a general appearance similar to the Ford Tri-motor. It carried twelve parachutists and a modest load of equipment and was used for training. Containers were slung under the fuselage on bomb-racks, but the machine never went into action. Later in the war it was replaced by the Caproni 148, which was a more modern version of the same design fitted with more powerful engines and a larger fuselage. Sixteen parachutists could be accommodated in the 148, and 850 lbs (385 kg) of containers slung underneath, but it too was only used for training and would have stood little chance of survival on an operational drop since it was too slow and had no protection at all.

For operational use, though there were no actual operations, the faster and stronger three-engined Savoia-Marchettis were employed. These were bombers, though there were also civilian versions used on the air routes, and the accommodation in the large fuselage was quite good. The SM 81 was based in Libya from 1937 onwards until replaced by the SM 82 in 1940. The SM 82 was a better machine in almost every way. Although it still had three engines, the undercarriage was retractable, the speed consequently improved to 235 mph (378 kph), and the load of parachutists was now twenty-eight with a maximum of five containers on the bomb-racks. This machine stayed in service in Italy until after the war, though there were not many left by then, and it was replaced by the C-47 in the

immediate post-war years. In the 1950s the C-47s were phased out in favour of the C-119 and this remained the backbone of the parachutists' transport until the C-130s came in in the 1960s. Another modern transport plane is the Fiat/Aeritalia G 222 which is somewhat like the Transall or the Caribou in general appearance. It carries forty parachutists and has a tail-loading door/ramp and the ability to carry and drop both heavy loads and men from its pressurised fuselage.

Britain

Britain started her airborne forces in a haphazard manner, not the least part of this approach being the provision and use of aircraft. There were virtually no civilian machines that could be used for parachuting. The old Imperial Airways had used either a short-range high-density carrier for the London–Paris route, or a low-density flying boat for what were called the Imperial or Empire routes, and neither was suitable for carrying parachutists. All other passenger machines were in private hands and tended to be small load-carriers for predominantly summer use. With a small country and an excellent network of railways there was no need for an internal air service, and any aircraft suitable for conversion to military use were almost without exception American. In any case there had been an idea that the way to carry freight was in gliders, with a tug pulling a long line of laden gliders and slipping them off one by one as the string passed tug pulling a long line of laden gliders and slipping them off one by one as the train passed

Top Left   *The Italian Fiat Aeritalia G 222 today serves Italy's parachute and air-landing forces.*

Left Centre Top   *The Vickers Valentia transport aircraft came into being in the 1920s and was still around at the beginning of World War II. The SAS made their first training jumps from Valentia and Bombay aircraft in Egypt in 1941.*

Left Centre Bottom   *The Bristol Bombay was used for parachute training in the Middle East and in India.*

Bottom Left   *British parachute trainees with one of the original Armstrong Whitworth Whitley carrier aircraft in the background at RAF Ringway, 1940. The Whitley was a bomber-reconnaissance aircraft converted for parachuting in the early years of World War II.*

over the relevant airfield. It was a curious combination of a goods train idea mixed up with canal barges. Luckily it was never tried, but the germ of the idea remained and it must have influenced the early thinking on military transports, since it can be detected in one form or another in the propositions put forward for flying parachutists into action.

The Air Ministry seems to have had the idea in 1940 that the way to take parachutists to battle was in gliders towed by bombers. The bombers would be loaned from their more normal duties, and would return to bombing afterwards; while towing the gliders they could offer protection from their guns, and the load carried in a glider would be several times more than that which could be packed into the restricted space of a bomber. The argument was certainly true in the last fact and it was later shown that bombers

Top Left   *The Vickers Vimy transport aircraft was originated in 1917 and saw service into the 1920s carrying military personnel.*

Top Right   *Armstrong Whitworth Albemarle Mk V, a bomber-reconnaissance aircraft converted for parachuting and as a glider tug.*

Right Centre Top   *Handley-Page Halifax, a heavy bomber, was used in airborne forces mainly as a glider tug but it occasionally flew as a paratroop aircraft from some overseas stations.*

Right Centre Bottom   *Short Stirling Mk IV. Both the Mks IV and V were support aircraft; a large opening in the underside of the rear fuselage being introduced to drop 24 paratroopers. This photograph is of a standard Mk IV glider tug and was the 1000th Stirling built by Short and Harland of Belfast and completed on 6 December 1944. The Stirling perhaps achieved its greatest success as a parachute supply aircraft.*

Bottom Right   *The Curtiss C-46 Commando was the first parachute aircraft adapted for simultaneous exits from port and starboard doors. Employed on the Rhine-crossing by the US 18th Airborne Corps in March 1945, the C-46 was prone to bursting into flames when hit. This photograph was taken after the war States-side.*

The Douglas C-47 flew in many foreign colours both during and after World War II. These C-47s are on active service in Indo-China with the Armée de l'Air *in the early 1950s.*

were excellent tugs for gliders, even going so far as to tow more than one at a time, but it was wild optimism to imagine that parachute troops could be successfully launched in that way. However, it is a measure of the general ignorance that ran through the senior military and aviation departments at that time. It was also partly generated by the fact that with no transport aircraft and with an industry geared to desperate measures to make enough fighting aircraft for the country to survive, towing gliders with loaded bombers was the only gesture that could be made towards this new and expensive-looking force. The same thinking discarded the DC-3 when it was suggested on the grounds that it was unarmed and unarmed transports would inevitably be shot down by fighters!

A few weeks later six Whitley bombers were handed over to the Parachute School at Ringway, and for some time these six were the only parachute aircraft in the country. The Whitley had already proved itself to be ineffective as a

bomber, so the offer was not over-generous, and like every bomber-conversion it had severe drawbacks, not least being the lack of space inside. However, there were a few compensations. The fuselage was long and narrow, but it had a flat floor, and there was just enough room to sit up straight against one wall and stretch out one's legs to touch the other wall on the opposite side. Headroom was about 4 feet (1.2 m.), which meant that everyone had to crawl, and in flight piercing draughts whistled down the length of the entire tunnel-like passenger compartment. There was very little space to move about, and once inside no man could shift without crawling over those next to him; after half an hour or so it was not uncommon for everyone to have twinges of cramp.

The method of jumping from the Whitley was bizarre in the extreme. The first ones followed the example of the pre-war biplanes which provided parachute instruction for the RAF by flying with men on the wings, who then 'pulled off' by releasing their canopies. The rear gun-turret was taken off the Whitley and a plywood platform put in its place. A strong bar was hinged across the opening from the fuselage and the instructor

The Franco-German Transall has seen service with both the French and West German Air Forces.

stood on the safe side of this. The pupil crawled under the bar and stood facing his instructor, and incidentally the slipstream, until the instructor told him to pull his ripcord. He was then plucked off into space and the instructor went back for another victim. Unwilling pupils were likely to have their ripcords pulled for them by an impatient and frozen instructor and the entire performance was hated by all concerned. The difficulty with the Whitley was that there was no practical door and the only opening in the rear fuselage was the hole in which the first models had fitted a retractable lower rear gun. This had been mounted in a metal 'dustbin' which was lowered beneath the floor to protect the tail from belly attacks. It was a failure, but the floor holes remained in all early Whitleys, and this hole had to be used for parachuting.

The hole was almost exactly 3 ft (0.91 m.) in diameter and was a short cylinder where it went through the lower part of the fuselage. The parachutists shuffled up to the hole and sat on the edge one after the other, with their feet dangling over space below. On the command 'Go' each man pushed off the edge and fell through the hole at the position of attention. Too vigorous a

shove and his face hit the far side. Too feeble a shove and his pack caught the edge he had been sitting on and tipped him violently forward so that his face hit the other side again, only more severely. Five men sat forward of the hole, and another five aft of it; ten was the maximum that could be crammed in, and after a bumpy and cold flight in the half-light of the Whitley the co-ordination and judgement required to make a successful 'hole' exit was often more than some recruits could summon up. Unfortunately there was no alternative until late on in 1942, just before the North African invasion, when the first C-47s arrived and brought with them a dramatic change to all parachuting in Britain.

The Whitley was actually used for two operational jumps which were the night operations against the Tragino Aqueduct in Italy in 1941 and Bruneval in 1942. The lack of success of the Tragino operation was not really attributable to the failings of the Whitley, but the unfortunate plane added to its poor reputation by having flown the party and their equipment, and it was

79

The French Breguet Sahara transport aircraft in Cyprus at the time of the Anglo/French assault on Suez in 1956.

universally damned from then on. It was out of service by the end of 1942 and disappeared entirely within a few weeks so that not one now remains even as a museum piece.

The replacement for the Whitley was the Dakota, which is described in the American part of this section, but there were other aircraft given to airborne forces by a more or less generous Air Force when they could be spared, or when they had failed to measure up to the tasks required of them on operations. Thus, the Lockheed Hudson was made available in small numbers when it was phased out from maritime reconnaissance, though it only carried six men and they had to make their exit down a plywood 'chute leading through a hole in the floor. This curious method was necessary because the door was too small to stand in, the roof was too low to be able to stand by the hole, and nobody wanted to go back to the Whitley idea of sitting on the edge of the hole. In fact it was quite a big hole and those who have jumped from a Hudson describe the 'chute as one of the more pleasant ways of leaving a plane. Hudsons were used for a short time in Britain for training and experimental work and then the few that were in use were sent out to the Middle East and India. There they were used in some minor

80

operations, but they were not well suited to the work.

In addition to the Whitley, other bombers were handed over and one which came into general use in airborne forces was the Albemarle. It was a twin-engined machine which was first issued to the RAF in January 1943, but by that time the specification which had brought it into being was well out of date and there was no job for the Albemarle, so it was put to work towing gliders. For this it was quite good and it could cope with a loaded Horsa, which was a severe drag on its tug and often needed a larger four-engined bomber. The radius of action with a Horsa was 230 miles (370 km), quite enough to cross the Channel and reach into landing zones in Holland. The Mark V Albemarle was mainly used for dropping parachutists, and ten could be carried in the fuselage forward of a large dropping hole. This was an easy hole to jump through for there was room to stand up and step through it without trouble. The bomb-racks were retained and containers could be carried and dropped either with the stick or immediately after. The range was much the same as with the other marks and the normal cruising speed was a rather low 130 knots (240 kph).

Probably the most successful bomber conversion was the Halifax. The first machines were issued to 295 Squadron early in 1943 in place of

Junkers Ju 52/3m;

Armstrong Whitworth Whitley;

Douglas C-47.

their Whitley Mark Vs, and from then on Halifaxes took part in every British airborne operation until the end of the war. They then remained in service until completely replaced by Dakotas in the late 1940s. The Halifax was a most useful glider tug and it was the only aircraft in service which could tow the Hamilcar. It also undertook all the long-range ferry tows with Horsas, and towed Horsas to Norway for Operation 'Freshman'. The Marks AIII and AIX were intended from the design stage to be specialist versions of the bomber for work with airborne forces. Instead of Merlin engines they were fitted with the Bristol Hercules VI and XVI, and the two marks of aircraft were very similar in appearance and performance. They were for the most part used in the European Theatre where the maintenance back-up was based and few went overseas.

Not only could they tow a glider, but they could each carry a formidable load of containers, and they were used for the first experiments in heavy dropping with jeeps and trailers. For the heavy drop the bomb doors were removed and a long beam hoisted into the bomb-bay so that it ran the entire length up against the bomb releases. The load to be dropped was rigged with a complicated arrangement of crash pans and struts and brought up under the plane. The load was then winched up into the bomb-bay and hooked to the beam, the idea of the beam being to spread the load along all the releases. The jeep and its trailer were released as two separate loads, the beam staying in the plane. It was a complicated way of doing what is now a simple operation, but there was little alternative at the time, since there was no way of getting the load inside the plane; nor if there had been could it have been released in flight. The external load of

Vickers Valetta C Mk 1 of the RAF seen here despatching trainee parachutists into the Oxfordshire countryside in the early 1950s.

The Hastings Mk 2 of the RAF superseded the Valetta as a transport and paratroop aircraft and saw service into the 1950s. This Hastings shows troops ready for action and a jeep painted in desert colours slung below the fuselage.

a jeep and trailer hanging in the slipstream severely cut down the flying ability of even a Halifax, and it was never easy to get a clean release from the beam.

The Mark AIX Halifax was specifically meant for carrying parachutists in an effort to overcome the continual shortage of Dakotas. The other marks could only take ten men, but the mark AIX could lift sixteen, still not an economical number, but better than nothing. However, it was hardly used in this rôle as it did not come into service until the end of the war and only dropped parachutists during the doldrum years of the late 1940s. It was well liked for the fact that the exit hole was large and easy to jump through, but like all bombers it was cold and draughty.

Towards the end of 1943 the Short Stirling became obsolete as a heavy bomber and many were transferred to airborne forces early in 1944 and fitted with a glider tow hook and release gear. They were used as tugs on all the operations in 1944 and 1945 and by the end of the war the RAF had six squadrons devoted to glider towing. They steadily replaced the Albemarles as these went out of service and they were also converted to parachute dropping, in which rôle

they could carry twenty-two parachutists who jumped through another version of the large floor hole. However, the only operational service that they saw was as glider tugs and supply droppers.

In addition to the converted bombers there was a whole string of other aircraft which were allocated to British airborne forces at different times in the war for various uses, mainly glider towing, and the list reads like a roll-call of the aircraft in service in 1938. Most of these were only present in small numbers and as soon as they ran out of spares they were scrapped and something else taken in their place. 1942 was no time to be preserving old aeroplanes, and anyone who lived near to a glider-training airfield could watch a wonderful display of elderly tugs pulling the Hotspurs round the sky.

After the war the British cut back on their airborne forces like every other country, and for a time there were enough Dakotas for all their needs. However, the Dakotas were steadily reduced in numbers as they wore out and there was a continual attempt to find a replacement; indeed there still is since this remarkable plane has not so far been surpassed in ruggedness and reliability. The British designs were not particularly distinguished, and the first was the Vickers Valetta, a bulbous mid-winged twin with roughly the same load capacity as the Dakota, more speed and range, but a hideous drawback

DFS. 230;

Messerschmitt Me 321 Gigant,

Gotha Go 242.

Short Stirling;

Handley Page Halifax Mk III;

Armstrong Whitworth Albemarle.

in the shape of the main spar of the wing which ran across the forward end of the load compartment in a box about 18 inches (457 mm) high and 12 inches (305 mm) wide. Everything had to go over that box, and it made a nonsense of the possibility of dropping loads by roller conveyor.

The next post-war introduction was the four-engined Hastings, a plane with obvious ancestry going back to wartime bombers. The Hastings had much to recommend it and it has not long gone out of service, but it provided only limited help to a force that desperately needed to drop heavy loads from inside the fuselage. Both the Hastings and the Valetta were side-door planes with two-wheeled undercarriages, and loading them was a nightmare. Worse than that, the Hastings had to revert to the discredited dropping beam in order to carry a heavy load, and at Suez in 1956 while the French were flying in their tail-loading Noratlases, the Parachute Regiment actually had to go to an airborne museum and

The Blackburn Beverley in service in the late 1950s enabled the RAF to deliver heavy loads on platforms from the boom door. Alternatively four sticks of parachutists could be despatched simultaneously: two from the port and starboard doors and two to the left and right of the boom door.

Scottish Aviation Twin Pioneer CC Mk 1 was widely used to airlift troops during the Malayan Emergency in the 1950s. The SAS cut a hole in the fuselage for dropping through to parachute on to tree tops in dense jungle. In this photograph a party of troops emplanes at Seletar for Sarawak on operations against Indonesian insurgents several years later.

The Armstrong Whitworth AW 660 Argosy took on in RAF service where the Beverley left off.

The Short Belfast of the RAF was one of the major transport aircraft of the 1970s.

Airspeed AS 51 Horsa;

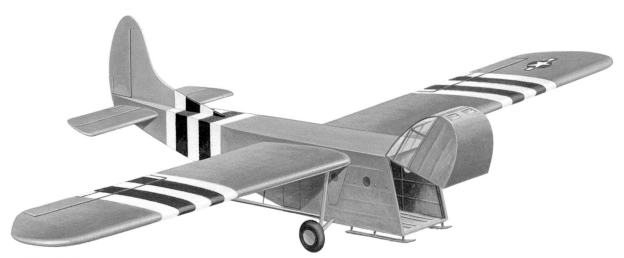

Waco CG-4A;

General Aircraft GA49 Hamilcar.

Aeritalia G.222;

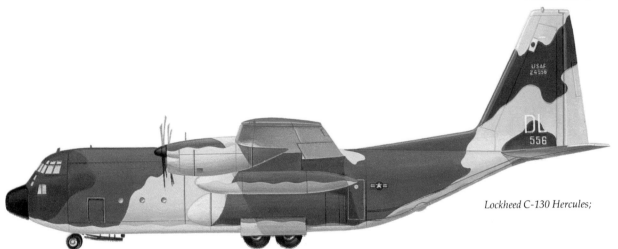

Lockheed C-130 Hercules;

Handley Page Hastings.

withdraw the dropping beam that was on display and use it to put a jeep and trailer down on El Gamil airfield. There can be no more damning example of short-sightedness than that; but the first tail-loading plane did not come on the scene until two years later, when the Beverley was introduced.

It is not now generally realised that the Beverley was first designed in 1944 for the expected airborne invasions of both Germany and the Far East in 1945 and 1946. The war ended sooner than was expected and the drawings were put away, to be pulled out again when the Korean War showed that airborne troops were still needed and that the lack of gliders was only made up by dropping from tail-loading aircraft. The Beverley was then hurriedly dragged out again, dusted off and put into production. Throughout its long life this huge and ungainly machine never properly fulfilled its rôle, for it had neither the range nor the speed to be a useful aircraft in the post-war world, but it is remembered with some affection by those who flew in it and jumped from it, not the least part of the nostalgia stemming from the extraordinary size of the main cargo compartment which resembled a small village hall. The severe limitations of range and pay-load that the Beverley suffered meant that any base for British airborne forces had to be within a few hundred miles of the dropping zone, and this was no better displayed then in the Jordan crisis in 1958.

The US had undertaken to keep the Lebanon under surveillance and to have an airborne force ready to intervene if there was a resumption of the troubles of the spring of that year. Britain agreed to do the same for Jordan. The US simply ear-marked some units in Germany and allocated the necessary C-130s to them. When called for they could fly all the way to the Eastern Mediterranean and jump straight into Lebanon in one hop, six hours' flying, and to prove it they flew all the way there, did not jump, and flew back. The British, with the same task, had to put a force into Cyprus and station the aircraft as well, because the Beverleys did not have the range to fly from any other available base.

The Beverley/Hastings combination stayed in service until replaced by the C-130 in the mid-1960s, and was assisted by another flying oddity, the Armstrong Whitworth Argosy, a twin-engined tail-loader which looked much like a C-119 and carried slightly less over a shorter

90

distance. Conceived as a commercial machine it had to be strengthened in the floor before it could carry military loads, and this extra strutting reduced the pay-load as well as the headroom over the cargo compartment. However, it was faster than the Beverley, though not as rugged nor as adaptable to unusual loads. Finally, it was expensive, and was in the end used only for training.

For the past ten years the standard aircraft of the British airborne forces, such as there are left, has been the C-130, and it is ironic that for the first time since the end of the war the units are now able to fly without stopping over large areas of the world, carry their heavy equipment within pressurised hulls, drop from any altitude, fly from unsophisticated airstrips and generally operate in a way which was vital to the success of many post-war police actions; yet what happens? The very force which has now reached a useful standard of value is cut back and reduced in all directions until it is virtually ineffective in its proper rôle.

USA

The United States had something of the same advantage as did the Germans when she started to form an airborne force. In Germany the parachutists had the Junkers 52; in USA it was the DC-3, or the C-47 as it became in the military version. In 1940 all DC-3s were civilian and the first jumps were made from borrowed Douglas B-18 bombers, but some DC-3s were soon provided and the first jumps were made from planes with most of the airliner fittings still in them. The military version started to roll off the production lines in January 1942, and it continued in a steady stream until the end of the war, and indeed in rather less quantity for some years after the war, for the C-47 is still in regular service with several airlines and a number of air forces and government agencies. It, more than anything else, enabled the Allies to form their airborne forces during the war, and it enabled these forces to be flown to battle. Without the C-47 there would have been no Arnhem and no Rhine Crossing, probably no Sicily drops, and only a very limited series of operations against the Normandy defences on D-Day.

The Dakota has become such a well-known aeronautical relic that there is little need to

Fairchild C-82 Packet of the US Air Force was described as a medium cargo assault transport. The C-82 was designed to meet the logistical needs of the immediate post-World War II years and was the pioneer of 'heavy drop'.

describe it in detail, but it may be necessary to remind the reader that the first models were laid down in 1932 as the DC-2 and the enlarged and improved DC-3 flew in December 1935 for the first time. It was years ahead of its time, yet at the same moment it was both simple and robust. The airframe and the two radial engines demanded a minimum of maintenance and the sturdy two-wheeled undercarriage would operate without complaint from the roughest of surfaces. As a troop-carrier it carries twenty-eight men; as a parachute machine it drops twenty. With a freight load the maximum is 7500 lbs (3402 kg) to 1500 miles (2414 km) at a speed of about 200 mph (322 kph) depending on the engines that are fitted. The dropping speed for parachuting is about 85 mph (137 kph) at which speed the slipstream is remarkably gentle and it is no trouble to jump through the door.

During 1941 and 1942 there was a rapid build-up in the production of the C-47 in the USA, and four transport groups of the USAAF arrived in Britain in the summer of 1942 bringing the first C-47s with them. There was an immediate demand for some for parachute training from Ringway, and in September a few were loaned so that the 1st Parachute Brigade could become familiar with the aircraft they would be using on Operation TORCH. The first few jumps showed a disconcerting habit of the British parachute to foul the tailplane and rip the apex to pieces as it came out of the bag. The easiest way to overcome

this was to lengthen the static-line, and an extra strop was hooked on to the existing line which had been long enough for the Whitley. All was now well, and the troops went off to Algeria having had at least one jump from a side-door machine. Equipment was still carried in containers because there had been no time to change the technique, but it was not long before experiments were being made with kit bags, and from then on the entire method of getting a parachutist's equipment to the drop zone underwent a major change, and it was all due to the Dakota.

For the US paratrooper the only aircraft was the C-47; he did not have to use another until right at the end of the war when the C-46 was introduced. All training and all operations were carried out from the same type of machine, and it considerably simplified the training and the equipping of the men. It was much the same sort of satisfactory position as the Germans enjoyed, and the US airborne were still using their C-47s in Korea in 1951, though they were already obsolescent by then. The only rival to the C-47 during its long reign as a transport was the C-46, a larger machine with a distinctive 'double bubble' fuselage in which thirty parachutists jumping from

91

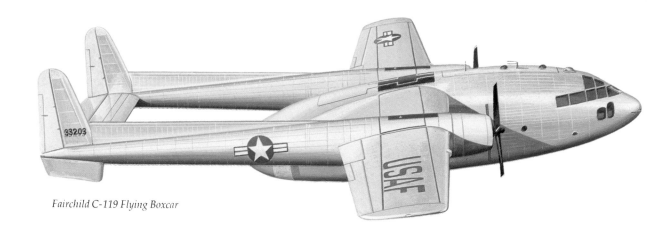

Fairchild C-119 Flying Boxcar

Nord N2501 Noratlas

Blackburn Beverley C Mk 1.

Above   *Dassault-Breguet Transall in German colours.*

Below   *Aérospatiale SA 320 Puma; the French Hotchkiss copy of the US jeep in foreground.*

The Fairchild C-119 Flying Boxcar was an excellent cargo and assault transport. This famous American 'work horse' of the late 1940s and 1950s saw active service in Korea and Indo-China. Popular with British paratroopers at the time as exits into the slipstream through the port and starboard doors in the rear were easier and produced fewer 'twists' than from the RAF Hastings.

both port and starboard doors or forty-air-transported soldiers could be carried. The C-46 was built by Curtiss and known as the 'Commando'; it was first used operationally for the Rhine Crossing operation in May 1945, and seventy-two Commandos carried the 513th Parachute Infantry Regiment over the river to Hamminkeln, but twenty-four were shot down by AA fire though the men jumped out of all but one. The trouble was that the fuel was carried in wing tanks which were not sealed and when the wing was hit the fuel ran out down the inside of the wing, and another hit set the whole lot ablaze. The morale effect of twenty-four burning

aircraft was so severe that they were not used again in the European theatre. They were sent out to the Pacific where they were invaluable. A very small number still exist as freight carriers in the USA, though it must now be difficult to find spares to keep them flying.

After the war the C-47 continued as the primary transport plane in the US Air Force, but it was apparent that something more modern was needed to carry the heavy equipment that had been lifted by gliders. One such machine was already in existence. In 1941 the US Army Air Corps had laid down a far-seeing specification for a new cargo aircraft. It was based on the concept of a large uninterrupted cargo hold, big enough for artillery and trucks, with a flat floor close to the ground. Fairchild undertook the detailed design and settled on a twin-boom tail layout with a high wing and twin engines. This allowed the required flat floor, and the rear of the

fuselage opened with clam-shell doors to allow a straight-low door-sill on which could be laid ramps for vehicles to run in and out. The mock-up was approved in late 1942 and the first prototype flew in 1944. The first production models were delivered at the end of 1945 and an intensive flight programme was put in hand. The plane was known as the Fairchild C-82 'Packet', and 220 were built up to 1948. With a capacity for forty-two parachutists or 20,000 lbs (9071 kg) of freight, it was the first practical tail-loading and tail-dropping aircraft to go into service with any air force. Troops jumped through two doors at the rear, but freight or heavy loads were dropped over the door-sill. Guns, jeeps and large loads were loaded on to wooden skidboards and pulled out by small parachutes, while bundles were hung from a strong monorail, run out over the sill and slipped off. Revolutionary though it was, the C-82 had some drawbacks: the radius of action was short and the take-off and landing ability on rough strips was not good; also the two engines were only just powerful enough and a greater margin of power was needed.

These requirements were built into the successor, the C-119, and it came into use in 1949. It was a much better proposition for airborne forces, carrying forty-six parachutists or 30,000 lbs (13,607 kg) of freight to a range of 1770 miles (2848 km), and capable of flying from the sort of strip that was normally met in overseas theatres. In 1950 it went to war in Korea with the 187th Regimental Combat Team, dropping both men and equipment in a way that was impossible only a few years before. The C-119 was bought by airborne forces all over the world, and it

Top Right *Fairchild C-123B Provider, stalwart of the Vietnam War.*

Centre Right *Lockheed C-130 Hercules of the USAF. This photograph issued by the Department of Defense on 16 February 1968, shows a 'Herc' dropping food and ammunition by the LAPES (Low Altitude Parachute Extraction System) to US Marines locked in battle at Khe Sanh, Republic of Vietnam. LAPES made re-supply possible without the aircraft landing. More than any other aircraft since the C-47 and Ju 52 the name of the C-130 Hercules is synonymous with Airborne Forces, troop movements and the flow of supplies. It is in service with the RAF and many other Air Forces throughout the world.*

Bottom Right *Lockheed C-130 Hercules of RAF Air Support Command.*

Top   *Sikorsky Skycrane in USAF service.*

Below   *Sud Aviation Super Frélon of the French navy.*

remained in use until very recently with several countries. The layout that it pioneered was copied by others, and the French Noratlas must owe a good deal to either the C-82 or the 119.

Tail-loading aircraft entirely altered the concept of an air assault. Whereas in World War II there had to be both dropping zones for parachutists and landing zones for gliders, with tail-loaders it is possible, though perhaps not always desirable, to put both men and equipment down on to the one space. In addition, a glider is a one-way means of travel, but an aircraft can make more than one journey, as was done in Korea. So not only is the tail-loader cheaper to use, but it is also more flexible and more 'cost-effective', to coin a current phrase. The twin-boom layout had several inadequacies and in 1957 the USAF started trials with the C-130 single-fuselage tail-loader. It has been a standard airborne transport ever since and is now as widely distributed around the world as was the C-47 before it. The great advantage of the C-130 and other machines like it is the fact that it changes an airborne force from being a tactical weapon to being a strategic weapon without losing its tactical ability. The C-130 has a pressurised hull and a cruising speed of 300 knots (556 kph), which allows a range of 2160 nautical miles (4000 km), carrying the maximum

pay-load of 44,000 lbs (19,950 kg). However, if the pay-load is cut down to 20,000 lbs (9070 kg), then the range goes up to 4460 nautical miles (8264 km).

For some idea of what this means, here are some examples. It is the same as flying from Copenhagen to Baghdad and back, or Madrid to Moscow and back, or a one-way flight from London to Delhi or London to the Bahamas, carrying a full load of parachutists. It puts a new aspect on the use of airborne forces, for they can fly in comfort in a heated and pressurised hull at an altitude which allows the aircraft to fly at its most economical cruising speed. When approaching the target the plane can come down to an operational jumping height, open the rear clam-shell doors, drop its load, close the doors, regain height and fly back again. It is a classic example of the effect that technology can have upon the effectiveness of military forces.

USSR

The last country to be considered in this rapid round-up of aircraft is the Soviet Union, which was among the pioneers of the airborne method of waging war, but which strangely faded out until after World War II. Originally the Soviet

A USAF C-5A Galaxy unloads at Fort Bragg, North Carolina. In five runs over the 'Sicily' Drop Zone at Fort Bragg, the number 8 Galaxy successively and successfully parachuted two dummies, 73 men, a 26,000-lb Army D-5 tractor, an armoured personnel carrier, and a 30,000-lb test platform. Left: A 22,150-lb M-113 armoured personnel carrier leaves the Galaxy, floats to the ground and drives off on its own power. Right: 36 paratroopers exit from the Galaxy's port door, and 37 leave from the starboard door. This test was conducted during July 1971.

The supersonic An-22 turbo transport plane, used by Aeroflot. The military version of the An-22 bears the NATO code-name 'Cock'.

parachutists jumped from transports which were the usual converted bomber of the late 1920s, and it appears as if there were few of these that they could call upon; though after the dramatic demonstrations of 1935 and 1936 things improved for a year or two, but all emphasis was lost in the purges of 1937 and 1938 when the top generals in the infant airborne force were executed by Stalin. At that time the plane which was used in all the public jumps was the ANT 6, a very large four-engined mid-winged monoplane of remarkably crude and antique appearance dating back to the 1920s. However, it must have been a giant in its day for it could carry about 10,000 lbs (4540 kg) to a distance of 500 miles (800 km) and the type was used for a record-breaking flight to the North Pole. The four engines were mounted on a huge wing covered in corrugated alloy sheets, much like the Junkers method of construction, and there was a large two-wheeled undercarriage between which some heavy loads were slung. There was even enough room between the wheels for a light tank

to be carried and put down on an airfield. The ANT 6 features in some memorable photographs of men jumping with ripcord parachutes and it is apparent from the way that they are scrambling about on the wing and out of hatches in the top of the fuselage that the dropping speed is modest indeed. This elderly and vulnerable aircraft remained in service in small numbers until about 1942, by which time the Germans had shot down several and there can have been none left.

The replacement for the ANT 6 was none other than the ubiquitous DC-3, either a licence-built version produced in the home factories or supplied direct from the USA under Lease-Lend. The first Soviet-built planes were flying in 1940 and by 1945 there were over 2000 DC-3s in use, carrying all manner of loads and operating from every kind of airstrip in all weathers. They all continued in use for some years after the end of the war in both civil and military capacities and no doubt there are still some of them flying today.

The DC-3, or Li 2 as it was known in the Soviet Union, resisted the same attempts to replace it as it did in the West. In 1948 the Ilyushin Il-12 was brought into military service, a slightly larger

Soviet parachutists boarding an Antonov An-12 paratroop and freight transport of the Soviet Air Force. Known in NATO as 'Cub', the An-12 has been supplied to India, Algeria, Egypt, Indonesia, Iraq and Poland.

machine with a tricycle undercarriage and a little better pay-load, and together with the DC-3 it provided the lift of the Soviet airborne troops until the middle of the 1950s.

Until 1956 the Soviet airborne force was little more than a light raiding force of parachutists with little or no heavy equipment, no ability to drop guns or vehicles, no gliders and only very limited re-supply arrangements. In 1956 this all changed with the introduction of the first Soviet tail-loading aircraft, the Antonov An 8. The An 8 could carry up to 10,000 lbs (4540 kg) or fifty parachutists. It was powered by two turbo-prop engines and was built in quantity. For the next ten years this plane was the main lift for the Soviet Army, and it made the airborne divisions into very different formations from that which they had been before. In the mid-1960s it was replaced by the An 10 and later the An 12, both of which were very similar to the C-130 with almost identical pay-loads, though shorter ranges. However, they have given the Soviet airborne divisions a capability beyond those of the West. The An 12 is now the standard transport and there are said to be enough of them to carry two or three divisions of airborne troops in one lift,

together with their equipment. So the wheel has turned full circle, in effect. Forty-five years ago the Soviet Union was the only country in the world with an airborne force at all, apart from a few Italian troops; her airborne force then all but disappeared and now it has come right round to being once again the largest in existence. It is unlikely to sink from sight for a second time.

Gliders

Military gliders are a feature of World War II alone. They have a short and clearly-defined history which ended abruptly in the late 1940s and will most certainly never be revived. The whole span of life of practical military gliding probably covers no more than twelve years, and that is stretching it to the limit. Gliders themselves are one of the oddities of the war, though they were serious military weapons and they contributed markedly to the success of the various airborne assaults that were made by each side.

The glider came into being because there was no way of delivering a load larger than a container on to the drop zone. Hence, unless the parachute troops could seize a landing strip of sufficient size to allow transport aircraft to land and discharge their cargoes, they had no chance of any support weapons and they became little better than a raid or a nuisance force. Once the defender could bring up some armour, no matter how light the vehicles were, the parachutists were helpless; and it was only a matter of time before they were rounded up. The Germans knew this full well and the pattern of all their early airborne attacks is the same: a parachute drop on to an airfield, the seizure of the field, followed by air-landing of infantry and light guns, often within less than an hour of the drop.

This was the formula for Norway, Holland and Crete, though the assault itself took slightly different forms. In the attack on the Belgian forts and bridges the use of gliders was a major factor in gaining them without loss of time, but this was a change in technique and it was brought about by the need to cross neutral territory in silence and make a surprise assault before there was time for the bridges to be blown. In the attack on the bridge over the Corinth Canal a variation of this idea was tried and the gliders landed only a few minutes before the parachutists. It very nearly failed, and after that gliders were only put down on to ground already occupied by parachutists.

The idea of carrying large loads in gliders was not new when the war started, but the trouble was that it was all theory and no real practice. Gliders were flimsy structures with long thin wings in which one man tried to find lift in the upward currents of air; but for military use a very different type of glider was needed. Sporting gliders were, and still are, designed to use the natural movement of the air and support themselves by picking up lift from rising thermal currents or by flying along ridge tops and being lifted up by the wind being deflected upwards at the crest. For this they need to be light and

The Battle of Crete, May 1941. A German DFS 230 glider on the edge of a roadside near Maleme.

A British Horsa about to be 'snatched-up' by a C-47 at an Army Air Base in North Carolina in 1943. This technique was used successfully operationally but with the American Waco gliders in Burma.

streamlined, and the man flying the glider needs to be a skilled pilot as well as a minor expert in meteorology.

A military glider is something quite different, almost as different as a cargo barge is from a sailing boat, and the outward appearance gives a clear indication of many of the differences. The sports glider is slender, graceful, beautifully smooth and rounded, and highly varnished to reduce all possible drag. The military cargo glider is large, usually square in section, fairly square in its wings and tail, with little concern for stream-lining, and often struts supporting the wings and tail. The fuselage is intended to carry bulky and heavy loads, and the outline of it is fixed by the size of the expected cargo. Sports gliders either have no wheels, or one only, and that sunk into the bottom of the fuselage; cargo gliders have a full undercarriage which is fixed and exposed to the airstream. Sports gliders have a gliding angle of over 20:1. At least in 1940 this was normal; now it is likely to be nearer 50:1.

Cargo gliders never exceeded 10:1. Sports gliders are launched by one or more means, mostly either by a winch launch from the ground or by an aerial tow using a light aeroplane. Cargo gliders could only fly with a powerful aeroplane towing them. Once the plane cast off the glider had to come down, and it generally did so quite quickly, in contrast to the sports glider which tries to keep up in the air as long as possible and

may even have to use some sort of deliberate device to spoil the flying characteristics in order to bring it down.

There are many other differences, and a few likenesses, but the main ones have been explained and it merely remains to record that, despite what must now seem to be fairly obvious large differences in the requirements and tasks of each type of glider when the first military gliders were being designed, it is quite obvious that the specification was muddled and the machines were too heavily biased towards the sports designs, with the result that they were of little use for cargo work, yet no good at all as free-flight gliders. This hiatus only lasted for the first models of each nation, but it shows how difficult it is to break free of convention, even in a war.

Gliders have not been used for military pur-poses for thirty years and it may be as well to remind ourselves of how they were actually operated when they were in their heyday during World War II. The following description applies to an Allied operation sometime around 1944, but when the Germans were launching their campaigns into Holland and Belgium they must have used a similar system. The first requirement was to load each glider with its operational cargo and secure the load to the floor with chains and lashings. It was essential that everything in the fuselage was tied down, including any passen-gers, because when a glider flew through the

101

Waco gliders thundering in to a well-prepared Landing Zone (LZ) with badly needed supplies for the Normandy beachhead (June 1944).

slipstream of its tug the movement could be quite violent, and there was always a chance that the landing would be even more violent. The load had also to be balanced about the centre of gravity, otherwise the glider flew tail up or tail down. The apparently simple task of loading was quite specialised and called for extra training from the men involved, and took some time to complete.

Next the glider had to be moved to its position on the airfield and lined up, and as it weighed anything from 3 to 8 tons (3–8 tonnes) or more, the amount of movement was usually kept to a minimum and the gliders were loaded as near to their take-off run as could be managed. Once in position the tow-rope was brought up and flaked out in a tight zigzag in front. The positioning of the gliders was a matter for careful planning as it had to allow each one to take off in its proper sequence in the flight stream, yet it must be possible for the tug aircraft to taxi round in front and pick up the ropes. One arrangement was to line up the gliders on either side of the runway and bring the tugs up the middle, but this took a lot of space and could not always be arranged. Once in the air the tug/glider combination circled until the formation was all airborne and then all formed a long stream heading for the target. Gliders flew in either a 'High Tow' or 'Low Tow' position, that is above or below the slipstream —but never actually in it because the slipstream induced the most violent turbulence and could actually break up the glider. On the Normandy invasion in June 1944 a Hamilcar carrying a Tetrach light tank broke up over the Channel and killed its entire crew and passengers because it was caught in the slipstream of its Stirling tug.

As the combination approached the target the co-pilot would check with the tug navigator and they would pick up the reference points on the ground. A mile or two from the target the tug would cast off, though sometimes he would take the glider right over the target (this depended on

the tactical plan), and then the glider would make its approach. If released right over the target the approach was simple enough: it was a more or less direct dive downwards from the release height using large flaps to slow down the speed, and a quick pull-out at just above ground level followed by a short landing run. If released some distance away the pilot would approach in as flat a glide as he could hold, his co-pilot calling out the height and looking for the ground markers, and at the right point it would be flaps out, a short dive and the same brief, bumpy landing run. There was no chance to go round again; the first approach was the only one, and if it was not right the pilot had to make the best of it. An appallingly high proportion of gliders crashed on landing, usually due to the fact that there were too many gliders in the sky at the same time and too many on the ground. With no freedom to manoeuvre, all that the pilots could do was to try and pick a clear patch of sky which coincided with a clear patch of ground and get down before someone else filled one or the other. It was not at all uncommon for a landing glider to crash into one already down, and on the landing zone everyone went round with one eye permanently cocked skywards.

Once down the next task was to unload, and since a stationary glider attracted bullets like flies to a honey-pot there was some urgency in the matter. Most military gliders had large doors in the front or rear of the fuselage and it was a matter of opening these, dropping a ramp, unlashing the load and driving it out. Crash damage could alter this simple plan, and the Horsa was unique in arranging for the tail section to be removable by unbolting if the nose was jammed. Should the bolts jam also, and this was common, there was a ring of cordtex explosive laid around the join—all the crew had to do was to light a short fuse and blow the tail off. Having got clear of their glider, the crew left it. The

wastage was amazing. If the operation succeeded and the battle rolled on well past the
landing zone, then special salvage teams came to
rescue what was left. Weather, looters and casual
damage all took their toll before the teams
arrived, and the usual return was less than 10 per
cent of the original flight. Gliders were expensive
things.

However, expensive or not, they did what was
required of them. They carried the artillery
pieces, the tanks, the jeeps and radios. They
became mobile headquarters, mobile repair
shops and mobile surgical theatres. They
delivered teams of men to one spot in one group,
which is something that a parachute cannot do,
and they enabled men to go and fight an airborne
war without the need to learn the special skills of
the parachutist, or run the risks of parachute
landings. Indeed, though it was considered
essential that parachutists should all be volunteers, in both the British and US Armies units
were designated to be glider-borne without
offering the choice, as it was considered to be just
another way of going to war. The recipients of
this casual honour were not always so appreciat-
ive, nor did they necessarily agree with the philosophy behind it; and to some extent they may
have been right, for any sort of airborne warfare
is a specialised skill which takes some time to
acquire.

Not all gliders were one-way machines. The
technique of 'snatching' allowed a glider to be
flown off without the tug having to land. This
was an Allied speciality which was only perfected late on in the war. A glider was positioned
in a clearing or on a flat piece of ground. A long
nylon rope led from the nose to a loop stretched
between two poles. The tug flew in low and
slow, trailing a hook. The hook caught the loop
between the poles and the tug immediately put
on full throttle and pulled away. The nylon rope
stretched out, taking the tension, and the glider
rolled forward to get airborne in 100 yards
(91.4 m.) or less, giving its crew a fairly sharp jerk
as it did so. The technique was used in the winter
of 1944 to fly wounded back from Holland to the
United Kingdom, in Burma to evacuate
wounded and equipment, and in both theatres
on occasions for mail.

Gliders were made in different ways. The
Germans, Americans, Japanese and Russians
looked upon gliders as being proper aircraft and
built them in aircraft factories. The British had no

spare capacity and from the beginning set out to
make their gliders in factories which were not
already on war-work. This fact forced them to
use wood, and the designs had to be simple so
that they could be built by unsophisticated
machines; in fact nearly all the British gliders
were made in furniture factories using plywood,
and even so there were never enough of them.
Despite the simplicity of the construction there
were other necessities in a glider which made
demands on all sections of industry, and which
also put up the expense. The pilots had to have
some basic instruments in order to be able to fly
at all, especially in cloud; wheels needed tyres
and controls needed wires and pulleys. Providing the tow ropes alone called for mile upon mile
of nylon from the infant nylon-spinning industry.

Germany

The Allies can probably blame themselves as
much as anything else for the fact that at the
beginning of World War II the German airborne
forces already had some transport gliders in service. The Treaty of Versailles had restricted the
building of powered aircraft in Germany and in
order to encourage any flying at all the German
Government was forced to use gliders. Gliding
was in its infancy in the 1920s, but in Germany it
gained impetus as more and more skilled pilots
were trained, and Germany began to take the
prizes in the international gliding contests. The
study of advanced aerodynamics was undertaken in universities, particularly Göttingen, and
by the early 1930s gliders were being towed quite
long distances by light aircraft. In 1932 the
Deutsche Forschungsanstalt für Segelflug designed
a glider for research into high-altitude meteorology, and most of the work was done by the
leading aerodynamicist of the day, Dr Alexander
Lippisch. A glider was chosen first of all because
it was cheaper and required less power to carry
the load of instruments and scientists, but also
because it was free from vibration and electrical
disturbances, which was important for the
measurements which were to be taken.

This meteorological glider was a significant
step in the production of the first military glider
for the airborne troops. The idea is traditionally

103

The DFS 230 military glider with a Ju-87 Stuka escort airborne for Crete, May 1941. The tow rope is clearly visible.

German troops debouching from a DFS 230 glider at a demonstration in Italy in 1943. Note the defensive armaments mounted behind the cockpit on top of the fuselage.

supposed to have come from Hanna Reitsch, who was one of the leading glider and aeroplane pilots in Germany, but it seems more likely that it originated in the fertile mind of General Ernst Udet, who was responsible for several aeronautical innovations. He saw that the meteorological glider was carrying about a ton of pay-load, and this was a useful figure for the new airborne forces to have at their disposal. The first military version was ready in 1937, and from then on there was a slow trickle of them. It was probably the first military glider in the world (there is a possibility that there were some in Soviet Russia before that date), and it was known as the DFS 230.

The DFS 230 (the letters stood for the *Deutsche*

Forschungsanstalt für Segelflug which designed it) was a simplified version of the original scientific glider, but it still betrayed its affiliations with the sporting sailplanes and gliders. The fuselage was square in section and built of steel tube covered in fabric. It was narrow and only deep enough to allow sitting headroom for a man. The wings were long and tapered and made from stressed plywood, braced by a single strut. The undercarriage was a pair of wheels under the fuselage with a long skid running from the nose under the belly. The wheels could be dropped after take-off and the landing made on the skid, if that was desired. Later models were fitted with braking parachutes and even retro-rockets in the nose in an effort to cut down the landing run.

The wingspan was 72 feet (21.9 m.) and the fuselage was 37½ feet (11.5 m.) long. Empty weight was 1800 lbs (816 kg) and the loaded weight could be up to 4600 lbs (2086 kg). Towing speed was between 100 mph (161 kph) and 120 mph (193 kph), landing speed was about 40 mph (64 kph), but depended to a great extent on the load.

The normal load was a pilot and nine men, all sitting in a line down the fuselage, the pilot and first five passengers facing forward, and the last four facing aft. The passengers sat astride a long bench with their rifles and carbines in clamps beside them. The first passenger could fire a machine-gun out of a slit in the fabric on the starboard side, but in later models he stood up and manned a proper defensive machine-gun mounting in the top of the fuselage. When cargo was carried it could be put in in place of the last four passengers, or all the fuselage space could be used. It was not an easy machine to get in or out of, as the only door was at the back on the port side; the pilot, however, could open his canopy.

The DFS obviously left a good deal to be desired as a military glider, but it was a deadly weapon, when used properly, in the early days of the war. The famous glider assault on Fort Eban-Emael in Belgium was carried out with ten DFS 230s and for this the feature which most contributed to the success was the flat gliding angle. The assault gliders were released at 10,000 feet (3048 m.) over Germany and glided silently over a part of Holland to land on top of the fort and deposit the engineer assault force and their demolition charges. It was a momentous and daring feat which deeply shook the Allies; and in size and scope it was never repeated, though the taking of the Orne Bridge in 1944 came very close to emulating Eban-Emael. Some DFS gliders were used by fighter squadrons in Russia as mobile workshops, and they flew with the squadron as it moved across the steppes, carrying repair equipment and spares. Many were lost in the assault on Crete, and in 1944 the numbers were further whittled away in Russia by re-supply operations and some reinforcement runs to the Army surrounded in Stalingrad. Altogether, 2230 were built in various factories and by 1945 hardly any were left.

They were towed by a variety of planes, but the most common were the Ju 52, which could actually take two (though it strained the engines

a little), the Heinkel He 111, Henschel 126, Messerschmitt Bf 110 and the Junkers 87. The Heinkel was often used in the latter years of the war and several experiments were undertaken with it. One was the first use of rigid tow-bars, using a steel bar only 6 metres (20 ft) long. The Ju 87 was used for training after it had been superseded as a dive-bomber, and it towed a number of gliders across the Mediterranean to Tunis when Rommel was being driven out of Africa.

Go 242

The limitations of the DFS 230 were apparent as early as 1940 and design work for a larger glider with a better load-carrying capability was put in hand. The machine was produced by the *Gothar Waggonfabrik AG* who had had long experience with aircraft, and the first models were issued to the *Luftwaffe* in the summer of 1941. The 242 was a high-wing monoplane with a central nacelle and twin tail-booms. The nacelle was made of tubular steel, fabric covered, and the rest of the machine was of wood. The first versions had a wheeled trolley for an undercarriage and dropped it on take-off, but later models had a permanent tricycle undercarriage.

The Gotha was large and ugly, but it was much nearer what a military glider ought to be. The pay-load was 8000 lbs (3629 kg) which equated to either twenty-three troops with all their personal gear, a light vehicle and a field gun, or the equivalent in stores. The wing span was 79 feet (24 m.) and the total weight of a loaded glider was 15,000 lbs (6804 kg), which was more than the smaller planes could pull. The flight characteristics were very different from the DFS-230. The Gotha made no pretensions to be anything other than a large, ugly freight carrier, and when the tow-rope was cast off it came back to earth fairly quickly. It was a rugged and roomy machine, and in 1943 attempts were made to turn it into a transport airplane by fitting two engines. For some reason this was not a success and the pilots reported that it flew badly and was unstable and the idea was dropped after a hundred or more had been converted from a total output of 1500. Another idea to improve the take-off run of the combination with a fully-loaded glider was to fit rockets to the nacelle. These rockets could take two forms. The first was a single Walter under each wing, the second a battery of four on a frame at the extreme rear of the nacelle. Both were perfectly practical, but the supply of rocket

105

Go 242 was introduced in 1942 partly as a freight glider and partly as a replacement for the smaller DFS 230.

Three Go 242As in tow by a Heinkel He 111Z (Zwilling).

A Go 242A, dropping its undercarriage dolly on take-off.

A Heinkel He 111Z (Zwilling) towing a Messerschmitt Me 321. The tug was constructed from two standard He 111-6's joined by a new wing centre section; the Me 321 (Gigant) was conceived for the projected invasion of Britain, (Operation 'Sea-Lion').

fuel was not good in Germany, and in the more distant airfields in Russia the availability of the rockets was generally poor, which placed greater strains on the tow-planes and made it necessary either to use a very long runway, which was not always possible, or to carry less pay-load.

Cargo was loaded into the Gotha by hinging up the rear of the nacelle and running the cargo up two ramps straight into the hold. Passengers could enter and leave by two doors in the front and the pilots sat in a glazed nose with an excellent view. Tow-planes were the Ju 52 or the Heinkel 111 and it was strong enough to be towed at speeds up to 180 mph (288 kph), though it was normally much less than this. As with the DFS 230, many Gothas were converted into flying workshops and stores and a few were turned into mobile field headquarters during the headlong advance into Russia in the autumn of 1941. Defensive machine-guns could be fitted and the pilots were armoured against fire from the ground by a steel floor to the cockpit.

All told, the Gotha was a practical and sensible design for a military glider. It was infinitely more useful than the DFS 230 and in general size and performance it was comparable to the British Horsa. It came too late for the airborne assaults at the beginning of the war and it spent most of its military life supplying units and formations on the Eastern Front.

Me 321

The Me 321 was the world's largest operational glider, and until the giant jets of the late 1960s it was also one of the largest aircraft that had ever been used operationally. It originated from an urgent need for a cargo carrier with a large capacity to support the intended invasion of Britain

in 1940. Apparently this was not actually realised until November 1940, by which time there was no hope of any crossing until the spring of the next year. The idea of a huge glider seems to have originated in the design department of the Messerschmitt factory, and Professor Willi had an audience with Rudolf Hess to test official reaction to the proposal. The reaction was strongly positive and Hitler gave his approval as well. A specification for the loads was given by the Air Ministry and work began at Messerschmitt. Incredibly, they had the first prototype ready for test-flying within fifteen weeks, in February 1941. They had built the largest military flying machine in the world at that time; the wings were 181 feet (55 m.) in span and the fuselage was 93 feet (28 m.) long and 19 feet (5.8 m.) deep. The two pilots sat in a glasshouse on top of the front of the fuselage no less than 23 feet (7 m.) above the ground. The monster was made from steel tube, covered in fabric and empty, and weighed 13 tons (13.2 tonnes). It was expected to carry 28 tons (28.4 tonnes) of cargo or 200 fully-equipped troops, all of whom could be loaded in through two enormous clam-shell doors in the nose.

Having built the monster the next problem was to fly it, for no real thought had been given to what should tow it. Flight trials used a Junkers 90, one of the few four-engined planes in Germany at that time, and with an empty glider it needed three-quarters of a mile (1200 m.) to get the combination into the air, whereupon it became clear that something better would be needed to tow the glider with a full load. The solution was the 'Troika' tow, a novel concept using three Messerschmitt 110 twin-engined fighters. The three were hitched to the glider by individual ropes of different lengths, the idea being to keep all four planes well apart. It was an impossibly complicated arrangement and called for an exceptional skill on the part of the three tug pilots, together with a good deal of luck, since the slightest failure on the part of one was immediately transmitted to all the others, sometimes with fatal results. It was a good enough method to get the glider flight-tested but it was plain that for operations something safer and more easily managed was going to be needed. It was General Udet, as we have already recorded, who had the idea of the *Zwilling* Heinkel, and once again the finished model was ready within a matter of weeks. It was just as well since the production of the glider had gone ahead and there were twenty-four by the end of the summer. Altogether 200 were built, but the majority were converted into transport aeroplanes by fitting six French Le Rhône radial engines. This reduced the pay-load, but it did mean that there was no need for a tug, and this was most important since there was only one squadron of *Zwillings*.

The 321, or Gigant (giant) as it was christened, used enormous quantities of material in its manufacture. The fuselage was steel tube covered in fabric, and when carrying troops a middle deck was put in to allow a complete German infantry company to be carried. The wings were steel tube also, triangulated into a complicated structure with ply covering the front half, as far back as the main spar, and fabric on the remainder. The wing plan was heavily tapered and was braced by a single strut each side from which ran auxiliary vee-struts. The single rudder and tailplane were also fabric-covered and again braced with struts. The undercarriage was originally two large wheels with two smaller auxiliaries and all were dropped after take-off, but this was found to be uneconomical on supply missions, and most of the flights were made with the undercarriage fixed. The 323, the powered version, needed a much stronger undercarriage than the glider, and it was fitted with what is probably the first multi-wheeled arrangement. Eight pairs of wheels were placed under the forward half of the fuselage and faired in with side bulges, and this allowed it to operate from rough surfaces without too much trouble.

In flight both the glider and the powered plane were reasonably stable but very heavy and sluggish to control. The pilots had no auxiliary power and had to rely on their own muscles to move the control surfaces, and some manoeuvres required considerable exertion. The first Gigant only had a single pilot, but this was rapidly changed to a two-man cockpit so that both men could push on the controls when it was necessary. The long wing made it a difficult machine to turn in the air, and once set on a course both glider and plane were best left alone to fly in a straight line with minimum effort from the pilots. Take-off was a continual problem throughout the life of both versions. The Heinkel *Zwilling* was hard-pressed to pull a loaded Gigant into the air and it required all of the 1200 metres that the first flight trial had used. To cut this down to a length that would suit a military airstrip, take-off rockets were used, and for a maximum load a Gigant fitted eight 1200-lb (544-kg) thrust rockets in a special rack under the wings. These made an awesome noise

An Me 321 (Gigant) towed by a trio of Me 110s in the so-called Troikaschlepp, *a hazardous three-point towing operation resulting in the death of many pilots. The Gigants proved useful for transport operations in Russia.*

Messerschmitt Me 323 (Gigant). A super-transport developed from the Me 321 glider and introduced in 1942. Crew of five. Powered by six Gnôme-Rhône radial engines. Me 323s appeared during the Tunisian supply operation in 1943 and fourteen fell prey to Allied fighters due to their low speed. Also served in Russia.

and smoke when they were ignited and for the passengers who were inside the fabric fuselage the memory of a take-off must be something that is with them still. Once clear of the ground the rocket frames were dropped, using a small parachute. The 323 used rockets also, particularly in Russia where it sometimes had to operate from short runways.

The pay-load of these large machines was not a precise figure and the normal glider load was rather less than the planned figure, though this may have been due rather to take-off difficulties than flying ability. Certainly, on one historic occasion, which is vouched for by the designer himself, a 323 flew from Tunis to Italy carrying 220 men; 80 sat inside the wings and 140 were in the cargo compartment. The take-off run is not recorded.

Other Gliders

As might be expected, there were many different ideas and designs for gliders in Germany, but none came into service apart from the ones already mentioned. One severe drawback to the use of more gliders was the lack of suitable tow-planes, and though the Ju 52 was an ideal machine for the job, it was desperately needed as a transport in its own right, and there were not enough obsolete bombers to allow much of an extension to the glider fleet. When the Me 321 was being built, a similar design was commissioned from Junkers as a back-up in case the Messerschmitt failed. Rather unfairly, Junkers were told to use wood which severely limited the

designer's freedom of action and he set out to build an enormous flying wing, a daring undertaking in itself since flying wings were quite novel and the stability of them was not entirely determined. Had the Junkers worked it would have carried 20 tons (20.3 tonnes) of cargo, or the equivalent in men, but it was a total failure. Several factors contributed to this. One was that the design and production departments did not work together, in contrast to Messerschmitt where the 321 was produced by an integrated team. When the shop floor came to build the machine they found that the designers had specified exotic woods and other materials which were not available in Germany in wartime and the production department had to substitute softwoods which added to the weight. The first time that a tank was driven into the completed cargo compartment it fell through the floor, and the design of an undercarriage to carry the all-up weight of 45 tons (45.7 tonnes) was most difficult. Finally, in April 1941, the first flight trials of what was known as the Ju 322 or Mammut (mammoth) began. There were two prototypes by that time, and ninety-eight others were already laid down before even one flight had been made. Two attempts were made to get the first prototype into the air. On the second try the Junkers 90 which was acting as the tug did get it

Two views of a Kokusai Ku-7 Japanese military glider. Allied code-name 'Buzzard'.

Japan

airborne, but it proved to be almost beyond control and the glider pilot cut loose and landed just beyond the runway. Both prototypes and the skeletons in the factory were broken up and used for firewood.

Both DFS and Gotha brought out improved versions of their standard gliders, but as the DFS was too small and the Go 242 was perfectly adequate neither of the ideas was taken up, and the few other designs that were drawn up were put aside for the same reasons. All told, the German glider story is one of success, with the industry concentrating on three sound designs; though one of them was really too small to be of much tactical use after 1940, and the 321 despite its later value was too large for the existing tugs.

Japanese gliders suffered from the same diversity of effort as did so many Japanese weapons in World War II. It seemed that the military were never content with what they had and were forever asking for something more, oblivious to the fact that Japanese industry was quite incapable of making what was called for in any quantity. Gliders are a good example, for there were many designs, all apparently blessed by the government, but none actually used operationally. Specifications were issued in 1941, a few earlier still, yet it was 1944 before any were flying in more than ones and twos; and by then the idea of airborne assaults had long since been shelved. A further difficulty which permeated everything in

Kokusai Ku-8.

the military field was that the Army and the Navy pursued separate developments and placed separate contracts, so that there was a good deal of duplication of effort at all stages.

Ku-1

The Ku-1 was laid down in 1940 as an Army design and was built in modest numbers though never used for anything other than training. It was a high-wing twin-boom layout not unlike a smaller version of the Gotha 242. The wing span was 55 feet (16.8 m.) and the pay-load was a crew of two and eight men or 1300 lbs (590 kg) of cargo. Maximum towing speed was a modest 80 mph (129 kph), and it had a fixed two-wheeled undercarriage with spats over the wheels.

Ku-7

The best of the many designs for an Army glider was the Ku-7 of 1942. It was known to the Japanese as the Manazuru, the Japanese name for a crane, but to the Allies it had the less attractive code-name of Buzzard. The idea was to build a glider big enough to carry a light tank or the equivalent load in troops, guns or stores. A considerable amount of design effort went into this glider, perhaps more than was justified by its future use, and the result was a most efficient machine with an excellent lifting capacity and good flying characteristics. However, as with so many Japanese gliders, all this took time and it was 1944 before the first one flew.

The layout was somewhat like a grown-up version of the Ku-1, with the same twin booms and central nacelle for the crew and cargo; in fact in side-elevation the Ku-7 looked very like the Gotha 242 which had almost certainly inspired it, though the wing plan was different and was heavily tapered. There was a fixed five-wheeled undercarriage and the pilots sat in a glazed nose with windows well round to the sides. Loading

was through the rear of the nacelle, the whole end piece swinging to one side on hinges. The wing span was 114 feet (34.7 m.), the empty weight 10,000 lbs (4536 kg) and the pay-load 16,450 lbs (7462 kg) or over 7 tons (7.1 tonnes). In fact it could just carry an 8-ton light tank, or thirty-two troops, or a 75-mm gun and towing vehicle and it had to be towed by either the Nakajima Ki-49 (code name Helen) or the Mitsubishi Ki-67 (Peggy); presumably there were the usual troubles over finding sufficient tugs, because it was not long before two engines were being mounted, turning the Ku-7 into a slow but successful transport. The Ku-7 came into being far too late; as a glider it was a doubtful asset from the start because there were not enough tugs to pull more than a small fleet of them, but as a twin-engined transport it could have given good service had it been in existence in, say, 1941 or 1942. By 1944 Japan was already thinking in terms of Kamikazes and similar desperate ideas. About 50 Ku-7s were built; most of them were converted to power, but few were put into service.

Others

There were at least three other glider designs which were all tried out and made in small numbers. None of them came into service and all were found in various stages of production when the war ended. The Navy ordered one design which showed some promise, and also appeared at the right time for operational use. The MXY5 was ordered in 1941 and flight-tested early in 1942. It was a well-designed and well-built glider capable of carrying two pilots and eleven troops, or one ton (1 tonne) of cargo.

The fuselage was tubular steel covered in fabric-covered plywood. The wing had a dural main spar and complete ply covering. There were flaps and spoilers, dual controls, retractable

111

Trainee glider pilot in the cockpit of a Hotspur training glider.

landing wheels and built-in skid on the underside of the fuselage. It was a most advanced glider and performed very well on test, yet only twelve were built in three years and none were used for operations.

Britain

The British glider programme is one of the best spots in the otherwise not very distinguished beginning to their airborne forces. From the first tentative planning stage, a sensible and restricted set of specifications was drawn up; and once agreed they were to stand for the rest of the war. In recent years it has not been fashionable to credit the 1940 War Office with much prescience, but there is no doubt at all that the combined planning staffs of the War Office and Air Ministry who laid down the British glider requirements were both far-sighted and hard-headed. When one considers that they were working in the hectic and slightly panic-stricken time of late June 1940 their achievement becomes even better.

What was decided was simplicity itself. There were no transport aircraft in Britain that could be used for carrying airborne troops and the only practical way seemed to be to use gliders. These, it was thought, could take both parachute troops and air-landed troops, and would be towed by bombers loaned from their proper duties. The

112

Air Ministry favoured gliders in any case because it was thought that they called for less training from the troops and they might also be useful for bomb-dropping and refuelling aircraft in flight. The glider committee therefore concluded that there should be four different types of glider built, and no more. All were to be made of wood and capable of being built in factories not used to the aircraft trade, the preference being for furniture firms who at that time were not involved in work of national importance. The four types were to be:

1. An 8-seater, subsequently to be known as the 'Hotspur' and intended as a silent assault glider similar in use to the DFS 230 in its attack on Eban-Emael.

2. A 25-seater, later to become the 'Horsa'.

3. A 15-seater, to be an insurance against failure by the 25-seater, for the committee had no idea if so large a glider could be made to work.

4. A very large glider for carrying tanks. This was to be an experimental project. It later became the 'Hamilcar'.

This was all. No encouragement was to be given to aircraft firms to indulge in private design exercises, and the development of the prototypes to fulfil these simple specifications was given to firms who were not at that time too heavily involved in building or designing operational aircraft and who could thus be expected to have some effort available.

Having made these decisions the Air Ministry lost little time in putting them into effect. The first contracts were out to industry by the end of June, and the initial order was for the smallest of the series, the 8-seater.

Hotspur

The Hotspur was the first military glider to be built by the Allies and the first one was flying on 5 November 1940, just four months after the order had been given. There is not the slightest doubt that the design was heavily influenced by both civilian sailplane design and the DFS 230, but to be fair to the designers the specification was equally biased. It called for an 8-seater, the equivalent of an infantry section of the day, capable of a very long approach flight so that it could be cast off at a respectable altitude and glide in to its target in silence, the tug having turned for home before being detected. A gliding angle of at least 24:1 was called for, and the requirement was for one flight only. The glider therefore needed to be both cheap and expendable, yet it had to exhibit considerable aerodynamic refinement. The General Aircraft Company was remarkably successful in interpreting this difficult requirement, and the first Hotspurs gave a performance very close to that called for. The pilot was in a glasshouse cockpit in the nose, and the passengers sat astride a long bench running up the centre of the fuselage. Later models changed the seating to a side bench. It was mid-winged, which meant that the main spar cut the passenger compartment in two, but the Mark I had no doors and the passengers entered and left by lifting the top half of the fuselage clear of the boat-shaped bottom half.

The Mark II Hotspur was introduced soon after the first flight of the Mark I and it differed in having small doors in the fuselage to allow the passengers to parachute from it. The lifting lid was abandoned. Another change was a smaller wing and a much stronger construction, leading to greater weight and the loss of the good aerodynamic qualities. However, this did not matter as it was beginning to be realised that the best way to use gliders was to make a dive approach to the landing zone and not try to glide for a long distance. Another factor in the change was the realisation that with gliders made for one flight only it was difficult to train pilots. Finally there was a Mark III which was a trainer pure and simple. This was a complete change in the specification since a trainer has to be very strong indeed to accept continual landings and take-offs, and once again the construction was different.

Hotspurs were only used for training and so far as is known no operational flights were ever made with them. In 1944 there was a scheme to use the remaining ones as a freight train for quick re-supply of the Normandy invasion, but it was never tried and the little glider rapidly faded out of sight as the wood and fabric deteriorated with storage in the open. There were none left in 1946. Pilots who were trained on Hotspurs all remember them with affection. They were easy to fly and when empty could be soared on a good day. They were towed by a variety of small military planes, often pre-war two-seater day bombers, such as the Hawker Hector and Audax, and so made only minimal demands on the hard-pressed RAF for tug aircraft. About 1000 were made.

Horsa

Horsa was the proposed 25-seater operational glider, and the idea was that it should increase the capacity of a bomber to carry parachutists. A Horsa would be towed behind a bomber on the approach to a parachute assault, and both bomber and glider would drop their men together. The men from the Horsa were to jump from two doors simultaneously, a brave idea in June 1940, and so two doors were cut in the fuselage, well staggered so that the two sticks would not interfere with each other. The actual doors ran up into the roof on slides, and they could be opened in flight; another reason for opening them was to allow the passengers to fire a machine-gun from each door in defence against fighter attack. There were also two other positions for defensive guns, one a round hole in the roof just aft of the wing, and the other a hole in the lower floor of the tail to deter attack from below the belly. None were ever used, but in this context it is worth mentioning that the Me 321 had fittings for several defensive guns, and all passengers were encouraged to fire their small arms at attacking fighters. They always did, and they never had the slightest effect on the fighters, who shot them down just the same.

The wings were given strong points for carrying containers, and as four of these containers would be over the wheels it was necessary to

A GAL Hotspur Mk II, which was the operational training glider.

The Airspeed Horsa, Britain's principal troop and freight carrying glider of World War II. The Horsa flew under both British and American colours during the Normandy invasion. The Mk II Horsa had a hinged nose to permit front loading of light ordnance and vehicles.

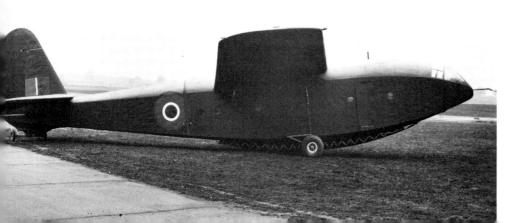

The experimental Hengist Mk 1.

A Horsa takes off on a night exercise towed by a Whitley Mk V.

drop the wheels after take-off and land on skids. In fact these strong points were never used, and were discontinued on later marks. Apart from the two parachuting doors there was a freight-loading door on the port side just abaft the cockpit. It was quite ingenious in its application since it was appreciated that all loading would be with the wheels in place, and so the floor line would be high. For loading the door hinged downwards and all cargo was run in on two long ramps. When unloading the glider would be on its skids; the door was dropped down and two short ramps taken from the floor and laid on it, making a short and wide ramp down which all the cargo could be rushed. It ruined the door, but for an operational flight this did not matter. The cargo door was not large as it had been intended that only motorcycles and combinations would be taken on airborne assaults, a direct copy of the German habit. It was one of the great strokes of luck of the war that the jeep fitted round the

doorpost and could be pushed in, but getting it out was too slow for an operational landing zone and a modification was made to allow the tail to be removed and the cargo run out over the sill. The earliest way of doing this was to blow the tail off with cord explosive, but the RAF Technical Development Unit devised a way of holding the tail section with six large bolts, and these could be released quickly without damaging the structure.

The Mark II Horsa overcame most of the loading difficulties by having a hinged nose which allowed very rapid loading and unloading. The entire cockpit with all the controls was swung to one side, but as it was apparent that the nose gets the worst of any rough landing, the removable tail was kept for emergencies.

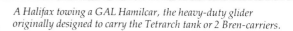

The Horsa was built in much the same rapid way as the Hotspur. The mock-up was produced in January 1941 and the first prototype flew in September. First production models were issued in June 1942 and by the end of the war more than 5000 had been built. Some were flown to North Africa in November 1942, others shipped to India, and, as the wood shrank in the tropical heat, 'renovation kits' were made up by the manufacturers to keep them flying. They were used in all the British airborne assaults after 1941 and many were used by the US divisions. They were both strong and practical and without them the great airborne assaults of Normandy, Arnhem and the Rhine would have been very different.

The Horsa was a high-wing monoplane of very plain appearance being almost the complete antithesis of the graceful Hotspur. It was made of plywood with not one surface of more than a single curvature. The fuselage was a long cylinder with an angular glasshouse nose roughly rounding off the front. The tail was a plywood cone, bolted to the cylinder. The wing ran out from about half-way along the top of the fuselage. It was enormous, and very thick; it was the most prominent feature of the glider when it was flying and its sharp leading edge taper was apparent no matter from what angle one viewed it. A tricycle undercarriage stuck out from the centre of the fuselage and there was a large and prominent rudder. The feature that surpassed all others in size, and also in effect, was the flaps. These really were 'barn doors' and they were forced down by compressed air carried in bottles. On the dive approach to the landing zone, the pilot lowered these large flaps and the entire glider seemed to stop dead in the air and then simply flop on to the ground in the most docile manner. Viewed from the landing zone itself, there are few more terrifying sights than a Horsa with full flap quite literally whistling in to land, the air shrieking round the whole structure.

The Horsa carried either twenty-eight fully-equipped men or a jeep and trailer, or jeep and

75 mm gun, or two jeeps, or 3½ tons (3.6 tonnes) of cargo. The Mark I was towed by a single rope to the underside of the nose. The Mark II had to change this because of the opening nose, and the tow rope was a 'Y' shape and ran to the wings. One or two were fitted with engines and tried as transports, but were not a success, perhaps because the only engines that could be spared and which the wing could accommodate were Armstrong-Siddeley Cheetahs of 375 hp (278 kw) and 750 hp (556 kw) which was scarcely enough to pull that large structure through the air.

Hengist

Hengist was the back-up 15-seater ordered by the 1940 committee. Only eighteen were built since it was soon seen that the Horsa was going to work. The contract for the Hengist was given to Slingsby, the only large-scale manufacturer of gliders in Britain before the war. The resulting machine was graceful and smooth despite the fact that most of the surfaces were either flat or straight lines. It towed well and flew easily, calling for little effort on the controls. Once it was seen that all was well with the Horsa design the remaining Hengists were broken up and all effort put into the larger model.

Hamilcar

The Hamilcar was the tank-carrier that the 1940 committee bravely called for, incidentally at about the same time as the Germans decided they too needed to fly tanks in gliders. Hamilcar was the largest glider built by the Allies, and the only one which actually carried an armoured vehicle. It closely resembled the Messerschmitt 321 in general outline, though it was only just over half the size and carried one-third the load. On the other hand, it had the great advantage that it could be towed by the existing bombers of

A striking view of a Hamilcar on tow.

A Hamilcar dispensing the Airborne Tetrarch tank. The Tetrarch had a speed of 25 mph. A few of these lightly armed tanks were landed from Hamilcars in Normandy to support 6th Airborne Division's Recce Regiment where they saw service for only a matter of days before being replaced by more heavily armed tanks arriving from the beach-head.

the RAF and did not need the complicated and expensive tug arrangements that the 321 called for. Nor did it need rockets for take-off, though it was never operated from other than good aerodromes with hard runways, and it might have been a different story if there had been a need to use it from rough strips.

The design was not settled until early 1941 and the contract given to the General Aircraft Company who set about building it at their works in Birmingham. Because the whole idea was such a novelty two half-scale models were made first, but the first one flew so well that the second was never made, and the next version was the first full-size Hamilcar. The entire structure was of wood, and in order to gain the

necessary strength and aerodynamic efficiency the wing loading had to be higher than any previous glider, and at 21.7 lbs/sq ft (106 kg/m²) it was higher than the Whitley, which was only just obsolete as a bomber at the time the design was conceived, and fractionally lower than that of the Dakota. The entire glider was covered with plywood and on the fuselage the ply was used as a stressed skin to take some of the load of the floor. The big square section cargo compartment was reached through the nose, the entire front of it swinging to starboard. Passengers could enter by small doors at the rear, but the main load was either driven in or pushed over the sill. The two-wheeled undercarriage was suspended on oil-damped struts and these could be released to

117

An American Waco CG-4A in RAF colours. The British name for the CG-4 was 'Hadrian'.

allow the fuselage to sink down on to its skids and so bring the floor close to the ground. A vehicle could then bump over the sill without needing ramps. In fact the vehicle was usually started up while the glider was still on the approach, the exhaust gas being piped out through the side. As soon as the glider had stopped the lashings were released by pulling wires and the vehicle moved forward. A mechanical catch released the door lock and pushed it open and the vehicle ran out, barely stopping at the sill. It was reckoned that a vehicle could be in action within twenty seconds of the glider stopping on the landing zone if this method was used.

The two pilots were in a long glasshouse above the cargo space and they had no direct communication with the passengers. They reached their 'office' by climbing up the outside and had to use telephones to speak to anyone. They had a none too easy task since the controls were anything but light, but they caused nowhere near as severe a strain as those in the Me 321. However, an hour or two was as much as most crews could take without becoming tired. The first prototype flew in March 1942 and was found to be successful without modification. Production on a modest scale began shortly afterwards and over 400 were completed by 1945. They only ever flew in Europe and were not shipped overseas. The chief reason for this was that the tugs were all UK-based four-engined bombers and the overseas bases were not equipped to service them. Another reason was the fact that by 1944, when the Hamilcar was available in numbers and when its light tanks were also available, these same tanks were becoming less and less useful on the battlefield as the size and effectiveness of battle

tanks and other armoured vehicles steadily improved, and light tanks were more and more at a disadvantage. The designed load was for one Tetrarch light tank, or one M 22 Locust light tank, or two universal (Bren) carriers, or two scout cars, or a 25-pounder field gun and tractor, or any similar combinations. Each load called for a different system of floor strengtheners and lashings, and the specialised back-up for the Hamilcar was quite large.

As with other gliders the Hamilcar was fitted with engines, but in this case the idea was not so much to make it into an aeroplane capable of solo flight, although that was achieved, but to assist the take-off and flight of the combination in the less favourable flying conditions which could be expected in the Far East campaign against Japan when Germany was defeated. Two engines were mounted in the wings and were meant to be run throughout the towed flight, and when this was done there was no reduction in the maximum load that could be carried. However, if the machine flew on its own then the pay-load dropped by 82 per cent with a full fuel load. This did mean, however, that the empty glider could be moved from place to place under its own power, which was a useful feature and eased the burden on the tugs. In the event the powered Hamilcar was not needed and only ten or so were converted.

The wing span of the Hamilcar was 110 feet (33 m.), the empty weight was 18,000 lbs (8160 kg) and the pay-load 17,500 lbs (7940 kg), or almost exactly the same weight as the empty glider. This is a mark of its efficiency, for the only other wooden glider to carry its own weight in pay-load was the Hotspur.

USA

The American glider effort is one of the epics of the war, and it is relatively unknown. It started in February 1941 when General 'Hap' Arnold, Chief of the Army Air Corps, demanded a specification for a military glider, and it ended in 1946 when the production lines closed after 16,000 gliders had been built. The cost was phenomenal even for a country accustomed to large sums of money, and more than 500 million dollars were spent on gliders and the various programmes associated with them. Quite literally, dozens of manufacturing companies were involved in the programme, and gliders were built all over the USA.

There were the usual false starts and the usual wrong assessments of the requirement. Some effort was wasted for instance on building specific training gliders, in much the same way as training airplanes are used, but gliders never seemed to need a special trainer, though it obviously helped not to have to use the operational models. Another blind alley was to call for an 8-seater, a fixation shared by all other glider-building countries at that time, and an aberration that was inspired by the success of the DFS 230. The Army Air Corps had some trouble in deciding on what was actually needed, and while it was making up its mind development contracts were let out to many companies. Within a few months there were already scores of different gliders in existence, all conforming to different ideals, and all more or less practical designs. The large peacetime light aircraft industry in the USA was responding to the needs of war with a will, and as a result the Army Air Corps was able to examine every likely combination of size and shape and select the most likely ones for its programme. This is an expensive way to draw up a specification, but it is a most successful one and it saves a great deal of time. By a happy chance the leading specification was given to the Waco Aircraft Company of Troy, Ohio, and Waco proved more than equal to the task. The first contract was with them in June 1941 and was for an 8-seater and a 15-seater. By September Waco reported that they had completed wind-tunnel tests, and the flight-test models were delivered in December. In April 1942 it was accepted and production got under way immediately. Shortly afterwards it was realised that an 8-seater was no use for operations, and the contract changed; but 100 were built and used for training. However, valuable experience had been gained and it was used in the construction of the next larger size, the 15-seat Waco CG-4, which was to become known to the British as the 'Hadrian'.

A Waco CG-4A in North Africa assigned to British glider troops of 1st Airborne Division for the Sicily lift in July 1943. The Wacos had arrived in North Africa in packing cases and British Horsa pilots played a big part in manning the Wacos for this operation, which because of the weather conditions on D-Day (9/10 July) proved to be a disaster.

Three views of the Waco CG-4A after completion on the factory assembly lines.

CG-4

The CG-4 was a larger version of the 8-seater CG-3 and it was utilitarian to a degree. Dyed-in-the-wool airmen were horrified when they first saw it and called it a 'box-car' (and less polite names). It certainly never looked beautiful, but it was less ungainly than the Horsa, even if it was never actually graceful, and it was easy to fly and easy to maintain. It soon became apparent to the Army Air Corps that none of their other development contracts were going to produce a better design than the Waco, so it was chosen as the standard cargo glider, and went into mass production with many different companies without delay.

The CG-4, and its variant the 4A, was conceived with the main intention that it should carry either fifteen men or one jeep and crew. It was a strut-braced high-wing monoplane which could actually carry more than its own unladen weight. The square fuselage was made from steel tubing, and from the beginning of the design one consideration had concerned access to the interior. The nose was designed to swing upwards and give a clear entry and exit for the load, shifting the entire pilot's cockpit area with it. Fabric covering was used for the fuselage and the floor was a plywood honeycomb which gave good rigidity. Wings and tail surfaces were made of wood covered with ply and fabric and the whole emphasis was on simplicity and robustness. As an example of the simplicity of the design, the first ones to be flown in action were shipped to North Africa in late 1942. They had to go in crates on the decks of merchant ships; and when they reached their airfields the flight crews had to unpack the crates (they generally lived in them afterwards) and assemble the gliders, using only written instructions that came with each glider. They managed this on the dusty and bare airstrips of Algeria, and the gliders flew with no reported troubles using hand tools and no lifting gear.

The undercarriage consisted of two wheels suspended on oil-damped legs, backed up by a central skid. The two pilots sat side by side in the glazed nose and the tow rope ran to an attachment point above their heads. It fastened on to a

120

steel member which ran across at the nose hinge point and the release lever hung straight down from it between the pilots. Later models, from about mid-1944 onwards, were given a protective structure of steel tubes in front of the nose to protect the pilots from the effects of a heavy landing, and in particular the effects of hitting the anti-glider poles put up in Normandy by the Germans.

The total number of CG-4s and 4As that were built was 13,900, and about 8500 were sent to the various theatres of war, the large majority going to Europe. CG-4As were flown all over the world at various times, and this was the only glider to fly in Burma when the Chindit operations needed to fly behind the Japanese lines. It was an excellent cargo carrier, but was slightly handicapped by the fact that it could not carry a jeep and its trailer or a gun, and two gliders were needed for a 75 mm gun, its crew and its towing jeep. Another slight difficulty was that fifteen men did not constitute a tactical sub-unit with the Allied armies; but these were small criticisms of a first-class flying machine which did much to assist the Allied victory. The tow plane was generally the ubiquitous C-47, and a C-47 could 'snatch' a CG-4A with little difficulty even when the glider was loaded. It could also tow two CG-4As on a double line, though there was not a large reserve of power for this and when it was done in Burma the tugs could scarcely clear the hills on the Indian border. However, in kinder climates the Army Air Corps actually tried parachuting from the CG-4A with two on tow behind a C-47, and it worked well, but it was decided that this was not an economical use of the three aircraft.

CG-10A

Late in 1941 the Army Air Corps began to realise that to sustain large airborne operations it was going to need a bigger glider capacity than that provided by the CG-4A. At that time five airborne divisions were being organised and, if they were to have a proper back-up on the ground, a glider with a much larger lift was going

The Waco glider was designed by the Waco Aircraft Co., Troy, Ohio, and manufactured in fifteen factories in different parts of the United States. This gives a view of the cockpit of the CG-3A, which was small compared with the CG-4A, which was to be the USA's battle glider.

to be needed. A contract was awarded to the Laister Kauffman Aircraft Company of St Louis to design a glider that would carry a load of 8000 lbs (3630 kg) or thirty troops with as much of the construction as possible being of wood. The result was the CG-10A, a design well ahead of its time, but in the end too late for the war and destined only to be built in small numbers.

It was a large high-wing monoplane with a single fuselage upswept to the tail and rear-loading doors and ramps just like the large transport aircraft of today. It had an enormous rectangular cargo compartment 30 feet (9.1 m.)

Top Right   The Waco CG-4A about to embark fifteen fully armed men.

Centre Top Right   Here the Laister-Kauffmann designed CG-10A troop transport glider is being towed into the air by a Curtiss C-46 Commando.

Centre Bottom Right   One of the first Waco-designed CG-13s takes to the air on tow by its tug aircraft at Laurinburg-Maxton Army Air Base, North Carolina.

Bottom Right   Waco CG-15A, another improvement on the CG-4A went one better in that this 'big motorless craft' could carry one more man than the CG-4A.

long which could carry a 2½-ton truck, or two 105 mm guns, or one gun and its towing vehicle, or forty troops. The wing span was 105 feet (32 m.) and the total loaded weight 23,000 lbs (10,430 kg); even so it could be towed by the C-46 and later on the C-54. However, it was never used in action.

CG-13A

The success of the CG-4A and the Waco company design team inspired the Army Air Corps to call for a larger version of the CG-4, and the company was given the same specification as for the CG-10. Waco stuck more closely to their brief and built a larger CG-4A, and they had it flying successfully by March 1943. Apart from a tricycle undercarriage the similarities with the CG-4A were very close and the construction was also the same. The CG-13A was accepted in the summer of 1943 and production orders given, but less than 150 were made, and of these eighty came to Europe and five went to the Pacific where they actually flew in the last airborne operation in the Philippines. A few CG-13As were flown in the Rhine-Crossing operation, but the remainder were used for supply missions. The load capacity was sufficient for a jeep and gun with crew, or thirty troops, but a loaded 2½-ton truck was beyond the abilities of the machine. It is interesting that these large gliders were becoming expensive to make and maintain, and the CG-13 used hydraulics to work the flaps and to open the nose.

CG-15A

The CG-15A was an improved CG-4A, and despite its advantages it never reached more than small production figures. The specification and the design were agreed in mid-1943 and put out to factories straight afterwards, and the first production versions were delivered in early 1944. The greatest change was in the wing, which was 40 per cent less in span and correspondingly reduced in area. There was better crash protection for the pilots and passengers, a better view from the cockpit, a higher towing speed and a better landing speed by the use of flaps. The weight went up by 400 lbs (181 kg), but the load capacity went up by 500 lbs (227 kg), and it was an easier and safer glider to land.

Others

There were so many other designs of gliders that

there is not space to mention them here. The usual inventiveness and enterprise was exhibited by the many firms who accepted design contracts. There was at least one flying wing, which was not a success, and the US Navy called for gliders that could land on water. Several were built, but the idea was dropped when landing craft became available in quantity. Another Navy idea was to have 'bomb' gliders which could carry explosives and be guided into such targets as submarine pens, using TV and radio. Nothing came of this, nor did anything come of an Army idea to have what were called 'Assault Gliders' which were meant to be much like flying pillboxes and were to land on landing zones ahead of the parachutists and provide fire-support for the drop. Some models were made, but were hurriedly abandoned when the implications were realised. Training gliders have been mentioned; there were seven different types and over 1200 were built altogether.

USSR

There is some evidence that Soviet Russia may well have had the first military gliders in service in the world, but with the usual secretiveness of that country this fact is almost impossible to verify. However, in 1935 when the first mass parachute demonstrations were being given there was also a fly-past by large cargo gliders, and at the same time it is known that there were experiments with what we now call powered gliders in an attempt to carry freight over the huge distances inside Russia. It is unlikely, however, that any of these ideas actually came into military service, and the first Soviet glider seems to have been the Antonov A-7.

A-7

The first models of the A-7 appeared in 1939 and were not far different from a DFS 230 in general size and outline. It was a graceful light machine with clear family connections to a sailplane and good flying characteristics. It carried a pilot and eight men or 1 ton (1 tonne) of cargo. The fuselage was more spacious than the DFS 230 and there were two landing skids placed side by side underneath the forward end of the fuselage. It was used to supply the partisans operating behind German lines.

Views of an Antonov A-7 Russian transport glider.

numbers, and was also supplied to the Czech forces when they started a post-war airborne army.

TS-25

The Ts-25 appeared at the same time as the YAK-14, and was a little smaller in that it carried twenty-five troops or about 5000 lbs (2270 kg) of cargo. It was broadly similar to the YAK in appearance and may have been a back-up design called for at the same time.

IL-32

The Il-32 was probably built to the same specification as the YAK-14 since it carried thirty-five men. It was very square and ugly, a high wing design with a very box-like body. Its claim to fame is that both the tail and nose section were hinged to open and had internal ramps. It was only built in trials numbers and was not put into production. The Soviet gliders appear to have continued in service until the first tail-loading transport aircraft arrived, and they must therefore be the last military gliders to have been in service anywhere.

Oddities

There have been aberrations of design in gliders just as there have been in all other aircraft, but there are two which are worth mentioning because they clearly show the attitude of mind of some men, perhaps many, at the beginning of World War II. This was the time when there was virtually no experience of gliding among the military leaders and only the haziest idea of what could be done with an unpowered plane. The great preoccupation at that time was to get vehicles down to the drop zone so that men, guns and ammunition could be moved about. Without vehicles the airborne force was no more than a collection of foot soldiers with no greater mobility than had Julius Caesar or Napoleon. There had been some abortive experiments before the war with flying cars. The idea was that a car had detachable wings and a propeller at the

YAK-14

There were plenty of glider designs in Soviet Russia during the war, but the need to move factories to the East to avoid the German invasion and the subsequent desperate need for operational airplanes meant that there was no chance of any being built in quantity, and in any case there were few tugs to pull them. When the war ended gliders were once more started, in contrast to the Western Allies who virtually dropped them once the war was over. The first Soviet glider to appear was the YAK-14 and it was produced without warning at the Tushino Air Day in 1949 when six of them flew over the crowd. It was a highly sophisticated and modern design with many good features, among which was the fact that the pilots sat above the nose and did not move with it when it opened. The wing was obviously well designed and efficient and the load capacity was 7700 lbs (3500 kg) or thirty-five fully-equipped troops. It could also drop parachutists and could be towed at 180 mph (290 kph). The YAK was apparently built in some back. The wings were bolted on, the drive connected to the propeller, and Hey Presto! you had a small four-seater aeroplane. Back on land the wings came off, the propeller was disconnected and you were back to a car again. It was a sure publicity attraction and there were several attempts to make it work; this must have inspired the attempts to make military vehicles fly. For some reason it was thought that wings on a vehicle would be easy to control and that the driver would need no special training at all, a view that no airman would ever have endorsed.

The Flying Jeep was a British idea, and when the first jeeps appeared in Britain one was solemnly fitted with not wings but an autogiro rotor. It also had to be given a tiny fuselage and a tail unit, so that the resulting conversion kit was a little complicated and must have been more than the originators had bargained for. A control column came from above the driver's head, and with it he could alter the angle of the rotor and so affect the glide angle. Only one flight was made; the jeep was towed off the ground and it undoubtedly flew, but the pilot had little control and it was scrapped. The idea, however, persisted, and in 1942 General 'Hap' Arnold, usually the most level-headed of men, wrote the following passage:

'I would like very much to have a small light jeep constructed . . . to carry two men and have light armour and guns. This jeep should be designed and constructed with a view to fitting wings to it so we can take off as a glider and land as a glider. Having dropped as a glider, it lands on a field somewhere, sheds its wings and goes around as a jeep.'

So the British were not so foolish; but what Hap Arnold got was not a flying jeep but a Waco CG-4. It was a better answer.

The Russians went one better than either of these and decided that what they needed was a winged tank, and they made one. It also flew. The facts about this winged tank are few and sketchy. It seems likely that the idea was first put forward in 1939 or 1940 and the aircraft designer Antonov was put in charge of a team to make the T 60 light tank actually fly. They succeeded in 1941, using a special set of biplane wings and a twin tail boom with a biplane tail. The entire construction was of wood, and the tail boom bolted on to the top of the tank hull along its rear half. The front half of the tank stuck out in front and the turret was turned round so that the gun faced to the back. The wings weighed 4800 lbs (2177 kg) and the total load was 18,000 lbs (8064 kg) or 9 tons (9144 kg).

For the first and only flight test a four-engined TB-3 bomber was used, with Sergei Anokin in the tank. The TB-3 managed to tow the huge load into the air, though we are not told if the tank ran on its tracks or whether, as would seem advisable, there was a trolley under it. However, it flew; but the engines in the tug overheated and the tank had to be cast off. Anokin glided down, starting his tank engine as he did so, and he landed the machine with his engine racing and the tracks flying round as fast as they would go. He brought it to a stop without mishap and was able to shed his wings, but though this could be taken as a highly successful test flight the experiment was not repeated, and shortly afterwards the Germans invaded and such bright ideas were shelved for ever.

Another oddity was the American XCG-17 which arose from a need in late 1944 to improve the tonnage that could be flown over the 'Hump' from India to China. There were not enough cargo planes in the theatre, but some of them were the powerful C-54, and someone hit upon the bright idea of taking the engines out of a long-suffering C-47 and turning it into a glider. It was done, the empty nacelles being covered with aluminium cowls and the cargo compartment lengthened to include the navigator's position. Thus lightened, the C-47 or CG-17 as it was known could lift 15,000 lbs (6800 kg) and the conversion was surprisingly easy to do. In the end the need lessened as the Allies advanced into Burma, and the C-47 was not called upon to suffer the indignity of being towed; but the idea was highly ingenious and typical of the sort of thing that was tried in times of stress.

THE BATTLE OF ARNHEM—
17–26 September 1944

Top Right
Men of the British 1st Airborne Division emplane.

Centre Right
A windmill in Holland.

Bottom Right
Arrival of the first lift west of Oosterbeek. The dropping zones were located on islands of heathland in a heavily wooded area 9/10 miles to the west of Arnhem on the Neder Rijn (Lower Rhine).

Bottom Left
The bridge-objective at Arnhem. This was the most northerly of a series of bridges in Holland to be seized by General Browning's 1st Allied Airborne Corps to facilitate the advance of the British XXX Corps through Holland. 'Boy' Browning was of the opinion before the operation commenced that 1st 'may be going a bridge too far.'

Top Right
3-inch Mortar team in action.

Centre Right
A 6-pounder anti-tank gun in the woodland typical of the area. The gunners were no match for the German tanks however.

Bottom Right
A Dutch nurse attends to the wounded in Oosterbeek.

Bottom Left
The German opposition. The leading man has an MP 40 Sub-Machine-Gun at the ready.

Top Left
Burning Arnhem.

Centre Left
Wreckage on a glider landing zone.

Bottom Left
Wrecked jeeps and trailers; the shortage of which being the reason for the failure to capture the bridge on the first day of the operation.

Top Right
British prisoners bring in their wounded in the area near the Rhine Pavilion in Arnhem where 1st, 3rd and 11th Parachute Battalions as well as an element of 2nd South Staffords were virtually decimated.

Bottom Right
A meaningful gesture of defiance.

Helicopters

The helicopter is in many ways a military phenomenon, if only for the manner in which it appeared on the airborne scene. It is not generally realised that there were a few light helicopters as early as 1945 and in 1950 when the Korean War started the US Army had fifty-seven, of different types, on the books. These were mostly under-powered passenger carriers with a limited range and payload, but they were quickly built up in numbers and throughout the three years of war the little Bells with the bubble canopy and lattice-work tail girder were flying liaison missions and evacuating the wounded. Apart from these activities and reconnaissance missions the small number of helicopters made no real impact on the war which was fought in a very similar way to World War II for the most part. Only at the very end was there a hint of what could happen if someone wanted it to. The US Marines had different funding and different ways of procuring their equipment and they had a Sikorsky helicopter with a lift of about six fully equipped men, depending on weather conditions. In 1953 there was a complete helicopter company in the Marine Division and they began to accept larger tasks.

One such was the lifting of defence stores up to remote hilltop positions. Without the helicopters the troops in these posts either went without any fixed defences, or they built a track for trucks.

This limited the positions that could be held, but with a helicopter to drop the sandbags and bunker timbers the whole area of operations opened out. The next move was to put OPs and listening posts on to hilltops where there was no route at all and where the only possible way in and out was by air. This dramatically altered the use of OPs and brought a new range of sites into use. But the final experiment showed the way ahead more clearly than any of these tentative moves. In February 1954 a complete marine battalion was changed over in the front line using helicopters. It took most of the day, and it could never have been done in the face of enemy opposition, but it was by then peace-time and the Sikorskys shuttled to and fro, their only problem being that they had to return to their company base to refuel. The message was not lost on the marines, who had in any case used the vertical lift technique to a small extent in the Inchon landings.

Two years later the US Army began the first of what became many experiments with military helicopters and the first tentative lessons were learnt. A year later, in 1956 at the annual Tushino Air Display the Soviets landed a complete assault force by helicopter, including light vehicles and small guns; very nearly a repeat of the 1936 parachute assault. Meanwhile the French were deeply involved in Algeria and they quickly found that their greatest need was for mobility of a different order than that offered by jeeps or trucks or even conventional aircraft. Within a few months the French Army had bought US helicopters and had become the leading authority on the practical use of rotary-wing aircraft in a hostile environment. They quickly found that once their enemy had got over the shock of being chased from the air he fired back at the unarmed helicopters and easily shot them down. The French also found that it was not sufficient to put a few tripod-mounted

French troops embarking in an Aérospatiale SA 320 Puma on a training exercise in France.

machine-guns in the open doors of the helicopters as a way of protection and they systematically began to put together the world's first practical armed helicopters. The results were not all that impressive, but they were adequate for Algeria. The best machines were the Piasecki 'Flying Bananas' which could lift rockets as well as machine-guns. In addition the first Alouette models were given SS10 wire-guided missiles and though they never fielded very many of them they gained a reputation that gave them a moral ascendancy over the rebels. In particular, the SS10 could be flown into strong points such as bunkers and also caves. The Algerians had used caves as bases throughout the campaign and without helicopters the French could scarcely ever dislodge them, but an SS10 missile exploding at the entrance, or worse still, in the entrance, had an appalling effect and the story grew with the telling. It was the start of gunships.

Elsewhere there were similar experiments, though few had the stimulus of battle to urge them on. In Malaya in 1951 and 1952 very small numbers of light helicopters were used to insert and extract British foot patrols from the jungle, and the immense advantage that this gave over the conventional and exhausting technique of long approach marches was immediately apparent. At Suez in 1956 a few British marines flew ashore in helicopters and in 1958 there were some half-hearted experiments in Britain with the arming of Whirlwinds, apparently in ignorance of the progress already made in France.

The 1950s were the years of experiment, some bold but most cautious and all severely limited by the capabilities of the equipment currently available. The truth was that the piston-engined helicopters did not have enough power to lift a worthwhile payload and the next significant step could not be made until the jet engine could be

Top Right   *An Alouette III in Algeria mid-1950s.*

Centre Top Right   *French Légionnaires alight from a Boeing-Vertol OH-21 Work Horse/Shawnee in Algeria.*

Centre Bottom Right   *A winter training exercise involving the Bundeswehr and a Bell UH 1D helicopter.*

Bottom Right   *A Westland Puma of the RAF flies in supplies during a NATO exercise on Salisbury Plain in southern England in 1977.*

Fallschirmjaeger in Crete, May 1941. This photograph has been taken from the wartime Signal *magazine.*

130

US paratroopers of the 82nd Division emplane in a C-47 for the Salerno drop, 13 September 1943.

harnessed to the rotors. It was not long in coming about and the 1960s were to be the years of development and consolidation. Development could not happen without a suitable vehicle and this was provided by the Bell Company of America. Called at first the XH-40 it soon became the Iroquois and later the UH–1, the immortal 'Huey' in its various forms. Like the Liberty ship, the jeep and the Dakota before it the Huey was robust, straightforward and, by the end of the decade, available in large numbers. Its users could afford to overlook its failings and it became the cornerstone of the airmobile concept. A typical version was the UH–1B which had an engine of 1100 shp, a crew of two and a passenger capacity of seven troops, or three stretchers, two sitting patients and a medical orderly, or 3000 lbs of freight; over a range of 360 miles.

The architect of the US helicopter concept was Lt Gen. Hamilton Howze and he headed a Study Group set up by the Secretary of Defense with the clear injunction to recommend the use of air mobility on the army battle fields of the future. Howze set to with a will and the result was the Airmobile Division, the Air Cavalry Combat Brigade and the Air Transported Brigade. By using these formations, backed up by logistical heavy-lift helicopters and STOL fixed wing aircraft the field commander was to be given unheard of additional mobility and the ability to by-pass obstacles, surprise and disrupt the rear areas and concentrate and disperse as quickly as the machines would fly. It was an exciting prospect, and sufficient experiment had been done to prove that it was all perfectly possible. The financial clearance was voted and Howze went to work with a will, his efforts being given especial impetus by the growing Vietnam War. It was a happy combination of circumstances for Howze. He had the right backing in the government, the right climate of opinion in the army, the right machine to do the job and on top of it all there was a low-intensity war in which to put all his theories to the acid test. Few men are given such a chance in a normal life. The 11th Air Assault Division was formed in January 1963 and it immediately started full-scale trials to determine just how large an area it could cover and what administrative procedures were needed, particu-

Men of the 2nd Bn Kings Own Border Regiment abseil from a Huey UH-IH near Fort Campbell, Kentucky in 1978.

Top Left   *New Zealand infantry about to board an RNZAF UH-IH Iroquois during a training exercise in the Waiouru training area.*

Bottom Left   *A Lynx Infantry Support helicopter of the British Army Air Corps on border duty; the fence dividing East and West Germany can be seen below.*

Top Right   *A Bristol Belvedere on active service at KroKong, Borneo, 1965.*

Centre Right   *A Westland Wessex of the RAF lands a 105 mm Howitzer to British troops manning a mountain outpost in the Radfan, West Aden Protectorate, 1963/64.*

Bottom Right   *A new Westland helicopter revealed to the public at Farnborough in 1980, the WG 30 lands with a 4-Man Mortar Section.*

Above: *German all-terrain vehicle in service with the modern Bundeswehr.*

Top: *US paratroopers with M-60 machine-gun.*

Right: *SAS trooper in the Borneo jungle, early 1960s.*

134

United Nations troops descend from a Westland Whirlwind in Cyprus in 1964.

This US Army Mojave (Sikorsky S-56) helicopter lifts a 5-ton M-56 tank at Fort Benning, Georgia. The S-56 can carry 36 combat troops in place of cargo.

The US Army Sikorsky CH-54A Skycrane, which saw service in Vietnam.

Sikorsky UH-60A Black Hawks of the US 101st Airborne Division at Fort Campbell, Kentucky, in Autumn 1979. The equipment can be identified as a Vulcan 20 mm Multiple Barrel AA gun and 'Gama Goat' tractor/trailer units.

Boeing-Vertol Chinooks in Vietnam.

A Sikorsky CH-53A. The Marine riflemen in the foreground are armed with M14s.

Members of a South Vietnamese 'Brown Team', one carrying an M16A1 Rifle, and US Raiders boarding a UH-1D Helicopter prior to a recce mission near Lai Khe, South Vietnam, July 1971.

US Army Sikorsky H-37B (Mojave) moves a 12-Channel VHF Radio Terminal on an exercise in the United States in 1972.

Above: *French para in action in Zaïre. 81 mm Hotchkiss mortar in evidence.*

Above: *Cargomaster*.

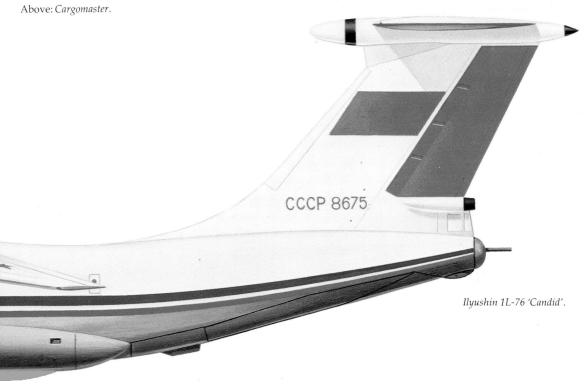

Ilyushin 1L-76 'Candid'.

US Army Huey UH-1D.

larly for refuelling. At the same time experience with transport helicopters used by the Vietnamese Army was taken together with the experimental results and built into operating procedures. By 1965 it was obvious that the airmobile concept could be enormously successful and the 1st Cavalry Division (Airmobile) was formed from the 11th. By September it was in Vietnam.

Meanwhile there were other developments in different parts of the world. In Borneo a small British and Gurkha force of troops held off an Indonesian invasion in daunting country. The border was nearly 1000 miles long; there were pitifully few helicopters and what there were came largely under control of two other services, the RAF and the Navy. Even so by careful planning and imaginative daring the units fought a successful campaign, learning much about airmobility at the same time. It was in this theatre that such phrases as 'mobility is range' were first heard (applied in this case to a pack-howitzer), and 'with helicopters a hundred men can do the work of a thousand'. The British Army became enthusiastic about helicopter mobility and many sacred ideals were sacrificed. It was found that the artillery could deploy siege guns into distant fire bases with complete success, while infantry patrols learned to cut LZs in jungle and rely entirely on being picked up from their radio call. Halfway across the world from Borneo similar lessons were being learnt in the savage mountain desert of the Radfan, north of Aden. Here the helicopter showed that it could transform the old Indian Army technique of 'picketing the heights'. In many ways it was a return to the Korean War method of lifting small patrols to inaccessible hill tops and bringing them back when they needed to move.

The French, no longer embroiled in Algeria,

were working out their own ideas on the use of helicopters and they were imaginative enough to be the chief progenitors of the idea that light helicopters had replaced cavalry in the traditional horseman's role of medium reconnaissance and harassment of the flanks. The Alouette was developed into a fast and agile machine that suited the air cavalry idea as if it had been made for it, and it was compatible with the SS 10 and SS 11 anti-tank guided missiles that were mounted on it. The French were the first to see that the combination of light helicopter and anti-tank guided missile was ideal for the European battlefield and they were for some years the leaders of the art. But they lacked one thing, and so did all the other nations except the Soviets and the Americans, they had no practical heavy-lift machine, nor could they really afford one.

At this time, the mid- to late 1960s, the Soviets were quietly carrying out their own experiments and to a great extent watching what happened elsewhere. All the activity was in Vietnam and it was here that the ideas were getting the battlefield trials and it was here that the mistakes were made and the lessons learned. The first lesson was that of security and safety. The early airmobile operations amply brought out what everyone had said for years—that a helicopter near the ground is vulnerable and the Viet Cong shot down a good few before the armed escort machine was introduced and in time a column of heli-borne troops moved in much the same way as had a naval convoy. The troop-lift moved in a long line with escorts on each side and these escorts had the specific job of protecting the convoy and engaging any hostile fire from the ground. To do this their armament became steadily more sophisticated and effective until these machines resembled naval destroyers or perhaps

A Sikorsky UH-34 helicopter of the US Marine Corps.

A US Army Sikorsky S-58 Helicopter taking off.

air force fighters.

But Vietnam taught more than equipment and weapon design, it taught the absolute necessity of proper procedures, proper communications and above all, proper drills for air crew and troops. By the time the war was over a force of twelve UH–1s could land their troops and be climbing away within two minutes from a small jungle strip just over one rotor's width in diameter.

The experience was not bought cheaply. Air crews flew at an intensive rate almost from the day that they arrived and casualties from enemy fire as well as from exhaustion were commonplace. Vietnam also taught that a medium-lift helicopter is vital to any airmobile force and luckily the US Army had the ideal one, the CH-46

Chinook. It could carry a 105 mm gun underslung and the crew and some ammunition inside. This provided the fast-moving artillery that the airmobile force needed and before the war ended it was not untypical for a gun-crew to make 20 or more moves in 24 hours when there was an intensive operation. This ability to bring artillery to the battle, as well as the continual improvements in the 'strap on' weapons steadily improved the hitting power of the division and overcame the main criticism of the airmobile idea, that it lacked a worthwhile punch.

The price for all this was in the support. Helicopters are not cheap machines to buy or to operate. They require continual and expensive maintenance from skilled crews and the more types there are, the more weapons there are and

141

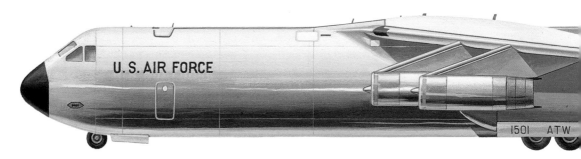

Lockheed YC-141B Starlifter;

Lockheed C-5A Galaxy.

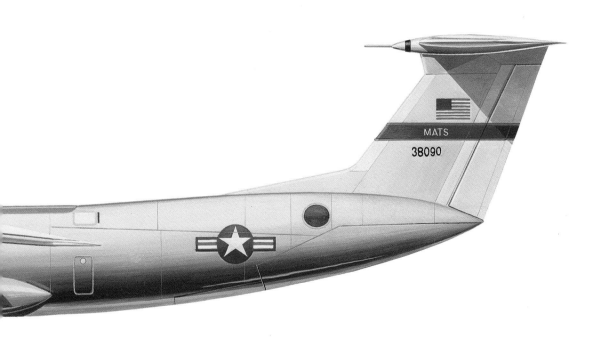

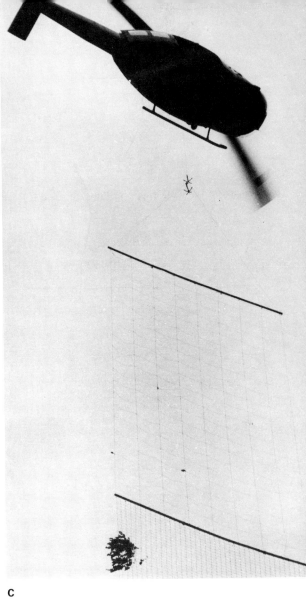

A

B

C

D

Opposite and Right *A New Idea in the Helicopter War. A) A Huey UH-1D loaded with steel mesh netting which is designed to be dropped on jungle tree tops forming a landing stage for machines and men. B) The helicopter lets down its steel netting. C) Two men leap out from the hovering 'chopper' on to the steel mat. D) Sergeant Bennie Braswell US Army calling his base camp on the radio. E) Men of the US 1st Air Cavalry Division arriving in a Huey UH-1D are about to perform the tricky task of landing on the steel mat.*

E

the more communication sets there are, so also is the maintenance load increased. There is no adequate substitute for the skilled man and in Vietnam they were grossly over-used. Helicopters also use fuel in an alarming way. Their range is relatively short, though this was never much of a trouble in Vietnam, but if they are to operate away from their fixed base they need to have forward re-fuelling points. The best way to set these up is to use the medium of heavy-lift machines to bring in flexible tanks, 'blivits' and put them on the ground somewhere behind the forward defence area. This, of course, uses helicopters that might be moving guns and since a helicopter that is out of fuel might well be out of ammunition also, it seems sense to stock some ammunition at the same re-fuelling point, or near it. Once again the heavier lift machines have to be used to bring up the ammunition and the juggling with loads, schedules and flying hours becomes a nightmare.

It will be interesting to see if the Soviet Army can sustain airmobile operations as successfully as has the United States. Certainly they have the machines for the job, but there is some doubt as to whether they have the structure and experience to use them in a prolonged assault. The main use would seem to be more modest and linked to the Soviet policy of the 'Desant', the long distance raid into the enemy's rear areas. This is not quite the same thing as an airmobile assault as it envisages the helicopters carrying the troops into the assault area, but so far there is no clear indication that they would set up a forward base and provide the sort of short-range mobility that the US used in Vietnam, but that may come. Machines such as the Mi–24 Hind are not only useful load and troop-carriers, but they also convert into formidable gunships and carry a very frightening variety of weapons. It is quite clear from observed strikes against the guerrillas

in Afghanistan that the Soviets are learning how to use helicopters for low-level attacks in much the same way as did the Americans. The normal technique for any gunship strike against the Afghans is for one machine to stay up high and provide observation and command for a flight of three armed helicopters which fly low to the target. This has largely negated the Afghan AA fire which at first was quite successful when the strike was launched by one or two gunships alone.

Reports of troop assaults from helicopters in Afghanistan are confusing and not very helpful. It seems that they are used, as indeed would be entirely sensible, but the terrain is so difficult that they cannot do much when they do land and apart from dealing with some small local centre of resistance they are more liable to become targets for concealed snipers. Hence the massive battalion-sized assaults and extractions that characterised much of the Vietnam fighting have not been seen in the mountains and valleys of Afghanistan.

In Israel and in Europe although there may be an obvious need for airmobile formations of all kinds, and not every military commentator will agree that the need exists, there is not the money to either provide or support them. Most countries are contenting themselves with a small troop-lift and a few gunships. The latter are generally a modified troop-carrier, just as were the first Hueys in Vietnam. The Israeli Army has a Rapid Reaction Force on permanent stand-by with at least a lift for one infantry company and on several occasions in the past fifteen years it has shown that it can scramble within a quarter of an hour and be on its way to an objective, taking an operational briefing by radio while in transit. No other country can match this sort of readiness, but few other countries need to. In the Federal Republic of Germany the airmobile

A Soviet M1L Mi-4 helicopter, whose NATO code-name is 'Hound'. The tank is a PT-76 Amphibian.

Japanese airlift. A Boeing-Vertol KV-107-11A.

concept has found the most backing and there are three airmobile brigades which are both para-trained and helicopter-borne. France has a single airborne division which is similarly dual-rôled, but neither country has the massive support backing needed for a full helicopter assault. The main idea is to move troops rapidly around the European battlefield, particularly anti-tank teams. Indeed, it does seem that in any future war the helicopter is going to play a significant part in the anti-tank defence, both with gunships and by shifting ground fire-teams from one place to another to meet varying threats. No other vehicle can match it for speed and cross-country mobility.

Vehicles

The great handicap of any airborne force is that once it is on the ground it is far less mobile than an ordinary infantry battalion. The dashing paratrooper flying for hundreds of miles to his drop zone, parachuting into battle with rifles, pistols and knives hanging all around him, lands on the ground and finds that he is no more mobile than a Roman legionary. Indeed he is usually in a worse position, since the Romans were sensible about the way they loaded their soldiers and for the most part they carried a reasonable weight which did not exhaust the man after a day's marching. Throughout World War II, and to a great extent today, the speed of a parachute force once it hit the ground was limited to that of the marching man, and from the very start it was realised that this was a drawback that needed to be tackled seriously. Because the force was going to be flown into enemy territory there was always a tendency for commanders to pile in every possible requirement and to pack as much ammunition as the planes would carry. Indeed there were a few occasions when the pilots found that they were overloaded and they had to take strong measures to dump some of the cargo before they could take off.

The Germans seem to have been more reasonable in the way that they loaded their soldiers, but they always banked on being able to operate an airfield within a few hours of the assault, so their need was a little less pressing. They also dropped near to their objective, a lesson not entirely absorbed by the Allies even four years later. Tactical mobility is essential to the parachutist for he has to make up for his lack of heavy weapons, and one way to do this is to keep moving and not get pinned down. Once the parachute force is hemmed in it is only a matter of time before it will be overrun, unless the ground forces follow up quickly. History is full of examples of the times when the ground forces did not come up and the luckless airborne men had no option but to fight against steadily increasing odds and heavier and heavier weaponry until they were overwhelmed. Without tactical mobility the airborne force cannot fight a battle of movement, cannot withdraw from attacks and cannot follow up advantages when they are offered, except of course that it can do all these things at the speed of a walk.

Today the position is much better, due mainly to modern aircraft and their extraordinary load-carrying ability; but in relying on aircraft for delivery the modern airborne soldier has almost gone back to the German technique of 1940, for now these planes need to land to unload and so once again the force has to capture some sort of airstrip or landing field. The light vehicles can be dropped by parachute, but light vehicles do not win battles. The whole story of ground mobility is tied up in the problem of delivery to the drop zone, and it sometimes looks as though the ideas are going slowly round in circles.

Germany

The Germans never actually designed any vehicles specifically for airborne use, which is in a way surprising since they tried special airborne versions of practically every other piece of military equipment. From the start, however, they were hampered by the fact that they could only bring vehicles into the battle in a DFS 230 glider or in a Junkers 52. The glider was clearly quite impractical. This left the Ju 52, which, though not impractical, was not too much help. The loading door and cargo compartment were both small and the floor was high off the ground. Any vehicle had to be run up a long ramp to get it up to the door, and once there it had to be turned through 90 deg., the curse of all two-wheeled undercarriages, and manhandled forward into the centre of the plane. It took a long time to load and quite a time to unload, and the size of the load was relatively small. The only German Army vehicles which could be flown in this way were motorcycles and sidecar combinations. There were no four-wheeled vehicles small enough to go round the door, and if there had

An air-lifted DKW Volkswagen staff car en route to North Africa.

191.

An Me 323 Gigant dispenses a carrier in Tunisia, February 1943. The vehicle is a German conversion of a captured French Renault Model UE tracked infantry carrier.

been it is doubtful if they would have been of much practical use for they could never have carried more than two men and virtually no other load.

So, having to make do with sidecars, the Germans put them to the best possible use. The motorcycle was the BMW, Model R 75, or the large Zundapp KS 750. Both were heavy and strong 750 cc machines with a single-seater sidecar, a tough engine and large wheels with big tyres. They both weighed 400 kg which made them difficult to manhandle, but they could carry a machine-gun or a mortar and both were equipped with a towing hook so that they could take a trailer if need be. These machines were carried in the Junkers and run out of the door on long ramps. They were used in all the airborne operations of 1940 and 1941 and remaining photographs show them chugging along carrying appalling loads and even towing the 3.7 cm anti-tank guns with the crew clinging on to the sidecar. Quite naturally the cross-country ability of that sort of vehicle was poor, to say the least, but it provided a minimal motor transport, and that was far better than none at all.

The next vehicle to be tried was a logical development of the sidecar, the Kettenkrad built by NSU. This was a small semi-tracked tractor with a single motorcycle wheel in the front and handlebar steering. The crew was three men, but it had a 1500 cc four-cylinder engine and the main use of the vehicle was to tow guns or trailers. It was slow and rather noisy, but it only weighed 1200 kg and it could tow a pay-load

Mopping up after the Battle of Crete, 1941. Three Fallschirmjaeger mounted on a BMW motor-cycle combination.

became a small cart and could be dragged off a normal flat drop zone without too much effort, but it could not be taken too far since the wheels were small and not very efficient and pulling was tiring for the men. The usual solution to this difficulty was to commandeer local transport and Norway, where the battalions took any vehicle that could move, was the best example of this. In Holland and Crete the fighting was too local and confined for there to be much need of transport until after the battle was virtually over.

Another peculiarly German idea was to use ponies. The mountain divisions carried their gear on Haflinger Alpine ponies and it seemed natural to use them for the airborne troops. They were flown into the battle areas in the Junkers, but, although this worked in peacetime, when it was tried in Holland the shell-fire on Waalhaven airfield caused the first plane-load to panic as they were being led down the ramp, and after that the idea was discreetly dropped. Nevertheless, the rest of the German Army used horses right up until 1945, and while the Haflingers were cutting loose at Waalhaven in the north of Holland a whole German cavalry division was moving up to the top end of the Zuyder Zee pushing the Dutch defenders before it.

The modern German airborne force has what is probably the best light carrying vehicle of any in the world. This is the Faun Kraftkarren or Kraka, a small flat-bed vehicle with the driver sitting on the front edge and the wheels below the load bed. The engine is a BMW twin cylinder motorcycle type tucked under the rear floor driving direct to the back wheels, and the whole outfit weighs 1300 kg and carries 800 kg. The surprising thing about the Kraka, however, is that it folds up. Just in front of the engine, and about two-thirds of the way back from the front is a hinge running right across the frame. The whole of the rear end can be swung down and tucked under the front so that the back wheels nearly meet the front ones and the overall length is reduced from 2.75 m. to 1.75 m. A Transall can carry sixteen Krakas when they are folded, or ten unfolded ones, and a CH-53 helicopter takes five folded ones. Of all the specialised carrying vehicles that have been envisaged or made for airborne use, the Kraka is the only one that actually works and works well. Since production started in 1972, 762 of them have been issued to German airborne and helicopter-borne units and they have been a complete success.

weighing the same. A few were tried in Crete, but there is no record of how they reached there, and one assumes that they were flown in inside a Junkers and somehow packed into the cargo compartment. It sounds a difficult operation and the Kettenkrad had to wait for the Gotha 242 glider before it could be flown with any simplicity. By the time that glider was in service, however, the airborne operations had ended and the little tractor became a normal infantry vehicle.

The main administrative problem facing a German airborne commander in 1940, once he had found all his men, was the collection of the containers of ammunition, supplies, radios and all the other impedimenta of war which had arrived with his parachutists on the drop zone. The weapons were for the most part easy, because each one belonged to somebody and he collected it from the container itself and carried it away. Reserve ammunition, however, was less straightforward since it was going to be needed soon, and when it was needed it would have to be some distance away. So the container carrying it had to be moved, and it could only be moved by hand. To solve this difficulty each container had a pair of wheels packed inside the lid, and a handle. The wheels clipped on to the sides and the handle allowed two men to pull. Like that it

A similar vehicle, though not so useful, is the Belgian FN AS 24. This came from the same drawing-board as the Kraka, but was several years earlier, and the first issues were to Belgian Parachute Commando units in 1959. It is a three-wheeler with the single wheel in front, and the structure is built of steel tube. The engine is between the two back wheels and the whole frame folds in to reduce the size. Extended, it carries four men seated abreast or a maximum load of 340 kg for an empty weight of 224 kg, which is a good pay-load ratio, but unfortunately the little FN can easily be overloaded and its virtues swamped. However, it is a brave attempt to produce a really light parachutable load-carrier and with sensible handling it gives the parachute units the sort of short-range tactical mobility they should have had many years ago.

Britain

The British realised from the start that any airborne force was going to need transport, but that there was little chance of providing more than a token strength on the drop zone. This sharply coloured the view of the uses of airborne troops and made it seem highly probable that they would be unable to be much more than a nuisance force or saboteurs. The idea of using airborne forces to seize and hold some position did not appear feasible at that time, or at least it did not to the men in the War Office and the Air Ministry, so despite the clear and sensible thought that went into the glider programme,

Top Left *Field Marshal Festing inspects an SAS Land Rover team at Hereford c. 1960. A Browning .30 Machine-Gun is mounted forward.*

Centre Left *The British Welbilke 2-stroke motor-cycle conveniently fitted into an equipment container. It measured 4 ft 3 ins long × 15 ins broad: maximum speed 30 mph; range on one filling of 6½ pints of petrol 90 miles. The Welbilke created a trendy fashion in motor-cycling in the post-war years.*

Bottom Left *A jeep lashed to a platform for dropping. The photograph is dated 28 January 1944. Jeeps were dropped on platforms from Stirling Mk Vs to the SAS Brigade operating behind the lines in France in the autumn of 1944.*

A jeep loaded into a Holland-bound Waco: 'Operation Market-Garden', September 1944.

An experimental drop of a jeep mounted on a platform using a GQ designed 'chute on Salisbury Plain in England in 1943.

those gliders were only meant for troop-carrying.

True, the Hamilcar was foreseen as lifting a tank, but none of the others was planned to take a vehicle of any size. There was no provision for even the lightest load-carrier beyond motor-cycles and sidecars. Once again the German experience coloured the British thinking entirely and, when the planning committee was first asked what load the Horsa could carry besides men, they replied that it was one motorcycle combination. Later this was modified to four sidecars, or one scout car, or one 3.7 in. howitzer. Anything else, such as a 15 cwt truck or a Bren carrier was out of the question until the Hamilcar had proved itself, when it was proposed to mod-ify it slightly and turn it into a general-purpose heavy-cargo glider which could take these larger vehicles. It was a fairly depressing prospect

really, for it meant that the War Office could see no more use for its airborne forces than that of raiding—a sudden drop on to an unsuspecting enemy, a savage beat-up, and a quick with-drawal either by sea or by air. It is interesting that the idea of withdrawing the force by air was in the minds of the planners, because that was the German idea in 1939, though they had seen the almost insuperable difficulties of it by 1940. However, in this plan there was no hint of the force staying and fighting it out, and so no heavy vehicles were needed. Later on, when it was realised that airborne troops could actually fight a battle on more or less even terms with the ground defenders, the absence of a proper heavy lift for the vehicles and guns became a severe handicap.

Luck played its part, as it so often does, and we have recounted already how the jeep fitted into the Horsa without difficulty, though with not much room to spare. So the British airborne forces of World War II were based entirely on the jeep, and the jeep showed itself to be well capable of coping with the demands made on it. By and large the jeep itself was not a carrier. It was too small, but it could tow almost anything. The idea was to put as much into the jeep itself as it would uncomfortably carry, and then hook on a trailer. For the drive off the drop zone jeeps were usually expected to tow a couple of trailers, leaving one at the RV (rendezvous) or the gun lines. Many gliders carried an extra trailer for this purpose and there was a special light trailer also which will be described later. The full story of the jeep belongs to the American section, and to a great extent the British used the US modifica-tions and variants; though there were many local modifications and additions built on to allow different loads to be carried.

The motorcycles of 1940 were largely civilian types impressed into war service, or built to WD orders on the same pattern. They were smaller and lighter than the German models, being for the most part single-cylinder, 500 cc Norton 16 H or BSA M 20 with a single-seat sidecar. A wartime Norton specially built for the Army was the Model 633 with a 633 cc engine and a shaft-drive to the sidecar wheel, the only British bike so equipped. In fact none of these combinations were ever used in anger by airborne forces, though solo motorcycles did prove to be quite valuable. There is always a need for single men to move around the battlefield; usually they are the local commanders, and if the battle area is fairly large, as it sometimes was in Normandy or Holland, a solo motorcycle can be most useful. It can also take the inevitable messenger with documents and maps, though perhaps not too much emphasis ought to be put on this task since the rider is so vulnerable to ambush.

The airborne motorcycles came in two sizes. The first was a 125 cc lightweight of conventional design and usually made by the James Company. It had a three-speed gear box, large wheels and only weighed 70 kg so that the rider could manhandle it over obstacles without too much effort. For cross-country use they were often better than the large ones and they were easier for inexperienced riders to master. This sort of motorcycle was used in many of the operations after 1943 and they proved to be quite useful. The main trouble with them was that they were ridden to death on the airfields and in the mounting camps before the operation ever took place. They could be dropped from the door of the C-47 with a single parachute, or carried in a crate in the bomb-bay of a Halifax, or pushed into an odd corner in a glider.

The next model was better known but tactically less successful. This was a folding motorcycle which went into a container and could be dropped from the wing pylons of the C-47, or the Whitley, or any other machine which could hook a container on. It was the 'Welbike' or 'Parascooter', specially developed for airborne forces by the Research Station at Welwyn in Hertfordshire. It has a place in history because it must be the first motorcycle ever to be designed for airborne use, and the emphasis was on size rather than performance. It had a tiny 98 cc engine with a single-speed and small wheels. The central frame was small and the handlebars and saddle-pillar folded down on to it making a bundle 1.30 m. long by 30 cm wide by 38 cm deep, weighing 32 kg. One man could lift it out of

a CLE container, unfold it and ride off within a few minutes of it landing. The frame was particularly rugged in order to withstand the shock of landing and the rough treatment that it got when being ridden, but the Welbike was not a great success. It was too small and the little wheels fell into potholes or stuck in shallow mud. The rider was very much perched on top of it and could not carry anything with him. Indeed even his personal weapon was an embarrassment, and most of the machines were found to be more use for message-carrying around the dispersed transit camps and mounting airfields. After the war they were marketed with some success as the 'Corgi' civilian machine, and were given a two-speed box for road use.

Another obvious way of improving a man's mobility on the ground is to give him a bicycle, and military history of the late nineteenth and early twentieth centuries is full of accounts of cycle battalions and cycle units. The idea is quite sound provided that one can be sure that all battles will take place on level flat ground with a firm surface. Under these conditions the bicycle is a useful way of getting about, and for town-fighting or in a country such as Holland and Denmark where there is a dense network of good roads they are perfectly practical. It is when the rider wishes to go off the roads that their limitations begin to show. The modern sport of cycle-cross is a sort of cross-country race on bicycles and it is instructive to watch the competitors, since they actually carry their machines for rather more than they ride them. Soldiers soon found the same thing, and once again they tended to use them in barracks and not in battle. Even so, there were folding airborne bicycles, and quite a bit of effort went into finding out how to drop them by parachute. A bicycle does not take kindly to being dropped, and after some experiment it was found that the best way was to arrange for it to land upside down on its handlebars. If it landed the right way up the wheels bent immediately into a banana shape.

None of these solo two-wheeled machines, however, were much good in the military sense. The man riding a two-wheeler is pre-occupied with steering and keeping his balance, and has little time for looking about him and keeping a sharp eye open for possible enemy action, whereas in any four-wheeled vehicle one man can drive while all his passengers are looking around and even firing. Except for special uses

Armoured jeeps with Browning .50 Machine-Guns at Bastogne, Battle of the Bulge, 26 December 1944–2 January 1945.

such as convoy-patrolling or despatch-carrying, the two-wheeler is not really practical as a military vehicle.

Realisation of this dawned early on and from 1941 onwards the private motor firms of Britain were seeking a light vehicle suitable for the new airborne troops, and capable of being carried in the gliders yet to be built. There were several which reached the prototype stage before the jeep effectively killed them, probably the most promising being the one designed by the Standard Motor Company. This was an ultra-light four-wheeler driven by their 8 hp four-cylinder car engine. The wheel base was 3 feet 11 inches (119 cm) and the track was 3 feet 4 inches (102 cm), and the easiest way to describe it is to call it two motorcycles joined together by an engine between the front wheels. The two front seat passengers sat in some discomfort on saddles on the back wheel mudguard, their knees well up towards their chins, one of them driving with a skeleton wheel and hand controls. The two other passengers sat on motorcycle pillion seats above the rear wheels, their feet resting on a piece of tube, and looking over the heads of the front two men. It must have been an uncomfortable ride, but it was better than a sidecar. The weight of this car was only 672 lbs (305 kg) and it

could carry the same weight. More importantly, it could also tow the same weight in a trailer, and it was good enough to be considered as a special vehicle for the Far East in a version known as the 'Jungle Bug'. It even went so far as to have a one-piece floatable trailer in which the empty Jungle Bug could be floated across rivers.

Swallow Sidecars, now the Jaguar Company, joined in with their SSVA in 1943 which was made to much the same formula as the Standard car, but had a rear-mounted air-cooled JAP Vee-Twin engine driving by chains. This was a slightly larger and heavier machine but only had room for two. It was developed into the SSVB with a Ford 10 engine, but that was still too heavy, though it did have an auxiliary gear-box to give a lower range of speeds. The last machine was another Standard offering, this time a slavish copy of the jeep but lacking the four-wheeled drive. All of these vehicles looked promising as possible airborne carriers, but they were swept away by the flood of jeeps from the USA and none went into even limited production.

World War II ended with the British airborne forces entirely based on the jeep. Large trucks came in the follow-up force which it was intended should catch up as soon as possible, and when it did so it more or less converted

The first airborne manoeuvres to take place in England after World War II (September 1947). This platform-mounted jeep is slung beneath a Halifax IX aircraft.

jeep-borne units into normal infantry. The artillery stayed as light gunners because they could not change their guns, but all the logistic support units were given proper trucks and could lift the normal daily requirements for the formation. However, it was realised that the jeep had definite drawbacks, among which was its weight. Empty, it was just over 1 ton (1 tonne), and to parachute that size of load required a fairly complicated platform and dropping gear. On the ground the jeep used rather a lot of fuel and jeep drivers were always a little bit anxious to know where the next fuel dump was to be found. In the post-war years there were several attempts to find a substitute for the jeep, but the British never actually managed it. The Land-Rover, when it appeared in 1950, was an ideal airborne vehicle with its better load-carrying and equally good towing capability, but it was still quite big and quite thirsty.

Most of the post-war airborne experimental vehicles used motorcycle engines and carried three or four men, but had little or no ability to tow trailers. The main idea was to provide some means of carrying machine-guns, mortars and ammunition, but the requirements of light weight, low silhouette and small size were all mutually conflicting and the usual result was that the vehicle broke under the strain or it bellied in the first stretch of mud and had to be unloaded and lifted out. One little vehicle which did quite well provided that it was treated with care was the Citroën 2 cv, and in the early 1960s the Royal Marines slung the 2 cv pick-up under their helicopters and used them in Malaya and Borneo. Today the British airborne units are in much the same position as they were in 1945.

They are now based on the Land-Rover, which is scarcely different from the jeep, and all the attempts to find a suitable replacement have only gone to show that the basic idea of the jeep was correct right from the start.

There was a special trailer developed for airborne troops, in fact for glider troops, because it could only be carried in a glider. This was a smaller and lighter version of the standard jeep trailer, made of thinner steel and without any springs. The wheels were ordinary motorcycle types and there was a combined handle and hook on one end. These trailers were loaded with standard loads of ammunition and if there was any spare carrying capacity in a glider one or more was pushed in. On the landing zone they were either pulled by hand to the RV or hooked on to a passing jeep, and once at the RV they were left, to be taken to wherever they were needed. There was never any intention that this trailer should do any more than one trip, and once the load was used up the trailer was dumped.

Nevertheless, none of these vehicles, useful though they were, altered the fact that the great majority of the men who parachuted into action walked on their own two feet from the moment they landed until the battle was over. The arduous physical training that all the recruits had to undergo had some basis.

The Hamilcar had been specifically designed to carry a light tank, though there is some doubt as to whether there was any particular tank in the minds of those who drew up the specification. There may have been because since 1938 a recce tank had been slowly coming to fruition in England, and, though it was realised that the day of the light tank was over for normal armoured warfare, it could offer some useful protection to an airborne force. The A 17 was originally intended for reconnaissance, but it got side-tracked after the start of the war when the policy concentrated on heavier fighting tanks. Then it was found that armoured cars could do the reconnaissance job, and then the A 17 contractor was bombed and his factory damaged, and in the end it was not until late 1940 that the first one came off the line. By this time it was no longer the A 17 but had become the Mark VII, and it was a bit of a Cinderella in the tank world. By 1943 177 had been made and that was the end of them; but the Hamilcar could lift one quite easily, and the name was changed to Tetrarch and it was adopted as an airborne tank. 6th Airborne Division formed an airborne reconnaissance regiment equipped with Tetrarchs, and a squadron went to Normandy on D-Day. A few more went on the Rhine Crossing, but that was all, and none went to Arnhem where they might have done well.

The Tetrarch was a truly light tank, weighing only 7640 kg when fully loaded. The crew was three men: a driver, a gunner and a commander. The commander must have earned his pay since he not only had to direct the driver, find targets for the gunner to engage, operate the radio and fight the tank generally, but he was also the loader for the 2 pounder main gun.

Weight was mainly saved in the armour, which was only 14 mm thick at the vital places. Elsewhere it was 4 mm, which was only enough to keep out small arms fire and shell splinters. The main recognition feature of the Tetrarch was the four large road wheels which steered slightly so that they bowed the flexible track for small changes of direction. It was quite a fast little tank; 40 mph (64 kph) was claimed on hard roads and it went well across country. The unfortunate thing was that it never really got a chance to put its virtues to the test.

There has been a need for something like the Tetrarch ever since 1945 and it has never appeared. The best that the British airborne troops have had has been a few armoured cars, but these are no good against armoured fighting vehicles, and like all airborne forces the British must protect themselves against enemy armour. Some sort of self-propelled gun with a reasonable performance from the gun would go a long way to redressing the imbalance that always occurs when the airborne unit meets the tank. It has not appeared yet, and now it may never do so since British airborne forces are once more in the doldrums of financial cutbacks.

USA

The US Army made the greatest contribution to the tactical movement of airborne forces with the jeep, and it did so without going through the motorcycle and sidecar phase first. The need for the jeep was foreseen before airborne forces were actually formed, and the two grew up together. Vehicle production was expanding at roughly the same rate as units were being raised. The first jeep was produced by Bantam in 1940 and a re-designed version was put into production in December 1941 by Ford and Willys, and some of the Bantam models were also taken. By 1945, 639,245 jeeps had been made, and a large proportion had been sent to the UK and the USSR. The jeep was undoubtedly one of the three war-winning weapons of the USA. The other two were the Liberty ship and the C-47. These three enabled the Allied Armies to move and fight, and the airborne Armies used two of them. It is very easy to over-dramatise the jeep simply because it did its job so well, but it did have its drawbacks and it is as well to recognise them. For one thing it was thirsty and needed plenty of petrol. About 10 miles per gallon (3.54 km/litre) was normal for a jeep with a load; less if it was towing a trailer. This is roughly the same as for a 3 ton lorry, and it meant that one feature of any jeep's load was cans of petrol.

Another fact was that despite the powerful engine there were only really seats for three men. If more than one man sat in the back they had to perch on the wheel boxes. There was not much room for kit and if a radio was put in the back it had to go on a special frame, and with the operator in place the back was full. Any personal gear had to be hung round the outside. It was also a cold vehicle. The hood, when it was left on, had no sidescreens and with no doors either the driver and passenger froze in winter. When it rained they got wet. The jeep was not built for comfort, however, nor was it meant as a family car. It was an utterly basic, tough, reliable and above all simple vehicle. If that was what you needed, then you had to put up with the

Top *A jeep and trailer off-loaded from a CH-53D Sea Stallion Helicopter of a US Marine Corps Heavy Helicopter Squadron (1972).*

Bottom *US paratroopers with camouflaged jeep and M 60 Machine-Gun on duty in West Germany.*

aircraft. This sort of light carrier begins to put a useful mobility into the ground force, even though the bulk of the infantry still has to walk.

The US Army had motorcycles too, the airborne one being a small Indian with a single-cylinder engine of 218 cc, but it seems to have had no more active service use than did the British ones.

One other vehicle that the US did produce especially for airborne use was the M 22 tank. This was actually the first tank to be designed for airborne use and the specification was laid down in 1941, at a time when there was no apparent way of carrying it, but it was probably intended to be lifted in one of the large gliders that were then in the design stage. However, the specification did actually call for a light tank that could be fitted inside an aeroplane, which was an ambitious idea at that time. The weight was not to exceed 8 tons (8.1 tonnes) and was to have a crew of three. The prototype was ready within nine months, and after severe testing it went into production. The first production models appeared in early 1943, but there was still no plane to carry it. As an experiment the turret was taken off one of the early models and the hull slung under the fuselage of a C-54. The turret was put inside and it took several hours of work at each end of the flight firstly to prepare the tank and secondly to put the turret back on again, so this idea was patently not an operation of war. The glider programme had settled on the small CG-4A, which could nowhere near lift 8 tons, so the tank had no way of getting to the battlefield. By this time more than 800 had been made and most of them were used for training in the USA. Some were given to the British under the terms of Lease-Lend and these went to the airborne reconnaissance units in the two divisions. A few of them were taken to the Rhine Crossing in Hamilcars, but they seem to have had little to do, and they never appeared in combat again. It was an unhappy end for the little vehicle.

The M 22 was built to almost the same specification as the Tetrarch and it was very nearly the same size, differing only in a few inches. The gun was virtually the same, the US 37 mm, and it had a single co-axial machine-gun. The armour was better; at its thickest points it was 25 mm and elsewhere it was 9 mm, so that it was probably a more efficient fighting machine.

Since 1945 the US Army has made several attempts, admittedly rather half-heartedly, to

discomforts and then make sure that you had enough petrol. Otherwise you could always walk.

Proof that the jeep was exactly what the airborne armies needed is the fact that it is still in service today, albeit in a slightly different form. Nevertheless, the general outline and the same design philosophy remain.

The present US airborne units back up the jeep with the Mechanical Mule, a light flat-bed carrier looking very like the German Kraka, with the same idea of an under-floor engine at the back and the driver sitting on the front edge. The Mule came into being long before the Kraka, so it set the pattern; and the Mule has one useful virtue in that the driver can control it when walking alongside, so that it can carry the absolute maximum load. Some Mules carry 106 mm recoilless rifles and others now have the TOW missile on them so that they are doing much the same job as the jeep for much less weight and bulk in the produce a suitable armoured vehicle for its airborne forces. The most notable one was the M 56 SP gun, a light tracked chassis with a 90 mm gun perched on top of the hull. It weighed 7045 kg and could be parachuted on a skidboard from rear-loading aircraft and went into limited service in the mid-1950s with the airborne divisions. Unfortunately the M 56 was not a complete success; the tracks gave continual trouble and the mounting did not stand up to the firing stresses imposed by the gun. It was also lacking in protection for the crew. There was only a small shield to give cover to the gun numbers, yet the whole arrangement was high off the ground. However, it was better than nothing, and perhaps it could have been improved and further developed. As it was, it was slowly phased out of service and ten years after its introduction it was listed as being Standard B, or in reserve.

Today there are no airborne armoured vehicles for the US airborne, and there is much reliance on the use of missiles and, possibly, attack helicopters. There is also the comforting knowledge that the US Air Force could provide massive air cover for any airborne assault and practically pulverise any resistance.

USSR

When the Soviets first revealed their post-war airborne forces in 1956 they also showed a specialised vehicle. This was the ASU 57 SP gun, and it was, at that time, the first SP gun in service with any airborne army. The ASU is an interesting and practical design, being little more than a rectangular box with a gun poking out of the front plate and no roof. It exists in two forms, a normal steel model which weighs about 5600 kg and is parachutable from a platform, and a lightweight version in which there is a great deal of aluminium and no doubt much less armour protection, weighing only 3400 kg, which means that it can be carried in the larger helicopters.

There are all sorts of drawbacks to this gun: the calibre is too small for effective use against modern tanks, the traverse of the mounting is very limited so that the whole vehicle has to be swung for a shift of more than a few degrees, and the armour will only keep out small calibre projectiles. Nevertheless, it exists in large numbers, and whatever the failings of the equipment it does provide a highly mobile armoured anti-tank gun which can arrive on the drop zone with the first parachutists, and within a few minutes of landing it can be in action giving covering fire against whatever opposition is contesting the landing. This is the sort of vehicle which would have altered the landings on Crete, Arnhem or Suez out of all recognition even if only five or six of them had been there, and it is quite obvious that the Soviets do not intend to have that sort of trouble if they ever have to launch an airborne attack now.

Top Right

On 20 November 1953 some 15,000 French regulars, Foreign Legion and indigenous troops were sent to fortify and hold an airstrip and village at Dienbienphu, situated 220 miles west of Hanoi and near the Laotian border. General Giap and four divisions of Chinese-trained Viet Minh troops surrounded the defended area and a bloody 5½-month battle ensued. The French were finally defeated on 7 May 1954 having suffered 15,022 casualties—dead, and taken prisoner. This photograph shows one of the reinforcement drops on the airstrip.

Centre Right

French paras in action in Algeria. It was about this time that the term 'para' came into usage in the English language for the first time; the toughness and élan of the French parachutist being much admired in the Armies of the world. The re-birth of French airborne forces owed much to the French SAS, which had provided two regiments to the war-time SAS Brigade and which had fought fiercely behind the lines to liberate their home country. The central figure in this photograph is Col. Château-Jobert, 2nd RPC, who under his war-time pseudonym 'Conan' commanded 3rd (French) SAS.

Bottom Right

Although the helicopter saw minor service in World War II, it was in Algeria that the potential of this flying machine as a gunship, troop and cargo transporter, recce and casualty evacuation aircraft was first realised and practised. Lessons thus learned stood the USA in good stead in Vietnam where the helicopter overtook the paratroop aircraft as the airborne assault weapon of the future.

Bottom Left

Beau Geste country but with a difference. Airdrop by Légionnaires in Algeria in 1956.

Heavy Equipment

It was only too well known to those who planned the first airborne forces that getting the man on to the battlefield was only half of the problem; the other half was to get his equipment, his weapons, his ammunition and better still his vehicles down with him. For, without any of these, all that they were delivering into the battle was a group of lightly-armed infantrymen. Nevertheless, at the beginning of airborne warfare, the problems of even delivering a man on to the battlefield were so daunting that the idea of transporting any equipment was quickly driven into the background whilst the first problems were tackled. In the end, as we know, throughout World War II the glider was used, but at the back of everybody's mind there was the thought that it ought to be possible to put the soldier and all his equipment in an aeroplane and get them down on to the ground by parachute. In fact this had already been done, albeit in a crude and elementary fashion, for in 1936 the Soviet army had a small range of perfectly practical containers and also a few very large containers (although now it seems as though these large ones were purely experimental). Nevertheless, there is a film clip in existence showing one of the ANT-6 monoplanes flying with a huge cylinder slung between the legs of its undercarriage. As the plane flies over the dropping zone, a parachute canopy deploys from the rear of the container (obviously manipulated by a manual release from inside the plane) and a second later the container is dropped and swings free to come down on its single canopy. This container was 18 or 20 feet (5.5 or 6 m.) long and 4 or 5 feet (1.2 or 1.5 m.) in diameter, which would certainly have allowed a fair-sized load to be carried, though it is unlikely that a vehicle was put inside it. After that there is no more mention of large loads being parachuted by aeroplanes until about the middle

Right *German paratroopers in World War II manning support and anti-tank guns, which could easily be air-lifted into battle: 75 mm LG Recoilless Gun: 105 mm LG 40 Recoilless Gun: 75 mm PAK 40 Anti-Tank Gun.*

of 1944, when experiments were being conducted in Britain with the intention of dropping jeeps and trailers from bombers.

There had been some attempts at getting large loads down by parachute by cheating slightly and dismantling the load into a variety of small components. The 75 mm gun that was used by the Allied airborne forces broke down into nine separate loads originally intended for mule transport. These nine loads were wrapped in quilted canvas covers and slung underneath the wings of the Dakota, and this sort of casually-wrapped load was known as a 'parapack'. Each parapack had a single parachute canopy with a static-line hooked to the plane. The navigator was responsible for operating the release and dropping the loads at the right spot on the drop zone. It was perfectly possible to get a 75 mm gun down in this way, though, of course, it took some time to locate the various components on the ground, bring them into one place and assemble the gun. Furthermore it still had to be moved, and at that time this meant that a jeep and trailer had to be brought in a glider. Nevertheless, it was a step in the right direction.

The British experiments were designed to drop the jeep and trailer in one piece, and this required rather more preparation than simply wrapping them in a quilted canvas cover. The vehicles were fitted with elaborate frames which were built around them. These frames took all the stresses of the parachutes in flight, and also some of the shock of the landing. Underneath were half-round steel pans which deformed on hitting the ground. From them ran steel tubular struts up the sides and over the top, so that the vehicle was quite literally crated. The parachutes were carried on a tray and the whole load was then taken to the airfield. The jeep and its trailer, or its gun, or whatever it was to tow, were then hooked underneath a long steel frame, known as a dropping beam. This beam had the release gear for each load, and it was hooked inside the bomb-bay of the plane. The beam, with its two loads beneath it, made a large and ungainly weight which was put on to a bomb-trolley and

wheeled under the belly of the plane. From there the normal bomb winches hauled the beam up and hooked it on. Obviously, only bombers could be used, but at the time there were no other planes with the lifting capacity. All the experiments were done using the Halifax IX.

At least half of the load hung out in the slipstream and seriously interfered with the flight of the machine. These early experiments were not always entirely successful. One great trouble was that the vehicle would somersault the

moment it was released from the bomb-bay, and it then either cut itself free from its parachutes or rolled itself into them so that they never deployed. Either occurrence meant an expensive failure and made a fairly large dent in the drop zone. It took a long time for an effective cure to be brought out, and it was generally accepted that a proportion of any heavy drop would actually smash itself on to the ground. When the Halifax was phased out in the late 1940s it was replaced as a heavy load carrier by the Hastings. This

machine had no bomb-bay, though it was strong enough to take an improvised release gear bolted on its outside. The unfortunate Hastings therefore flew with its entire load exposed to the slip-stream, making the maximum drag.

This method of dropping was a very clumsy and difficult way of taking a small gun or a vehicle on to the dropping zone. The business of rigging the load was highly specialised and took a long time using highly trained men; further-more it needed special equipment because the vehicle or trailer or whatever was being loaded had to be picked up by crane and lowered on to its crash pans. When it was finally rigged it then had to be picked up for the second time and carried by lorry to the airfield, where it was put on a bomb trolley, wheeled underneath the plane and finally winched up into place. On the drop zone de-rigging was not quick either, since the whole of the mechanism was quite compli-cated and took some time to strip off.

Worse still was the condition of the plane. Not only did it have to fly with an ungainly square shape sticking out underneath but, if there was a hang-up or if the drop was cancelled, it could not possibly land with the vehicle in place. It there-fore had to drop it somewhere, regardless of whether the parachute opened or not. In a real emergency the entire dropping beam, with or without its load, could be jettisoned as if it had been a large bomb. This crude and rather expen-sive way of heavy dropping was the only method which could be used until the tail-loading aircraft appeared. In Britain this was not until after Suez in 1956, and for the Suez operation the vehicles of 3 Para had to be slung beneath Hastings and dropped in this way. There was a great deal of last minute hurried improvisation in order to get the jeeps, trailers and the new 106 mm recoilless guns down on to the drop zone at El Gamil airfield.

By the time of Suez, both the American and French Armies were already well experienced in using tail-loading aircraft and in dropping loads from them in flight. The method which they used

Saladin Armoured Car, which is armed with a 76 mm gun with RAF Hercules in background has a similar mission to the Abbot SP Gun.

Top and Centre Right *Armoured Cars of the now defunct Royal Armoured Corps Parachute Squadron with air-landing capability: Ferret fires a Vigilant anti-tank missile: Fox equipped with Swingfire missiles.*

Bottom Right *A Scorpion of the 17th/21st Lancers being loaded on to an RAF Hercules for air-landing.*

was the skidboard. In its simplest form the skidboard is a wooden board with a load tied on to it and a parachute or a cluster of parachutes tied on to the load. The board is a convenient way of moving the load on the ground and sliding it into the aeroplane, and it also acts as a useful skid when the load is being pulled out.

However, we are perhaps getting ahead of ourselves by talking of skidboards before actually describing how a tail-loading aircraft drops its heavy loads. The essence of this operation is to arrange the load or series of loads inside the fuselage, each separate and distinct and each with its own parachute or set of parachutes packed on top. In the 1950s the technique was to fly with the rear doors off for the whole journey. On arriving at the drop zone the load is thrown out of the plane and its parachutes opened by a static-line. The first experiments in this way used gravity to deposit the load, and all the pilot did was to pull up the nose of the plane until the skidboard slid out over the sill. It was very quickly found that this was dangerous and most unsatisfactory, for it was quite easy for the plane to stall, and in that case it was uncomfortably

162

close to the ground to make a recovery. Occasionally gravity was not enough to pull out the load, and several porpoise-like motions were needed in order to dislodge it. Plainly something better was needed; the answer was to use an extractor parachute.

The extractor parachute is normally fairly small, only 2 or 3 metres across, and is deployed into the airstream behind the plane. It pulls out a long cable and then snatches the load out of the cargo hold while the plane flies along straight and level. It is safer and quicker than the gravity drop and it is universally used today for all heavy dropping from tail-loading aircraft.

All is not quite as simple as it appears, however, and the whole operation of dropping a heavy load through a tail-loading aeroplane resolves itself into four distinct phases. The first phase is the one which occurs when the load is pulled out. The plane is normally flying at something like 300 kph and even a quite small extractor parachute in the slipstream exerts an enormous pull when it deploys. It does this quite quickly and gives the load a very sharp snatch indeed, drags it swiftly backwards across the floor of the aeroplane and out over the door-sill into space, whereupon it all starts to fall under gravity. This then is the first phase: it starts with a sharp sideways snatch and the load must be so arranged that it can stand up to this sort of severe jolt.

Once over the door-sill the load starts to fall freely under gravity and the main parachutes are pulled out by the static-line. The static-line may be attached to the aeroplane but it is much more likely to be pulled out by the extractor parachute. It takes somewhere between 2 and 3 seconds to get the main parachutes out of their packs and fully streamed, and in that time the load has built up quite a high speed. It might be helpful at this moment to imagine that the load weighs about 10 tons (10.2 tonnes); there is, therefore, an enormous force pulling downwards on the parachute lines. What has to be done now in this second stage of the flight is to slow the load down as quickly as possible. If the parachutes are allowed to open in the normal way they give such a sudden jerk on the whole suspension system that something will have to break. Generally it is the canopies, which rip open into tatters. The most usual way of providing this gentle deceleration is to arrange for the canopies to be kept partially closed by some form of reefing gear, so that they provide a good deal of drag but are not actually fully open. This is sufficient to bring the load down to a safe vertical speed. The reefing gear then automatically breaks apart and lets the canopy or canopies open out. The usual way of doing this is to install a clockwork timing mechanism, which is started when the canopies are pulled out and allows for a delay of up to 3 seconds. So the second phase takes an appreciable time during which a considerable amount happens, and it takes 5 or 6 seconds from the

time the load drops over the door-sill to the moment when it is safely under its parachutes. In that time it has fallen about 300 feet (90 m.)

The third phase of the flight is the descent under control with the canopies fully deployed. The object here is to ensure that there is no swinging or oscillation, otherwise the load will hit the ground at an angle and smash itself to pieces. With a single canopy it is difficult to cut out oscillation, but a cluster of canopies nearly always falls absolutely truly; and provided that the wind is not too strong the load should be deposited on the ground completely upright. It usually comes down at roughly the same speed as a man.

The last phase of the flight is the actual landing and the casting-off of the parachutes. The first part is the arrival on the ground, and this is where some form of shock-absorbing has to be used. Shock-absorbing takes many forms. Loosely-packed bales of straw have been used, in the past, and for vehicles it is quite popular to use wooden struts which break under the impact. A useful material for awkwardly-shaped loads is a cellular structure made of either cardboard or plastic, which breaks down progressively as the load forces itself down on it. It is essential that whatever is used provides an even resistance to the motion so that the load does not tip over in those last few metres of movement. The final and most important action is to cast off the parachutes. If the parachutes are not released the instant the load touches the ground, they will pull it over to one side and drag it across the drop zone until they are stopped by hedges or trees. All heavy drop loads therefore have some form of automatic release which casts off the parachute cluster the moment the load touches the ground. Some of these are mechanical devices; others use a form of explosive bolt which is triggered off by the tension being released on the cables and which then fires a small chisel and cuts the main suspension wire. Whatever system is used, it has to act quickly and surely before there is any sideways pull. The load should now be standing on the drop zone upright with all its shock-absorbing material compressed flat beneath it, with its parachutes blown away somewhere downwind and the load ready to be unlashed and either driven away or picked up.

This, of course, is the description of an ideal drop—not all of them happen in that way. It might be appropriate now to return to the

Top Right   *A Bloodhound missile being loaded on to an RAF Beverley around 1960, for transportation to an Exercise area.*

Top Left   *The Douglas C-124A Globemaster II, which went into American service on 1 June 1950, is shown here with a typical cargo load: a 2½ ton 6 × 6 army truck and a light M 24 tank weighing a total of 49,000 lbs.*

Centre Top Left
Dropping supplies from an RAF Hercules to British Army Monitoring Posts in Rhodesia in the period leading to the emergence of the new Zimbabwe.

Centre Bottom Left   *This 105 mm Howitzer M 1 lashed to a platform prior to a successful drop to the 187th RCT of the US 11th Airborne Division at Sunchon near Pyongyong, Korea, October 1950.*

Bottom Left   *A Hercules C-130; transport flying at 200 feet above the ground demonstrates the parachute low altitude delivery (PLAD) system. After split-second suspension in mid-air the 1500-lb supply bundle, parachuted to earth in five seconds.*

When these photographs were taken around 1950 Heavy Drop techniques were in their infancy. Top left: C-82 Packet in flight. Top right: A 105 mm Howitzer bundled up on a drop platform receives a final check before take-off. A jeep in the front of the cargo bay is hidden from view. Note the rollers under the platform. Bottom: This split-second shot caught the howitzer having been despatched from the boom of the C-82 but before the main, static-line operated canopy 'chutes had opened to control the gun's descent.

skidboard and to explain what part it plays in this ideal parachute drop. Firstly, it carries the shock-absorbing material underneath the load and, secondly, it provides the skid for the load to be dragged out of the aeroplane. This latter purpose is very important, for any hitch in that vital short slide over the door of the plane could well result in the loss of the whole aeroplane. The final function of the skidboard is to provide the flat surface on which the load lands, and once the load has landed there is no further purpose for the skidboard at all. It is left on the drop zone and may, or may not, be salvaged later. Skidboards are cheap and they are usually a large piece of thick plywood braced by strips of softwood which act as runners. The essential point about a skidboard is that the load has to be attached to the parachutes; the skidboard takes none of the flight stresses.

The great advantage of the skidboard is that it is simple and there is not very much to go wrong.

Training is fairly easy but there is the drawback that whilst the board itself is cheap it puts all the strain of the flight on to the load. Where the load is a vehicle, it means that special suspension points have got to be built in and properly stressed to take the parachute lifting lines. Although this works quite well for light loads, the skidboard technique is not ideally suited to heavy weights, largely because it cannot provide sufficient shock-absorbing material for the landing, but it is immensely useful for re-supply drops where the load is in a large net or sling and the board is justified on to that.

There is another way of dropping heavy loads and this is the one favoured by the British and the

165

Another USAF Hercules C-130 transport flying at only a few feet above the ground demonstrates the '1528' Low Altitude Parachute Extraction System (LAPES). This method of resupply, which was used successfully in battle situations in Vietnam, did not rely on a suitable airstrip for the aircraft to make a landing and thus ensured its swift getaway from the battle zone. This picture was taken during the testing period, as a Hercules, piloted by Brig. Gen. Joseph N. Donovan, delivered 36,000 lbs of cargo to the Drop Zone.

Soviets. This method is known as the stressed platform, and there are few other countries which have not yet shown a great interest in it. In its essentials a stressed platform is just a very large skidboard made out of alloy girders. The difference lies in the approach to the whole operation. With a stressed platform the load itself takes no strain at all in the flight; the parachutes are attached directly to the stressed platform and the platform carries all the shock-absorbing equipment beneath it. So the load takes no shock beyond the bump of landing, and the advantage is that ordinary unmodified vehicles can be quite successfully dropped; and indeed very delicate loads such as crates of eggs can be put down on to a drop zone without any harm. The drawback to a stressed platform is that it is much more expensive, more complicated, and heavier than a skidboard, so that some of the precious aircraft pay-load is taken up in carrying the stressed platform. Another nuisance is that in peacetime, and probably in wartime also, it has to be recovered from the drop zone because it is so valuable.

The loading and the rigging of a stressed platform is quite an art. It takes a good deal of fairly careful training, because the platform has to be balanced so that it hangs squarely and directly beneath its parachutes. Nevertheless, the advantages do seem to be encouraging. Probably the most obvious one is that there is virtually no

restriction on what can be put on the platform so long as it comes within the weight and size limits, and it does seem that a stressed platform can carry rather larger loads than a skidboard. So far 32,000 lbs (14,500 kg) has been successfully dropped on a platform. The sequence of dropping a stressed platform is enormously impressive if watched from inside the plane in flight. The extractor is dropped from above the door and streams behind in the slipstream. Within a second it bangs open and immediately the platform jerks away towards the tail. It goes with a rush and a roar, always making a cloud of dust inside the plane, and by the time it falls over the door-sill it sounds exactly like an express train entering a tunnel—it is moving at nearly the same speed too. Once the platform is steady in flight, its shock-absorbing bags open out underneath. These are air bags made of a synthetic plastic material and they are shaped like short cylinders. They hang below the platform and there are usually eight of them, four on each side. As the platform lands, each bag bursts with a loud bang, almost exactly the same action as a small boy blowing up a paper bag and then banging it between his hands. The bags absorb practically the whole of landing and collapse quite flat so that they leave the platform standing on the drop zone with its load upright.

The Soviet Union also uses the stressed platform for heavy dropping, but in their case there are some differences from the British method. The first and most obvious one is that the Soviet platform has a rigid steel tubular structure above it to take the suspension lines. On the British the four main suspension lines run roughly from the four corners of the platform and so are likely to run alongside or even press into the load. In some cases the load has to be braced and strengthened to keep the lines away from it. With the

Soviet platform there is a girder built over the load with four robust tubular legs which are bolted to the platform. From this girder run two long wire strops up to the junction point with the parachute canopy or canopies. This considerably simplifies the loading of the platform because the load just has to be pushed under the girder structure and then lashed down. On the other hand, there is a distinct disadvantage in that it is of a fixed height, and so awkward-shaped loads cannot presumably be put on the platform without lengthening the support legs. It also adds height to the whole load and platform, although nowadays this is far less important than it was some years ago, because there is plenty of headroom to spare in a modern transport aircraft.

There are two interesting and unusual departures in the general Soviet platform. The first one concerns the parachute itself. Although it is difficult to know what is the exact standard system used in Russia, it has been noticed on many occasions that they prefer to use a single very large canopy, whereas this is never done in the West. The Soviet canopy is not exactly semi-circular, as is a normal man-carrying parachute, for it has a conical section in the middle rising up to the apex and this seems to make it very much more stable. A similar sort of canopy has been seen for the recovery of the Soviet space capsules, which are always dropped over land in Russia and seem to come down without any oscillation or without any severe landing shock. The main objection to the use of a large canopy, apart from the difficulties and expense of making it, would be that when packed in its bag it must be extremely heavy and clumsy and perhaps needs a small crane or some similar form of mechanical lifting to get it on to the platform.

The second difference in the Soviet platform is the way in which the landing shock is absorbed. Instead of using some form of shock absorber, such as the British air bags, the Soviets use an entirely novel and most successful retro-rocket. A retro-rocket is one which fires in the opposite direction to the motion, with the object of slowing something down. In the Soviet platform the

Soviet airborne forces leap from a ASU-85 Assault Gun during manoeuvres in February 1969.

Top Left *Italian paratroopers in the mid-1970s unpacking an air-dropped 105 mm model 56 pack howitzer. The men's personal weapons are BM 59 Mark Ital. Para. 7.62 mm rifles.*

Bottom Left *Soviet ASU-57 57 mm Self-Propelled Gun.*

vehicle springs bend at all.

The latest and certainly by far the most exciting form of aerial delivery is known as ULLAD, which stands for Ultra Low Level Aerial Delivery. It is a technique which was developed jointly in Britain and the USA and is specifically intended to be used only by aircraft with large rear doors; in particular, of course, the C-130. In this technique the load is not dropped by parachute at all; what happens is that the delivery aircraft flies across the drop zone as close to the ground as it possibly can and preferably within 6 or 10 feet (2–3 m.) of it. The doors are open before it starts its run and the load is pulled out by the normal extractor parachute and just dropped off the sill of the door down to the ground. It then bounces along for a short distance and comes to rest. Although this sounds quite horrifying and enormously destructive, in point of fact the shock is probably not much worse than that which would be caused if the load was on a platform and dropped in the normal way. With proper design the extractor parachute can be arranged to slow the load to such an extent that it hits the ground with very little forward speed, and the deceleration forward is not too severe.

The difficulty with this system is on the aircraft side. Firstly it is not easy to find a stretch of ground sufficiently flat and sufficiently clear of all obstacles to allow a plane to come down, make its run and pull away again. At night this becomes particularly hazardous. The next difficulty is that as the load is pulled out the centre of gravity of the plane alters and the pilot has to be very quick and very skilful in order to correct his trim when he is so near the ground. It is therefore not a technique which one would use for an assault landing but it can be extremely useful for re-supply drops or in some cases for putting a load down on to a very small and awkward drop zone which has broken ground all round it. By using ULLAD the load does not drift off the dropping zone and it can be put down very precisely within only a few yards of an intended point.

retro-rockets, either four or six of them, are in a small pack at the junction of the parachute cable and the suspension strops from the load, so that they are 20 or 30 feet (6 or 9 m.) above the load. As the load is in flight and coming down to earth a line automatically unrolls and hangs below with a heavy weight on the end. The moment that the weight hits the ground the rockets are fired and they burn for somewhere between 1 and 2 seconds, giving an extremely powerful upward thrust on to the main suspension strops. The effect of this is to slow the load down so that it touches very lightly indeed, and then the canopy is automatically cut away and leaves the load standing upright. It seems likely that this rocket system can be adjusted either in the size and the power of the rockets or perhaps by the number of rockets which are put into the pack, so that it can slow down loads of differing size and weight. There are no figures for the maximum load that can be dropped on a Soviet platform but they very successfully parachute the self-propelled anti-tank gun ASU 57 which weighs 12,000 lbs (5440 kg). Together with the weight of the platform and all the chains and lashings which have to go on it, this must be a load of nearly 7 tons (7.1 tonnes); yet a 1-second burst on the rocket pack is sufficient to touch it down and barely make the

168

With all these difficulties in the aerial delivery system it is not surprising that ever since the airborne forces were first developed there has been some interest in using a delivery system in which there is no parachute. So far no great progress has been made on this, but in the latter stages of World War II in India, Burma and later in Malaya in the emergency a lot of dried foods such as beans and rice, and sometimes fodder for animals, were thrown straight through the door of a slow-flying supply aircraft. The technique in this and in any similar system of delivery is to have the contents in two loose containers such as sacks. In other words a sack filled with beans would be put inside a very much larger sack and when it hits the ground the inner sack will almost certainly burst but all the beans stay inside the larger one. This system seems to be capable of development so that liquids can be delivered in the same way. Water or petrol can be put into a flexible plastic container which is then put inside a very much larger plastic container. However, what will work for beans and fodder will not always work for liquids; for sometimes the outer container is scraped or punctured by something on the ground and then the entire operation has been worthless, because the load leaks away. Furthermore, it is no easy matter to carry a large floppy plastic container with several hundred pounds of fuel when one does not have specialised equipment to lift and carry it. Strangely enough, after all these years, the easiest way of moving motor fuel or water when on the battlefield is still the old steel jerry can containing $4\frac{1}{2}$ gallons (20.4 litres).

Despite all the years of research which have gone into ways of lowering heavy loads on to the ground it still seems that the parachute is the most efficient and the most cost-effective way of doing it. There have been many attempts to produce such devices as folding wings or rotor blades, or even arrangements which depended solely on retro-rockets slowing everything down at the very last instant before touchdown, but all of these have been shown in the end to be more expensive, more complicated and far less attractive than the well-known and well-tried parachute. Nobody could pretend that heavy dropping using parachutes is a simple or cheap exercise, for it is a most complicated and time-consuming operation in the preparation, and it makes considerable demands in skill for the rigging and the setting up of the loads, the packing of the parachutes and the arranging of the whole of their complicated opening sequence. At the time of dropping they must be dropped from the right kind of plane, which has to be piloted with a good deal of skill and has to fly at the right height and speed while the load is pulled out. Once the load arrives on the drop zone there is a very fair chance that much of its expensive equipment in the form of the platform or the parachutes may be damaged and in wartime they will probably be totally lost, but it still seems worth while. Despite the expense, the effort, the dangers and the demands for skilled men, all the indicators are that the parachute is going to stay in service for the delivery of heavy loads for many years yet.

A recent photograph of BTR 50 Armoured Personnel Carriers crammed with Soviet paratroopers practising large-scale manoeuvres with giant transport helicopters overhead.

VIETNAM CONFLICT—
1964–1972

Top Left
Two members of the 2nd Bn, 327th Infantry, 101st Airborne
Division, direct UH-1D helicopters on to the airstrip at Ta
Bat.

Top Right
A US Army major, who acts as adviser to the 7th Vietnamese
Airborne Battalion, on the march in a Paddy field.

Centre Right
An adviser of the US Special Forces, the 'Green Berets',
checks the safety box of a South Vietnamese paratrooper's
parachute harness.

Bottom Right
US Navy SEALS in Vietnam. Their Sea, Air, Land rôle
give them a special place as the Elite Forces of today. Note
the ammunition belts for the Stoner MG worn around the
torso.

Bottom Left
A light-hearted photograph of the Australian SAS taken on
a survival exercise in central Australia. The 1st, 2nd and 3rd
SAS squadrons fought in Vietnam 1967–71.

Top Left
Air supply drop in South Vietnam.

Bottom Left
Two US Special Forces advisers work with the local irregulars in the Republic of Vietnam. The irregular in the foreground uses the M 79 Grenade Launcher, a popular weapon with the Special Forces, especially when loaded with anti-personnel ammunition.

Bottom Right
Although this photograph of a New Zealand SAS trooper on an exercise was not taken in Vietnam, it will remind the reader that the NZSAS fought in that war. A detachment of 30 men from the NZSAS Squadron served in Thailand in 1962 and in November 1968, 4 Troop NZSAS was deployed in an Australian SAS squadron at Nui Dak. 4 troop was withdrawn in February 1971. The NZSAS trooper in this photograph is armed with a Modified M 16A1 Rifle with a 40 mm Grenade Launcher under his barrel.

171

Mounting an Airborne Assault

This chapter is intended to outline the procedure for an airborne drop: the planning, the training, the briefings, the preparation and the actual drop itself. Those who have served in airborne forces will know it backwards and can skip to the next, but for those readers who have never been through an airborne drop and who have never been involved in the intricacies of mounting a drop this chapter may open a few eyes and dispel a few illusions. Parachuting is only a small part of the whole business, just as rifle shooting is only a tiny part of infantry warfare, and the main effort goes into all sorts of other things. Let there be no mistake, the management of an airborne operation is a highly skilled and demanding craft. It only comes after much application and experience. It is not something that is instantly picked up, nor is it always obvious. There is in this simple fact an explanation, at least a partial explanation, for some of the early failures and for some of the extraordinary successes of the first operations; for quite often ignorance is bliss, but it only works once.

Probably the dullest thing to write about in any military operation is the planning. The tedium of counting numbers, allotting spaces, weighing up possibilities, assessing chances, allotting ration strengths, and all the rest of the straightforward humdrum labour that goes into even the smallest military move is good for nothing more than inducing sleep, and an airborne operation has plenty of it; but it has a few brighter aspects too. The real question in any airborne assault is to decide where to go. Where will have the most effect? Where can the transport aircraft get to? Can the fighters support the fly in? (Today they almost always can.) Will the drop zone be right on the objective, or some way off? These are important questions, particularly the ones relating to the position of the drop zone. Nobody in Britain is ever going to forget Arnhem and the fatal mistake that was made in dropping well away from the objective. Is it always sensible, however, to drop right on the target? At the Corinth Canal in 1941 it certainly was; so it was in Entebbe in 1976 and in Zaïre in 1977. Provided that the ground is suitable and that the aircraft can fly in without being blown to pieces the motto of General Sherman must be the one. 'Get there fustest with the mostest', his biographer claimed that he said, and if he did he was absolutely right, for the fustest gains the surprise and the mostest wins. A 'Good Big 'Un' will always beat a 'Good Little 'Un' and let there be no doubt about it. So wherever possible one chooses the drop zone which is right on the objective and puts as many men down as can be done with the aircraft at hand and the size of the zone itself. A good big drop zone allows a plane to drop all its load in one pass, and that is almost obligatory; turning off and coming round again was acceptable for Corregidor and similar tiny DZs with no flak, but in any future war the surprise factor is not going to last very long and while it does the men must get on the ground and grab what they can.

The next major decision is to choose the time of day. Is it to be a day or night drop? Fashions change; the very first were all by day, but by 1945 they were mostly by night. Later, day came back into favour, particularly the ones against semi-regular enemies such as the Congo and Vietnam, but for general war in Europe it would certainly be night, with all the varying fortunes that that entails. Night makes it difficult to see the ground—not impossible, but certainly difficult. If it is to be night, then it is important to decide whether it should be at full, half or no moon. Who will gain by the phases? A simple raid is helped by total darkness because it only employs a small number of highly-trained and rehearsed men. An airborne invasion, on the other hand, might well need a half or full moon to guide the multiplicity of units on the ground, and it might even decide to go in at dawn and have the whole day to sort itself out and take the first objectives. In desert or on snow, night is never completely dark; but a background of European farmland and woods becomes a total blackness from the air after dark, and the luckless parachutist, looking down for the few seconds that he has in which to check his drift, spot the RV, gauge the wind and

172

generally prepare to meet the ground, is helpless. This is the moment when all the rabbits' feet, sprigs of heather, leaves of shamrock, girls' garters and other lucky charms have their brief moment of power. Within moments it is all over, and from then on it is training, stamina and sheer guts which win the day; but there are few more poignant memories than those flashes of time when one has left the dim light of the fuselage, punched through the black viciousness of the slipstream, felt the snatches of the canopy, and then looked down into a black and sinister void. For a few seconds, it is terrifying, full of unseen hazards, holes and stones and hummocks and hedges and trees and every other real and imagined horror that injures night parachutists.

Whether it is night or day the troops have to rally; they must collect into groups and move off together. In 1935 at the first ever public showing of a parachute assault at Kiev, Major General (later Field Marshal Lord) Wavell remarked that there were still men moving off the DZ (drop zone) an hour and a half after the drop. That was excusable for those times. Nowadays 30 minutes would be considered generous. The most obvious place not to hang about on is the DZ where one has dropped. It is the one firm location that the enemy has; it is the place that will be radioed and telephoned all over the district; and for the parachutists it is the place not to be, so all training and rehearsing has to be towards the best method of quitting it as quickly as possible. Daylight helps here, and night may confuse, but nothing confuses more than enemy interference. If the transports have been intercepted or diverted then individual training really comes into its own. Airborne drops rely for success on everyone arriving in a certain sequence, and nothing is more disconcerting than to pick oneself up on the black DZ in the middle of the night and look around for the familiar and rehearsed signals only to find none; and to realise after some time that one has arrived not tenth, or twelfth, or whatever it was, but first, the whole flight order has gone wrong and there is no signal, nor will there be until made by you, and the plan needs recasting urgently. Doctor Johnson said that it concentrated a man's mind wonderfully to know that he was to be hanged in a fortnight, but few things concentrate the mind better than standing in the middle of a strange piece of country in the middle of the night with the air full of one's comrades on their parachutes

with the knowledge that one has to rally them into one cohesive body.

By day the assault relies on speed and surprise for its success. The difficulties of flying a complete airborne assault into enemy territory have never been small, and today with the modern radars and missiles it would seem to be all but impossible to get through to the drop zone. This still remains to be proved and it obviously alters with each different operation, but it is a fact that the small airborne drops which have taken place in the last fifteen or so years, ones such as the Congo and the early ones in Vietnam, have all been in daylight. They have all, however, been against only light and unprepared opposition. By day, if the enemy has his wits about him at all, he can be expected to react fairly quickly and he ought also to have some idea of the size of the force dropped since he can see the planes flying in. For the parachutists a daylight drop is much easier. Whilst still in the air there is enough time to have a quick look around and pick up the salient points of the DZ and possibly to recognize the rendezvous (RV). This is most important, and we shall return to the matter of RVs later on, but just to know whether one is facing towards it or away from it helps tremendously in those first few seconds after landing. The important thing after picking up one's kit is to move fast, so everyone needs to get up and run, and it is surprisingly easy to run in the wrong direction at night. By day it is quite the reverse; one follows the crowd.

Clearing the DZ is the first vital action in an airborne assault. In the fateful Ardennes drop in December 1944 von der Heydte was still gathering stragglers in twenty-four hours after landing, whereas he had probably expected that it would have taken no more than an hour to rally the entire force. A good time for a battalion completely to clear a DZ is half an hour, with a maximum allowance of an hour, in daylight. At night it usually takes twice as long no matter how well everyone is trained, briefed and rehearsed. There are at least two ways of rallying an airborne force on the DZ. The first and most obvious is to use a single RV. Everyone goes to one place and is then sent out to their own company, battery or other sub-unit area. This way the force commander can keep a continual check on the number of men and the items of equipment that have come in and are available for action. He will have decided beforehand what proportion of the

173

force he needs to start his operation, and it is quite usual to send off the leading sub-units when they have half or two-thirds of their men present. The remainder are sent up to them later on, in a formed party. The commander has to balance the odds against waiting too long in order to get everyone on to the RV, and perhaps lose some surprise, or to go ahead with fewer men and risk the battle. In all the early German operations in 1940 the technique was to rush in almost without a pause, and it worked against light opposition. At Arnhem four years later there was almost too much emphasis the other way and time was lost in carefully assembling all the troops before moving off. By that time the enemy had pulled himself together and was ready for battle.

The second method of rallying is to use several RVs, one for each sub-unit. This means that rallying is faster, but it can also be confusing since there are several RV signals to choose from and several men inevitably go to the wrong one. It also makes the unit more vulnerable to attack during the vital rallying period, since it is more scattered; however, there are often good reasons for using more than one RV and it can work most satisfactorily. The essential part of rallying is to have good signals. This is where the wrong equipment can all but ruin an airborne assault before it ever gets started, and this is more likely to happen at night. By day the usual signals rely on something visual. A good idea is a fluorescent panel which can be seen by the men in the air as well as on the ground. Another is to fire small flares. Again it all depends on the opposition and the tactical situation. If the force has dropped right on the objective then some feature of the ground ought to be enough for everyone to run to. On a flat featureless plain, or one surrounded by woods with no obvious landmark, something artificial must be put out. Light signals are very good, because no piece of ground is completely flat and a man 700 or 800 metres away may easily be in a slight fold and not able to see right across to the other side, but he will not miss a light flare going up 200 feet (61 m.) above the trees. Such a signal is also useful for those (one hopes few) who for some reason have been dropped off the DZ and find themselves in strange surroundings.

At night some sort of light is essential. Flares are too bright for most operations, and the ideal is some sort of flashing torch or handlamp. In

World War II the British forces produced the Wald Light, a flashing green and red light on top of a 10 foot (3 m.) mast. It was most effective; but for some odd reason it was never modernised and passed out of service within a few years. It was heavy and bulky, but at that time there was nothing as good. Most modern lights are much smaller and use some electronic flasher, and there will be several of them with the force so that one will always survive and can be set up. When the Japanese started night operations they used sound as a rallying aid and took clappers, gongs, whistles and even, it is alleged, musical instruments on the drop. Apparently all these devices confused more than they helped, and noise is no use at all for bringing anyone in to one point (though a whistle can help at times). The eyes are better direction-finders than the ears.

Having decided on the time of day for the drop, the next matter is the number of men and their weapons and equipment. The usual limitation is not the manpower but the aircraft, for there are never enough. The force will therefore probably have to be tailored to suit the available lift, and the breakdown between man and equipment worked out from that. It is not the right way to go about a military operation, but, apart from the Americans and the Soviets, no army has enough aircraft to lift all its troops at one time, and often there are not enough aircraft to lift more than a small proportion. So the quart is juggled into the pint pot, and the planners can get on with deciding in what order everyone is to land. To minimise the damage wrought by one or more planes failing to get to the target, every sub-unit is split as far as it can be. Commanders never fly in the same plane as their seconds-in-command, and a company will be split between two or three aircraft so that a proportion of them can be guaranteed to arrive.

This impressive contemporary scene from the Russian steppes is typical of the type of photograph depicting the might of Soviet Air/Land manoeuvres that flow freely today from Information Services in Moscow. Although the photograph may have been 'doctored' to reflect such a huge concentration of military activity in one photograph, it succeeds in conveying, as is clearly intended, the immense potential of Soviet Airborne Forces on the conventional, non-nuclear field of battle.

Mounting an airborne assault in the 1980s involving the heavy drop and air-landing of equipment and supplies has come a long way from the days of the lightly armed airborne troops of World War II, 1939–45.

The next decision concerns a Pathfinder party. Pathfinders are a small group dropped a short time before the main stream to mark the DZ and generally ensure that the main body will find the right place. For a large drop Pathfinders are almost a necessity to make sure that every aircraft gets in over the DZ on exactly the right bearing, but with a small force of only two or three aircraft the navigators can be left to find the right place on their own. If a Pathfinder party is going to be used, it needs a special briefing, may need special aids, and takes one more plane away from the main body.

After the Pathfinder decision comes that for the heavy drop. The heavy drop involves any loads that will be dropped on platforms or skidboards. The planes carrying the heavy drop can only take the crews of the vehicles, and will use a different DZ or one end of the main DZ to put the vehicles down. The most difficult decision in any operation where aircraft are short is the one relating to the vehicles. There are some that for any infantry battalion are vital, and without them the unit can barely operate, and then at a very reduced efficiency. This essential list includes the following:

1. Commanding Officer's vehicle, carrying radio sets. The trailer usually has a small command post in it.
2. Signals vehicle and trailer, carrying all the spare radios and batteries.
3. Medical vehicle, including a small medical aid post in the trailer and stretchers on the vehicle.
4. Artillery vehicle, carrying the artillery officer and his radios. The observation officers will jump with the infantry companies they are to work with. Their spare radios are carried in this vehicle.
5. Engineer vehicle and trailer. This may or may not be taken, depending on the operation.

Number 6 and subsequent vehicles will usually be carrying support weapons and ammunition mortars, which while reasonably light in themselves and capable of being man-packed need plenty of ammunition, and a day's supply can easily weigh half a ton (0.5 tonnes) for two mortars. This has to be transported to the ground and then carried around the battlefield, and it is usual to allot one vehicle and trailer to each mortar. Even that is barely enough, but it

176

has to suffice, and if the mortars are having to fire for longer it may be necessary to fly a special sortie to drop ammunition to them. The same arrangements are made for the anti-tank weapons and of course the guns. An airborne force which takes its own airborne artillery with it is assured of instant fire support, but the price is a high one since the guns take up a lot of aircraft space and need continual re-supply with ammunition. In Korea in 1950 the 87th Regimental Combat Team dropped 3500 men on to the DZ north of Pyongyang and well into North Korean territory. The RCT took its own artillery with it and parachuted sixteen guns, four trucks, thirty-nine jeeps and trailers and no less than 584 tons of ammunition of all calibres, all on the same day. It may have been a bit lavish, but it ensured that there was no excuse for not shooting at any target that appeared. At Suez six years later there was much less emphasis on the heavy drop and many of the weapons were man-packed. Today it would be suicide to mount any drop without adequate, indeed plentiful, fire support and anti-tank defence.

The vehicles are rigged on to their platforms of skidboards on the day before the flight. The timing of the rigging is fairly tight since a rigged load is usually taken straight into the plane once it is checked, and the plane cannot sit about for long with a load inside it. Each vehicle crew rigs its own load, and having done that they have to join up with the rest of the unit for final briefing, rest, and move to the airfield. The heavy drop machines usually fly in together at the end of the flight stream, and drop more or less at the same time. The crews meet at a separate heavy drop RV and then go out to find their loads. This often takes longer than expected, especially at night, and the main body may easily have moved off from the main RV before the vehicles are all in. When that happens the vehicles have to be moved in a body to catch up. It is fatal to let single vehicles move on their own for they invariably get lost or ambushed.

It can be seen that a DZ is a busy place, with different activities happening all at the same time, and it takes much planning and rehearsing to get it all to work properly when it happens in pitch dark, on strange ground. This is one reason why all airborne forces make such efforts to choose men with initiative and drive. The entire business of taking part in an airborne drop is exhausting and sometimes baffling and it all happens right at the beginning before any of the fighting starts. It is vital that everyone keeps his head on the DZ and does the right thing, or the whole operation may go wrong before it gets into battle at all.

Communications are the life-line of any airborne operation. The mysterious wireless failures at Arnhem are well known and the result was a series of ghastly errors. Re-supply drops came in on to DZs held by the enemy, units and sub-units were out of touch for hours on end, sometimes days, and even the force commander was out of the battle for twenty-four hours because he had gone forward to make contact with a battalion which was off the air. At Corregidor a few months later the communications were perfect and the commander was circling above the DZ all the time radioing last minute changes of dropping point to the crews as they flew in. Communications mean air support at the right time on the right target; they mean re-supply at the time when it is needed and in the place where it is needed. They also mean that the force acts as a whole and not in splinter groups. Adequate radios and enough batteries to run them are every bit as important as weapons and ammunition, and re-supplies of batteries take priority over everything else.

Command of the operation varies according to national practice, but in NATO it is usual for the Air Force to command the operation until the troops are on the ground. After that it is an Army responsibility. This arrangement is designed to make sure that each specialist commands in his own sphere. The Air Force which flies the troops must be in command for the loading, flight and decisions on weather. Only an Air Force can make these decisions, but once on the ground it becomes a soldier's battle and the Air Force reverts to a supporting rôle. This may seem a trivial matter to mention, but the source of command can be important. The Germans solved it in a novel manner by making their airborne troops part of the *Luftwaffe*. This was an accident, but it was a happy one because it meant that the command of any airborne drop was in overall control of the Air Force who provided the planes and flew them. It meant that there was one planning staff, one command staff and one overall commander who was responsible for all aspects of the operation from start to finish. Nobody has since managed such a tidy arrangement. The German airborne troops were in fact a sort of airborne marine force, having the same relations to the Air Force as marines have to their navy, and it worked very well.

It is interesting to compare the Allied troubles with their aircraft allotments and joint command. The British had no suitable parachuting aircraft and relied on American C-47s. The United States divisions had barely enough C-47s for themselves and found that they had to give a proportion to the British. Quite naturally they felt that they had first priority, and this led to some embarrassing friction on several occasions. An elaborate Joint Staff had to be set up, which was expensive in skilled manpower and slow to make decisions.

As if the difficulties of the flight and the drop are not enough, the airborne force often has to fight with fewer weapons and different techniques from normal troops. Once into enemy territory there is no line of communication, except through the air. From the moment they land the force is effectively surrounded and fights on its own until the ground force catches up with it. This implies a rather different mental attitude; there is no going back, and often there is no rest because the initiative must come from the airborne all the time. Once the initiative is lost then everything is lost and the enemy can mop up at will; so everyone has to go forward continually and at the fastest possible speed. An airborne force that is surrounded and pinned down is useless, as Arnhem has shown for all time. The difficulty is to hit hard and keep on hitting when the enemy is almost certain to be better equipped with vehicles and to have heavier weapons. Airborne artillery has to be lighter and shorter-ranged than conventional guns because of the weight and size factor. Ammunition is always a headache because supplies are entirely dependent on aircraft getting through. Movement will always end up with foot-slogging for some men, and the speed of the column becomes that of the slowest marcher. It is a battle in which wits count every bit as much as muscle and there is only a limited time in which the airborne troops can expect to hold out; after that they must be relieved or the enemy will gain the upper hand and destroy them. The usual method of supplementing the support weapons on the ground is to use Fighter Ground Attack (FGA) aircraft, and in the past this has been done most successfully. Nobody knows how successful it could be in the future. The FGA would have

177

to fly from their bases behind their own forward areas and cross the entire combat zone before reaching the airborne battle, and it would not take an alert enemy too long to rush some anti-aircraft missiles into the space between. Nevertheless, for the early stages at least, the FGA can bring an enormous weight of fire to bear. This goes to emphasise that future airborne operations, in Europe anyway, will have to be much shorter than they have been in the past. Relief will have to come in half a day or so, otherwise it will be too late.

One way in which fire support may be provided, at least for a short time, is by using armed helicopters. This is still an area that needs to be looked at more closely; but the Soviets, for instance, have built many armed helicopters which can carry a considerable armament. It would not be impossible to fly armed helicopters in with the main transport stream and to use them to protect the DZ and support the assault. Fuel and ammunition for them could be dropped or air-landed on the DZ and for a short time the helicopters would have complete superiority over anything on the ground. After a certain time they would be outclassed by the enemy bringing up suitable anti-aircraft missiles and guns, but for the period of the assault they could provide almost overwhelming fire on immediate call to the assaulting troops. For a short-term assault, say the seizure of bridgeheads and other obstacles in front of a rapid advance, the use of such helicopters could be decisive; it would also be totally unexpected.

Re-supply is something that is not easily planned in advance, though some outline must be allowed for. The difficulty is to foresee what will be needed in the changing fortunes of battle, but if the current trend of thought is accepted the battle is going to be so short that re-supply and reinforcement will be hardly appropriate. Where it does have to be done radio communications are the key to success. The aircraft have to be guided straight in to the DZ without hesitation, and they must fly off directly after the drop. Nevertheless, the greatest problem facing everyone is the extraction of the airborne force. In the classic method of operating, the ground troops will come forward and pass through. The difficulty is to get the timing right. At Waalhaven in Holland in 1940 the Panzers were a day or two late, but it did not matter too much. A few more days might have changed things. At Arnhem they only got

there in time to rescue a few survivors. In Korea they got there almost as the drop was taking place and there was no real job for the airborne to do. In a future war the link-up will need to be very soon after the drop. A matter of hours seems reasonable, because with the amount of armour available to modern armies, even in the back areas, an airborne force is going to have a difficult time in holding out on an objective, and an even harder time if the objective is really important to the enemy (say a road bridge on a line of withdrawal or something equally sensitive).

So far no country has managed to devise a way for getting airborne troops out by air, but this ought not to be impossible given enough helicopters and given that there is no interference on the landing zone. Helicopters are supposed not to be able to operate over the enemy areas because they are so vulnerable to anti-aircraft fire of all kinds, but it might be possible to choose a quiet route for them and to saturate the ground with fire as they pass over. They could then do a quick swoop and pick up the force and return, but there would be no chance of a second lift; everyone would have to go in the one flight, and it could be a most expensive experiment. On the other hand, if these things are not expected, then they have a good chance of succeeding—for the first time. The early German thoughts on airborne forces envisaged aeroplanes landing and taking out the force once the operation was over, and this might just be done in modern war if the conditions are right. It would need STOL aircraft and a great deal of nerve on the part of the Air Force commanders, but a quick sortie with suitable fighter defence might easily succeed. There are plenty of suitable STOL transports flying today which could make this sort of flight: the Canadian Buffalo, the US YC series of prototypes or the Israeli 201 Arava to name a few. All of these are capable of landing and taking off within a few hundred metres, using flat grassland or a similar surface, and they could be loaded within a few minutes and away almost before the wheels had stopped turning. The greatest difficulty is not the flying, or even the anti-aircraft defences, but it is the making of a clean break from the enemy ground forces and disengaging for even a short while in which to make the pick-up.

Appendix

Airborne Forces of the World

The following survey lists the airborne forces which are claimed to exist by the various armies throughout the world. It is based on information published in the *The Military Balance 1981*, published by the International Institute for Strategic Studies, together with additional information gained from a wide variety of journals and government publications. The information is believed to be correct at the time of writing, but it is inevitable that changes will have occurred by the time that this book is published.

The number of countries which claim to have some sort of airborne force is quite astonishing, but it must be remembered that it is one thing to call a unit a parachute battalion, or a para-commando battalion, and quite another to actually train and equip it for that rôle. Many smaller countries use the title to indicate that the unit is considered to be of a higher standard than the others in the Army, and in some other cases it appears as though it is done to keep up appearances with the neighbours. The best indicator of the presence of an actual airborne force in being is to look at the list of aircraft in the Air Force; when there are only a token number of transport planes it can be safely assumed that the airborne force is really an infantry formation under another name. Should there be several squadrons of planes of all the same type, and all suitable for the carriage of troops and equipment, then the picture is different and it is obvious that some sort of airborne capability could exist were it required.

One interesting point which emerges from a study of transport aircraft in service today is the remarkable number of C-47s which are still flying and which are still listed in the Air Forces of quite advanced and wealthy countries. This amazing and much-loved aircraft continues to give good service almost forty years from the date when it first went into military use. Indeed there are a few countries where the C-46 Curtiss Commando still flies and that was first used in early 1945.

There are only a few countries which actually make and sell parachuting equipment and parachutes. The largest supplier is the United States, but others are Britain, France and to a lesser extent Germany. Practically every other national airborne force in the world uses equipment bought from one or other of these major manufacturers. The Soviet Union supplies the Warsaw Pact countries, but there has been little evidence so far of Soviet equipment being seen outside that area.

Algeria In 1962 Algeria became independent, and during the 1960s a modern Army was built up using Soviet equipment and advisers. A parachute battalion was formed and is said still to exist. There have been few reports of its activities, but it must be assumed that it still exists. There are sufficient transport aircraft in the Air Force to lift the battalion, though there is a mixture of types which would complicate any operation above company strength.

1981 Airborne units: one parachute battalion.

Argentina There is sufficient airlift in the Air Force to lift at least one battalion, though only in a mixture of aircraft. There is no mention of a parachute capability.

1981 Airborne units: one airmobile brigade.

Australia The Australian airborne capability is contained in one SAS regiment, which undertakes the usual SAS tasks. However, there is adequate airlift in the Air Force to carry at least one battalion of infantry, and parachute training is widespread among the Army. There is therefore a possible airborne capability beyond what is declared in the Order of Battle.

1981 Airborne units: one SAS regiment.

Belgium Since 1945 the Belgian Army has maintained a small airborne force, and this has been employed in the Congo area on at least two occasions in the last fifteen years. The battalion is highly trained and exercises frequently.

1981 Airborne units: one para-commando regiment (battalion strength).

Bolivia There is a claimed battalion of parachutists in the Bolivian Army, but the aircraft listed in the Air Force Order of Battle do not support this idea. It might be possible to mount a small operation using the mixture of elderly transport aircraft that are available, but that is all.

1981 Airborne units: one parachute battalion.

Brazil Brazil has a well-trained army, largely equipped with US material. It can be assumed that the parachute brigade uses American techniques and equipment and that it is maintained at a high standard of training. The heavy drop capability is not known, but there are over twenty DHC Buffaloes in the Air Force and these are aircraft with a very good STOL performance, so it is reasonable to assume that support weapons could be delivered with the brigade.

1981 Airborne units: one independent parachute brigade.

Burundi This East African state has one parachute battalion on record but only three vintage DC–3s.

1981 Airborne units: one parachute battalion.

Cameroun This West African state lists one parachute company amongst its Army units. The Air Force has only a few transport aircraft.

1981 Airborne units: one parachute company.

Canada Canada has been involved in airborne warfare since it started in Britain, and after 1945 a force of fluctuating size has been maintained. For some years economic reasons forced the Army to reduce to trained parachute companies within the structure of existing infantry battalions, but this has been seen to be uneconomical in the long run, as well as being almost impossible operationally. A feature of the Canadian airborne training is winter warfare, and the airborne unit is fully capable of parachuting operationally in the middle of the Arctic winter.

1981 Airborne units: one airborne regiment (battalion size).

Chad Chad has three infantry battalions, which include five parachute companies. The Air Force lists nine C-47s; the French influence in Chad being observed by the existence also of a Noratlas.

1981 Airborne units: five parachute companies.

180

China (PRC) Little is known for certain about the Chinese Army, but their claim to have three divisions of airborne troops is perfectly believable. The Air Force has a mixture of transport aircraft, about 400 in all. There are also said to be 300 helicopters. These do not make a large lift, especially since many of the aircraft are elderly and limited in their capacity, but it is likely that at least one regiment could be lifted in one flight. By making sacrifices in the transport fleet a division could be flown, but whether it could be maintained on the ground is another matter.

1981 Airborne units: three airborne divisions.

China (Taiwan) The Republic of China on Taiwan has a large army for its population and is almost entirely dependent on the United States for equipment and training. The airborne formations are likely to be using obsolescent US equipment and aircraft. The Air Force has C-119s, C-46s and C-47s among its fleet and over 100 helicopters of mixed designs. The operational capability of this force would be limited to a short-range assault, using techniques not far removed from those of World War II.

1981 Airborne units: two airborne brigades and four Special Forces groups.

Colombia It is known that the airborne battalion of the Colombian Army has been operating in the jungle against the guerrillas who are opposed to the government, and this may have affected their airborne training. The Air Force has a mixed fleet of transports which would gravely complicate any operation larger than a company assault.

1981 Airborne units: one battalion.

Congo Ever since independence in 1960 the Congo has claimed to have at least one airborne unit in the Army. It still does, but the few transport aircraft that are owned by the Air Force make it unlikely that they are at an adequate state of training, or that they could undertake an operation.

1981 Airborne units: one para-commando battalion.

Czechoslovakia Czech airborne units have been seen in publications and in ceremonial parades for many years and it appears that they are well trained and kept up to strength. The Air Force has a fleet of Soviet transport aircraft which is big enough to carry at least one battalion at a time for a parachute assault, and there are also about 100 helicopters.

1981 Airborne units: one airborne regiment.

Ecuador The one battalion in the Order of Battle is probably in the same position as that of Colombia. In the case of Ecuador there are apparently sufficient aircraft in the Air Force to take the entire battalion with light scales of equipment.

1981 Airborne units: one airborne battalion.

Egypt It is difficult to be certain of the state of training of the Egyptian airborne troops, for they have not been seen in action. The equipment is bound to be Soviet in origin and with the severance of military relations with Moscow the condition and general repair of it is unknown. However, the Air Force has about sixty transport aircraft and so could lift at least one battalion, if not more.

1981 Airborne units: one parachute brigade; two airmobile brigades.

El Salvador This South American state has one parachute battalion but this may be only of company strength. The Air Force has a small number of suitable transport aircraft.

1981 Airborne units: one parachute battalion (coy).

Ethiopia Although Ethiopia has a large and powerful army numbering 225,000 men, the formation of an airborne element is a new development. The Air Force is equipped with the latest Russian and American transport aircraft.

1981 Airborne units: four para/commando brigades.

France France has always maintained a strong airborne arm and it still does today. Traditionally the Foreign Legion has had a strong parachute element, and this is still so. A brigade of the division is made up of Legion battalions, now usually based in Corsica. The other brigade is in Metropolitan France. The Air Force has plenty of transport aircraft and can lift at least two battalions at one time. Training is good and the units exercise frequently. Heavy drop is sophisticated and the great majority of the weapons and equipment are French.

1981 Airborne units: one division of two brigades; one air-portable division (Marines).

Germany (FRG) The Germans were the first to use airborne forces properly, at the beginning of World War II. As the war progressed the opportunities for large operations decreased, though the number of special parachute formations increased steadily. This was largely due to the fact that they were recognised as élite troops who could be used at critical points in the battle, but it may also have had some foundation in the fact that a parachute division has a lighter scale of equipment and so was easier to form. After the war the German Army was disbanded and it was not until the late 1950s that the Training School at Stendal was reformed. Since then there has been a steady increase in the number of units, until today they form three airborne brigades of three battalions each. These brigades operate as a mixture of parachute and helicopter-borne units, trained in both skills.

1934–35. 22nd Infantry Air-Landing (*Luftlande*) Division formed.
1936. Parachute Training School set up at Stendal.
1938. October. 7th Flieger Division formed.
1943. 1, 2, 3, 4 and 5 Parachute Divisions formed.
1944. 6, 7, 8 and 9 Parachute Divisions formed.
1945. 10 Parachute Division formed in Austria from remnants of 1 and 4 Parachute Divisions.
1945. May. All parachute units disbanded.
1958. Parachute School reformed at Stendal.

1981 **West Germany** Airborne units: three airborne brigades.

1981 **East Germany** Airborne units: two airborne battalions.

Ghana Parachute training has taken place in Ghana since the 1960s, at one time supervised by the Canadian Army. One airborne battalion is in being and the unit is served by two Air Force transport squadrons.

1981 Airborne units: one airborne battalion.

Greece Greece has one para-commando brigade which has light scales of equipment and a mixture of French and US airborne aids. The Air Force is well equipped and should be able to carry two battalions at one time. The Greek airborne experience stems from World War II when the Greek Sacred Squadron formed part of the British SAS/SBS in the Mediterranean threatre.

1981 Airborne units: one para-commando brigade.

Guatemala This small Central American state claims to have one parachute battalion, but it is most unlikely that there is more than a small cadre of trained men in the entire country. The Air Force has no more than four or five transport aircraft and the chances of any significant numbers of trained parachutists actually serving in the Army is negligible.
1981 Airborne units: one parachute battalion.

Guinea A Special Forces battalion exists but it is poorly equipped with transport aircraft.
1981 Airborne units: one Special Forces battalion.

Hungary The Hungarian airborne battalion is probably more inclined towards helicopter operations than parachuting; however, pictures have been seen of parachutists and the Air Force has sufficient aircraft to provide an adequate lift for the complete battalion were that ever to be needed. The state of training of the troops is not known.
1981 Airborne units: one airborne battalion.

India The Indian Army raised a complete airborne division during World War II and has kept up the skills ever since. Although the Air Force has a mixed fleet of transport aircraft there are more than enough to make certain that a minimum of one battalion could be parachuted at one time, and two probably could. The state of training and the variety of airborne equipment is not made known, but it is likely that there is a good Heavy Drop capability.
1981 Airborne units: two parachute brigades.

Indonesia Indonesia claims to have a large airborne force in comparison to other countries in the Far East, but it is highly likely that they exist in name only. The inept performance of the two attempted parachute assaults during the 1964 Confrontation does not inspire belief that any adequately trained officers or men actually serve in these units. The Air Force has only a few transport aircraft which could be used for an airborne assault and there is one helicopter squadron.
1981 Airborne units: two airborne infantry brigades.

Irak This Arab nation has an army of 200,000 men but little is known about its two Special Forces brigades and what proportion of these men are parachute-trained. Two Air Force transport squadrons are well equipped with the latest Russian aircraft.
1981 Airborne units: two Special Forces brigades.

Iran Before the downfall of the Shah there were one parachute brigade and one Special Forces Brigade in Iran, both backed up by plenty of modern aircraft. These brigades are still reported to exist but there is little information available about them.
1981 Airborne units: one airborne brigade and one Special Forces brigade.

Israel The Israeli Army has given convincing demonstrations of its airborne capability often enough in the past twenty years and places great reliance on the use of fast-moving airborne troops to safeguard its frontiers. The Air Force has enough aircraft to lift two battalions in one flight, but the Israeli methods of using civilian equipment during wartime make it likely that the actual lift could be twice as great, by commandeering. The state of training of all units is always extremely high and the reaction time of the regular battalions can be measured in minutes.
1981 Airborne units: five parachute brigades (three are normally kept at full strength; two are made up with reservists).

Italy Italian airborne forces have suffered from a shortage of financial support throughout their existence; nevertheless, two small divisions were formed during World War II though they were never used in action as airborne formations. As with so many other airborne units, they were used as line infantry and wasted away. There were parachute units with both the Air Force and the Marines, though these were intended to be mainly sabotage and raiding forces rather than assault troops, and the units never reached a great strength. When Italy surrendered in 1943 some parachutists of the *Folgore* Division came over to the Allied side and were formed into 'F' Squadron of the British Eighth Army. When the war ended the few Italian parachutists still remaining were equipped with British equipment and were using C-47 Dakotas. Within a year a new Italian Training School was formed and SM82s brought back into service. From then on the training and equipment was purely Italian, and it is still so today.

1937. Training School started at Tarquinia.

1939. Two battalions of parachutists in existence in Libya. Total strength about 500 men.
1940. Libya. Another battalion formed at Castel Benito. About 300 men.
1942. 7 December. Florence. Formation of the *Folgore* Division.
1943. March. Formation of *Nembo* Division, incorporating Marine and Air Force units.
1943. Formation of 'F' Squadron.
1946. Reforming of Parachute Training School. Start of post-war airborne units.
1952. Parachute Brigade formed at Pisa.
1978. Parachute Brigade reformed to Airborne Brigade. Equipped with helicopters and fixed-wing transport aircraft.

1981 Airborne units: one airborne brigade.

Ivory Coast This small and backward African country claims to have an airborne force, which may be an attempt to keep up with its neighbours. Since the Air Force has less than half a dozen aircraft that could be remotely suitable for parachuting, and roughly the same number of helicopters, it is unlikely that any real capacity for airborne warfare actually exists.

1981 Airborne units: one parachute company.

Japan The first Japanese parachute troops began their training in 1940, and a year later there were more than 14,000 men either in training or fully trained. German instructors played a large part in this initial setting-up, though they had little influence over the tactical use of the units. An unusual feature of the wartime Japanese airborne formations was that they were sponsored by both the Army and the Navy, so that in effect there were two different systems. Even the training differed. The Navy parachutists were an adjunct to the Marine raiding forces and were not meant to engage in pitched battles. However, the army parachutists were always lightly armed, since there were no aircraft suitable for a heavy drop; and though they scored some successes in the first few months of the Pacific War their later use was marked by poor preparation and planning together with insufficient support.

The present Japanese Self Defence Force uses the airborne technique for rather different purposes, and though there is a force of trained parachutists, the more usual method of arriving on the battlefield is by helicopter.

1981 Airborne units: one airborne brigade.

Jordan Recent information reveals that there are three Special Forces battalions in the Jordanian Army.

1981 Airborne units: three Special Forces battalions.

Kenya This East African state is currently forming one air cavalry battalion. Two Air Force transport squadrons are equipped with Caribou transport aircraft.

Libya This North African state claims one Special Forces group and an assortment of Russian and American transport aircraft.

Malaysia One Special Services unit is reported to be in existence. As in the Libyan case it is not known how many men are parachute-trained.

Mali This poor and tiny African state claims to have one parachute company in an Army of 4000 men; the Air Force could at best lift only part of it.

1981 Airborne units: one parachute company and one Special Force battalion.

Mexico The Mexican Army claims to have a parachute brigade in its field element. These are the regular troops, the large number of conscripts being sent to garrison units which operate rather differently. The Air Force has a mixed bag of transport aircraft which could probably lift about 300 men. There is thus the ability to parachute reinforced company groups, though it would take at least two lifts to put a battalion on the ground.

1981 Airborne units: one parachute brigade of two battalions.

Morocco The Moroccan Army has shown itself to be a well trained and capable force on several occasions since the country gained full independence in 1956. It has played a useful part in the United Nations Peacekeeping duties, and is well equipped with mainly French weapons and vehicles. The two transport squadrons in the Air Force have sufficient aircraft to lift at least two battalions, and while the standard of training of the parachutists is not known it must be assumed that they exist and that they are capable of carrying out their rôle.

1981 Airborne units: one para/mountain brigade.

Nepal This small independent state in the Himalayas has one parachute battalion.

New Zealand The New Zealand Army maintains one parachute-trained SAS squadron.

Niger This small African state claims one parachute company and a few American aircraft.

North and South Korea Although it is now almost 30 years since the Korean War ended, the North Korean Army numbers approximately 1,000,000 men. The 22 Special Forces commando brigades will undoubtedly contain a strong parachute element. Russian transport aircraft are available in huge numbers. The South Korean Army on the other hand includes only seven similarly styled brigades; the US Army and Air Force maintaining a strong presence still in South Korea.

Oman Latest reports indicate the existence of one parachute company.

Pakistan The Pakistan Army includes a Special Service Group supported by two air transport squadrons and helicopters. The Army of Pakistan shares its Airborne heritage with that of the 44th Indian Airborne Division of World War II.

Peru The number of parachutists in the existing brigade is probably not large, and the Air Force has a mixture of aircraft in which to fly them. However, there are sixteen DHC Buffaloes in the inventory, and these ought to be able to lift a battalion when required.

1981 Airborne units: one para-commando brigade.

Philippines The Filipino Army includes one Special Services brigade.

Poland Although Polish parachutists played a significant part in the Allied airborne assaults in World War II and a parachute school existed in Poland before the war, the real history of airborne formations within metropolitan Poland is quite short and only started after the Soviet domination of the Polish defence forces. The Polish Air Force is one of the biggest in the Warsaw Pact, apart from Soviet Russia, and it has a modern, though small, transport fleet. This is backed up by 100 or so transport helicopters; the total lift available for airborne operations therefore amounts to something like a brigade or more. Although not often seen or mentioned, it must be assumed that, in common with all the other Warsaw Pact Armies, the Polish airborne units are kept up to strength and well trained.

1981 Airborne units: two airborne battalions.

Portugal The Portuguese Army supports only one commando unit, which includes parachutists.

184

Romania Romania possesses the almost obligatory airborne regiment, and from time to time pictures of the airborne troops appear in the press. The transport fleet is probably capable of lifting at least one battalion, but the heavy drop capability is not clear.

1981 Airborne units: one airborne regiment.

Saudi Arabia There are two parachute battalions. It is known that the equipment of these battalions is good, and there are ample aircraft to lift them as well as helicopters. Whether there is any heavy drop ability is not entirely clear, and if it exists what systems it uses are also unknown. Since the Saudi Army is remarkably well trained, it can be assumed that these two battalions are up to the same standard, in which case it represents a useful addition to the defensive forces of the country, and it might be thought that with such long frontiers it was worth while increasing the parachute element.

1981 Airborne units: two parachute battalions.

Senegal In common with its neighbours, Senegal claims to have a small parachute force. There are enough C-47s to lift one or two platoons, but the state of training of the men and their equipment position is not known.

1981 Airborne units: two parachute companies.

South Africa The South African Army is largely composed of conscripts and it is operating at full stretch at the moment in containing the guerrilla movements which press on its borders. In these operations there seems to be no use made of parachute units and it is likely that these units are now losing their combat effectiveness as airborne troops. The small South African transport fleet is fully occupied in supplying the border troops and in ferrying troops to and fro.

1981 Airborne units: one parachute brigade.

Spain Spain has had an airborne force since the late 1950s and this has been steadily building up in recent years. (Minute parachute units were first actually raised by both the Republican and Nationalist Forces in the Civil War.) The Air Force has a good selection of modern aircraft and could undoubtedly lift two battalions at a time without much trouble. There are also about twenty transport helicopters and six CH-47 Heavy Lift machines.

1981 Airborne units: one air-portable brigade; one parachute brigade.

Sudan Sudan has a small parachute force, largely using US equipment. The available airlift is restricted, but it appears to be adequate for the foreseen operational rôle of the parachutists, which is the rapid reinforcement of the frontier regions in the event of invasion or guerrilla risings.

1981 Airborne units: one parachute brigade.

Syria The Syrian airborne force does not appear to have been used operationally and it is not clear why it is maintained. Good lift capability is provided by Russian transport aircraft and helicopters.

1981 Airborne units: one parachute regiment.

Thailand The Royal Thai Army has had plenty of US aid and sends its men regularly to the USA for training. The small airborne force uses equipment and weapons from the USA, and though its unit training may be less than is needed to sustain a long operation it seems that there is sufficient capability to mount a small airborne assault.

1981 Airborne units: one airborne and three special forces battalions.

Tozo This state claims two parachute battalions but only a handful of aircraft.

Tunisia The Tunisian Army is not large and it is occupied in maintaining the peace along the borders of the country and also in training. Tunisia has had difficulties with both Algeria and Libya and the defence forces are kept at a fairly high state of readiness. The air lift is very limited, though it is possible that in time of real trouble other countries would be willing to lend aircraft, and the para-commando battalions must be restricted in what they can do on their own.

1981 Airborne units: two para-commando battalions.

Turkey The Turkish Brigade uses US equipment and training methods and it exercises frequently. It could be a significant striking force in the event of a war in the Eastern Mediterranean, and there are sufficient transport aircraft to fly it into battle and to maintain it once there.

1981 Airborne units: one parachute brigade.

United Kingdom The British were slow in starting their airborne force, and although the final result was a well-trained and capable body of troops there was never enough air lift to carry them all, and throughout World War II they suffered from insufficient aircraft. This continued into peacetime and is still true today. Britain has used airborne troops for many operations since 1945, though few of them—as in the recent Falklands War involving 2, 3 Para, the Marines as well as the SAS—have actually employed the parachute to reach their objective. The present strength of British airborne forces is such that they are scarcely a viable 'airborne' force at all.

1940. June. Prime Minister ordered the formation of parachute troops.
1941. September. 1st Parachute Battalion formed, incorporated into 1st Parachute Brigade.
1941. October. Air-landing Brigade formed. October. 1st Airborne Division formed.
1943. April. 6th Airborne Division formed.
1944. February. 44 Indian Airborne Division formed.
1948. 1st and 6th Divisions combined into 16 Independent Parachute Brigade. 44 Division became Reserve Army.
1955. 44 Division reformed into 44 Parachute Brigade (TA).
1977. Only one parachute battalion to be in the parachute role at any one time. Other two to be operated as infantry.

1981 Airborne units: three parachute battalions, one in parachute role at any one time, and one regular SAS regiment. Royal Marine Commando units also contain a strong element of parachute-trained troops.

USA The United States formed their first airborne unit almost as late as did the British, but they made up for lost time by quantity and by producing the aircraft to fly the formations. Altogether five airborne divisions were formed in World War II. The US divisions comprised both parachute and glider troops but the main emphasis was on parachuting. Gliders were only latterly used for heavy equipment. After the war there was a cut-back to two divisions and later to rather less than that. Today there is one fully parachutable division, the 82nd, and one air-mobile division with some parachute capability, the 101st.

1940. June. Test Platoon formed at Fort Benning.
1940. November. 501st Infantry become the first parachute battalion.
1941. 502, 503 and 504 Parachute Infantry formed.

1942. August. 82nd and 101st Airborne Divisions formed.

1942. November. 17th Airborne Division formed.

1943. February. 11th Airborne Division formed.

1944. 13th Airborne Division formed.

1945. Airborne Divisions cut to 82nd and 101st.

1968. 101st Division became Airmobile and was partly lifted by helicopter.

1979 Airborne units: one airborne division and one air-mobile division. The United States Special Forces as well as strong elements of the Marines and Rangers are parachute trained.

USSR The history of the Soviet airborne arm could be said to have gone up and down with the passage of time. The first parachute troops appeared in 1929 and were used in small numbers on an army exercise in 1930. Six years later there was the now legendary mass parachute drop of 1500 men before an invited audience of military attachés and observers. From then on little was heard of the apparently large parachute force until it was used in three disastrous operational drops against the Germans during World War II. These were poorly conceived and carried out and from then on the Soviet parachutists went back into obscurity again. After World War II it was known that some sort of airborne capability existed in the Soviet Union, but it was not until the Tushino Air Display of 1956, together with the Moscow Parade in the same year, that the truth dawned. The Soviet Union had rebuilt its airborne arm into a large and well-trained force with modern equipment. Since then it has continued with this policy and today the Soviet airborne army is the largest in the world and arguably the best equipped. Certainly it is the only one with self-propelled anti-tank artillery, and it is highly likely that it now has substantial numbers of missiles also. The divisions are trained continuously and use both parachutes and helicopters to reach the battlefield. The men are all volunteers and are usually long-service soldiers with a pride in their division and their airborne speciality. They are treated as élite troops and serve in Metropolitan Russia, only coming into East Germany or similar border regions when there is a large exercise. Even their precise numbers are not known with accuracy, but when there are so many of them this becomes a somewhat academic matter. The Soviet Air Force has sufficient modern aircraft to lift more than one division at a time, to a distance of 2000 miles (3220 km) or so.

1981 Airborne units: eight but may be as many as eleven airborne divisions.

Yemen (North) The North Yemen Arab Republic is one of the newest armies to claim an airborne force. The Air Force has however only twelve suitable transport aircraft, and these are a mixture of types. The facilities for training and maintaining a parachute force do not exist in the Yemen, so it is likely that training takes place elsewhere.

1981 Airborne units: one parachute brigade.

Yugoslavia The Yugoslav Army practises airborne movements and small unit actions from both parachute aircraft and from helicopters. It can be assumed that the brigade mentioned in the Order of Battle is up to strength and well trained. There is also probably a heavy drop capability. However, the transport aircraft, which include the venerable C-47, are a mixture of types, which limits the operational flexibility of the unit.

1981 Airborne units: one airborne brigade.

Zaïre Zaïre makes an extravagant claim for parachute-trained troops. But the Air Force has only a small number of transport aircraft, in a mixture of types, not all suited to parachute dropping.

1979 Airborne units: one parachute brigade, two battalions and one Special Forces brigade.

Zimbabwe The new Army of Zimbabwe consists of some 12,000 men. During the recent civil war the Rhodesians maintained two parachute-trained battalions of Light Infantry and three SAS squadrons. The new Zimbabwe in 1981 listed three infantry battalions and six independent infantry companies. It must be assumed that many of these infantrymen are experienced parachutists and a lift capability in the form of a transport squadron of C-47s and two helicopter squadrons remains.

186

Typical establishment of a British airborne division, 1944

Div. HQ

| Para Bde | Para Bde | A/L Bde | A/L Arty Regt | Engr Coy | Sigs Sqn | Recce Sqn |

Para Bn	A/L Bn	
Para Bn	A/L Bn	Pathfinder Coy
Para Bn	A/L Bn	

NOTE. A/L = Air-landing, i.e. gliderborne.

Italian Division (*Folgore*)

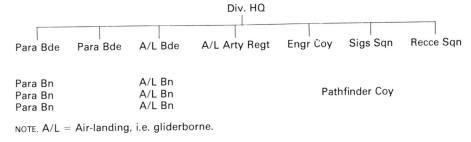

Divisional HQ

186 Regt	187 Regt	185 Arty Bn	Atk Coy	Mortar Coy	Med det	Sigs det
V Bn	VIII Bn
VI Bn	IX Bn
VII Bn	X Bn

Regiment: about 2500 men.
Battalion: establishment, 29 officers. 300 men.

Bn HQ

| Rifle Coy | Rifle Coy | Rifle Coy | Engr Pl | Sigs det | Med sec |

NOTE. The numbering of the *Folgore* battalions changed frequently during 1943/44, particularly in 187 Regiment. In 1944, 187 Regt is quoted in one source as having II, IV, and IX in its structure.
The numbering of the artillery battalion is the same as one of the Regiments in the *Nembo* Division.

Italian Division (*Nembo*)

Divisional HQ

183 Regt	184 Regt	185 Regt	184 Arty Bn	Mortar Coy	*M/C Coy	Sigs det
XV Bn	XII Bn	III Bn
XVI Bn	XIII Bn	XI Bn

*M/C = motorcycle.

NOTE. Each Regiment was formed from men from different arms of the service; Marines, Air Force and Army. There was no anti-tank company and it seems likely that the *Nembo* was more frequently used piecemeal for reinforcement. Some battalions went to Russia in 1943. Others fought in northern Italy with the Germans.

Typical German Parachute Division, 1944 establishment

Div. HQ

Rifle Regt	Rifle Regt	Rifle Regt	Arty Bn	AA bn	Atk Bn	Mortar Bn	Engr Bn
Bn			Bty
Bn			Bty		Recce Coy	Sigs Bn
Bn			Bty

Total strength: 16,000 men		Mortars:	125
Rifles:	9689	Hy Mortars:	80
Pistols:	3810	AA guns:	39
SMGs:	3026	Arty guns:	103
MGs:	1010	Vehicles:	2141

Japanese Organization (1944)

Raiding Group
Raiding Brigade   Raiding Flying Brigade

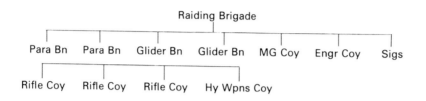

Raiding Brigade
Para Bn   Para Bn   Glider Bn   Glider Bn   MG Coy   Engr Coy   Sigs
Rifle Coy   Rifle Coy   Rifle Coy   Hy Wpns Coy

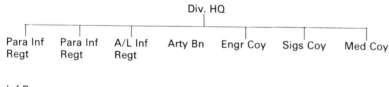

Raiding Flying Brigade
Flying Regt   Flying Regt   Glider Regt   Sigs
Sqdn   Sqdn   Sqdn

NOTE. 1. Raiding Group was 5575 all ranks when up to strength.
2. Only one Raiding Group was ever fully formed.
3. The Raiding Flying Brigade was never properly established, as there were too few aircraft.

US Airborne Division, 1944 establishment

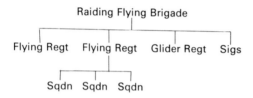

Div. HQ
Para Inf Regt   Para Inf Regt   A/L Inf Regt   Arty Bn   Engr Coy   Sigs Coy   Med Coy

Inf Bn
Inf Bn
Inf Bn

Total strength: 13,000 all ranks.

NOTE. 1. Original organisation was one Para Inf Regt and two A/L Regts.
2. The Arty Bn was enlarged in 1944 to include 105 mm guns. The parachute element was thirty-six 75 mm howitzers.
3. Original strength of a Para Inf Bn was 34 officers and 412 men. This was increased in the 1944 reorganisation to bring it more into line with the standard Infantry Bn.

188

Glossary

AIRBORNE Specifically, anything which is carried in the air, but by convention now taken to apply to troops and their equipment which are carried to battle by air and either parachuted or landed on or near the battlefield.

AA Anti-aircraft.

CANOPY That part of a parachute which is made of thin material and provides the resistance to the air. Originally of silk, now always of nylon. A canopy is made up of many smaller sections called panels and gores.

CONTAINER Originally a metal box which was parachuted with a stick of men, and in which they carried their weapons and equipment. Containers were carried on bomb-racks outside the plane and had a parachute on one end. The word now describes the personal pack carried by each man in which he takes his weapons and light equipment. This pack is a canvas wrapper slung on the parachute harness and dropped below the man on a nylon rope.

DESPATCHER A member of the crew of the aircraft dropping parachutists. The despatcher stands by the door and controls the departure of the men.

DROPPING HEIGHT AND SPEED All parachutes have a minimum height below which it is not safe to drop since the canopy will not have sufficient time to open, nor will the parachutist have enough time to react to any malfunction. Similarly all parachutes have a maximum speed above which they will not open easily and may tear. Thus the dropping aircraft has to fly above a minimum height and below a certain speed. This often places a considerable strain on the pilot.

DROP ZONE (DZ) The area in which parachutists land.

EXIT The act of jumping from an aircraft. Each aircraft requires a slightly different form of exit because of the variations in the size and position of the door, the strength of the slipstream going past it, and several other related factors. The exit is most important since a poor exit can cause the jumper to tumble and perhaps become tangled in his rigging lines.

GORE A parachute canopy is divided into a number of triangular gores, running from the apex to the periphery.

HEAVY DROP The equipment drop in a parachute assault. The Heavy Drop is often put down on a different DZ from the men, though it will only be a few hundred yards. Vehicles, guns and ammunition supplies will be carried in the Heavy Drop aircraft.

JUMPMASTER US term for a despatcher.

KIT BAG Originally a means of enabling a man to carry his weapon and personal equipment with him in the air. The kit bag was strapped to the leg and tied to the parachute harness by a line. When his parachute had opened the jumper lowered the bag below him. First used 1942 and became obsolete in 1956.

LANDING ZONE (LZ) The area of ground designated for gliders to land.

PANEL Part of a gore. A gore is usually divided into four panels, each with the weave running in opposite directions, and with strong seams. Thus any tear can only run across one panel and will not cause a noticeable loss of lift.

PARAPACK US term. A large canvas container carried on external bomb-racks. World War II only.

PATHFINDER A small force dropped shortly before the main assault. Pathfinders locate and mark out the correct DZ and set up beacons to guide the main stream of aircraft.

PERIPHERY The circumference of a parachute canopy.

PLATFORM A strong structure on which a vehicle, gun or similar large weight is clamped down. Parachutes are attached to the platform and it is carried in the Heavy Drop aircraft and dropped by sliding it out over the rear door sill.

RALLYING POINT See RV.

RENDEZVOUS (RV) The point on or near the DZ to which all parachutists in a military drop go after landing.

RESERVE An emergency parachute carried on the chest of all parachutists today.

189

RIGGING LINE The line which runs from the shoulder harness up to the canopy of a parachute.

RIPCORD The handle and attached wire which opens the pack of a manually-operated parachute. All reserve parachutes use a rip cord.

STATIC-LINE A line or webbing strap attached to the main parachute of a military jumper. As the man falls away from the door the static-line pulls out his canopy and deploys the parachute.

STICK A number of parachutists who drop from the same plane at the same time.

STROP An extension for a static-line. Different aircraft require different lengths of static-line in order to get the men well clear of the fuselage before the canopy deploys, and this difference is made up by strops.

TEE OR T A Drop Zone is usually marked with a large 'T' made of cloth panels, or by night, lights. This marks the beginning of the drop. The end is marked by an 'X' similarly laid out. Ideally, the first parachutist will land on the T.

Acknowledgements

Australian Army, 170 (bottom left). Bellamy, Chris, 13 (bottom right). Bundesarchiv, 8 (top), 9 (centre bottom), 15 (top right), 16, 17 (left), 21, 22, 25 (top), 25 (centre), 33 (top left), 35 (left), 37 (top), 38, 51, 54, 55, 60 (left centre bottom), 60 (bottom), 67, 68 (top), 70, 71, 100, 104, 106, 107, 109, 125, 126, 127, 129 (centre bottom right). Bundeswehr, 134 (bottom). Camera Press, title page, 42 (bottom left), 64 (bottom), 66 (left), 144, 145, 146 (bottom). Cowhin, Hugh, 108, 133 (bottom right). COI, 62 (top), 132, 164 (centre top left). ECPA, 13 (top left), 33 (bottom), 26, 30, 41 (bottom), 57, 93, 128, 129 (top), 129 (centre top right), 158. GQ Parachute Company, 46, 48. Haythornthwaite, Philip, 6, 7, 9 (top right). Heckler and Koch, 61. Hogg Ian, 35 (right). Irvin Parachute Co., 8 (right), 42 (top right). IWM, 8 (bottom), 13 (top right), 14 (top), 14 (bottom), 15 (top left), 28(top), 32, 34, 35 (centre), 37 (centre and bottom), 56, 62 (bottom), 114, 118, 150, 153. Munson, Kenneth, 74, 80, 110, 111, 123. MARS, 58 (top), 102, 130, 131, 137 (bottom left), 164 (centre bottom left). MOD (AIR), 9 (bottom), 13 (bottom left), 14 (centre), 25 (bottom), 42 (top left), 76, 77, 79, 82, 83, 86, 87, 95 (bottom), 101, 115, 116, 117, 119, 122, 129 (bottom left), 129 (top right), 129 (centre right), 136 (top left), 151, 154, 161. New Zealand Army, 41 (left), 133 (top left), 171 (bottom right). Novosti, 23, 98, 99, 146 (top), 167, 168 (bottom), 169, 175. Royal Armoured Corps, 164, (top left). SME-Ufficio Storico, 10 (bottom), 12, 33 (top right), 36 (right), 68 (bottom). Soldier, 41 (top right), 66 (right), 135. Spanish Army, 10 (top). Thompson, Leroy, 36 (left), 60 (left centre top). US Air Force, 91, 94, 95 (top), 95 (centre). US Army, 17 (right), 18, 19, 26, 28 (bottom), 42 (bottom right), 49, 58 (centre), 58 (bottom), 59, 60 (top), 63, 64 (top left), 64 (left centre), 64 (left centre bottom), 78, 97, 120, 121, 122, 134 (top left), 136 (centre), 136 (bottom), 137, 140, 141 (bottom), 136, 160, 164 (bottom), 165, 166, 170 (top left), 170 (centre right), 170 (top right). US Marine Corps, 141 (top). US Navy, 9 (bottom), 170, 171 (top left), 171 (bottom left).

Index

Figures in *Italic* type refer to captions of black and white photographs and line drawings; those in **bold** refer to captions of colour illustrations and photographs.